"Half philosophical *cri de cœur*, half political education, this book is a passionate call for the defense of democracy. Informed by a deep understanding of the Holocaust, Leonard Grob and John K. Roth call out the calculated incitements to hatred by Hitler, Putin, and Trump. This book is needed in our troubled times."

—**Björn Krondorfer**, professor of religious studies, Northern Arizona University

"Philosophers and Holocaust scholars, Leonard Grob and John K. Roth have drawn from all their accumulated wisdom and marshalled all their strength to offer insights gained from a lifetime and warnings learned from the Holocaust to understand the issues of our day—the Russian invasion of Ukraine, the Trümpian assault on democracy, the polarization of American society, the lure of authoritarianism, and the assault on truth. The result is challenging, engaging, illuminating, even foreboding."

—**Michael Berenbaum**, professor Jewish studies, American Jewish University

"Powerful, provocative, and challenging, *Warnings* is an important book. It is elegantly written and carefully argued. The authors remind us that democracy is fragile, that *American democracy* is fragile. They urge us to pay attention to history, to learn from the Holocaust. Read this book. Learn from it. Pass it on."

—**Carol Rittner**, RSM, professor emerita of Holocaust studies, Stockton University

" *Warnings* is a conversation between two philosophers, Leonard Grob and John K. Roth, with significant work on the Holocaust. Drawing on ancient sages and citing parallels to 1930s Germany, they discuss recent trends that threaten to destroy the foundations of our nation, and they call for courage to restore mutual respect, fundamental equality, and justice for all. *Warnings* is an urgent message to the nation to preserve the noblest and enduring ideals of America."

—**Myrna Goldenberg**, professor emerita of English and philosphy, Montgomery College

Warnings

Warnings

The Holocaust, Ukraine, and Endangered American Democracy

Leonard Grob and John K. Roth

 CASCADE *Books* • Eugene, Oregon

WARNINGS
The Holocaust, Ukraine, and Endangered American Democracy

Cascade Books
An Imprint of Wipf and Stock Publishers
199 W. 8th Ave., Suite 3
Eugene, OR 97401

www.wipfandstock.com

PAPERBACK ISBN: 978-1-6667-4396-8
HARDCOVER ISBN: 978-1-6667-4397-5
EBOOK ISBN: 978-1-6667-4398-2

Cataloguing-in-Publication data:

Names: Grob, Leonard, author. | Roth, John K., author.

Title: Warnings : the holocaust, Ukraine, and endangered American democracy / Leonard Grob and John K. Roth.

Description: Eugene, OR: Cascade Books, 2023. | Includes bibliographical references and index.

Identifiers: ISBN 978-1-6667-4396-8 (paperback). | ISBN 978-1-6667-4397-5 (hardcover). | ISBN 978-1-6667-4398-2 (ebook).

Subjects: LSCH:. Democracy—United States—21st century. | Citizenship. | Civil society. | Ethics. | Judaism—Relations—Christianity. | Holocaust, Jewish (1939–1945). | United States—Politics and government—2017–2021. | World politics—21st century. | Christianity and culture—United States.

Classification: HM766 .G50. 2023 (print). | HM766 (ebook).

06/29/23

To
Susan and Lyn

Women, if the soul of the nation is to be saved,
I believe you must become its soul.

—Coretta Scott King

Where you see wrong or inequality or injustice, speak out, because this is your country. This is your democracy. Make it. Protect it. Pass it on.

—Thurgood Marshall

Contents

Acknowledgments

THE FOUNDING FATHERS OF the United States get credit for establishing American democracy. But whenever democracy is endangered, as it is in 2020s, men—especially White men—do most of the damage.[1] Coretta Scott King was right. If our country's soul is to be saved, its democracy defended and expanded, American women, long left out and still struggling for their rightful places, will make the difference. We dedicate this book to two of them, our partners, who have taught us, as well as their children, students, and friends, what respect, friendship, and love—all essential for democracy at its best—truly mean and require. Susan and Lyn strengthen American democracy. Without them, this book would not exist.

American democracy depends on an amazing array of people. In authoring this book, we are indebted especially to journalists and scholars—many, but by no means all, named in the pages that follow. Their freedom of inquiry and speech, so crucial for flourishing democracy, gave us insight as well as information. Their courage and eloquence inspired us to try our best. Doing that, they helped us to emphasize, is necessary for democracy's health.

Our friends at Cascade Books and Wipf and Stock Publishers keep American democracy strong by using freedom of the press to publish meaningful books that advance dialogue, another key democratic practice. We are deeply grateful for the trust, also a fundamental condition for democracy, that our editor, K. C. Hanson, placed in us. His commitment conferred responsibilities upon us; his encouragement kept us striving to fulfill them. Democracy cannot be healthy without reliable guidance and sound

1. While affirming that race and ethnicity are human constructs, we—two White American men—want to advance the increasingly widespread practice of capitalizing *White* when the term refers to a person's or group's racial or ethnic identity. This step does not imply esteem or pride let alone superiority or supremacy. For more on our thinking, see note 12 on pages 16-17, below.

counsel that people give to one another. Emily Callihan, George Callihan, Jorie Chapman, Ian Creeger, Joe Delahanty, Shanalea Forrest, Jeremy Funk, Calvin Jaffarian, Zechariah Mickel, Mike Munk, Richard Shrout, Mike Surber, James Stock, Matthew Wimer, and the entire, highly capable team at Wipf and Stock Publishers supported us magnificently. We thank them all and our dedicated publicist-friend, Lorna Garano, as well.

Prologue

Old Friends, New Dialogues

Old friends—one a Jew, the other a Christian—we philosophers, Leonard (Lenny) Grob and John K. Roth, have spent decades learning, teaching, and writing about the Holocaust. That fact makes us deeply concerned about democracy. *Warnings* defends liberal democracy against 2020s threats and shows how to resist them.

Late summer 2022 found Americans in sour moods as the midterm elections approached. Ballots in twenty-seven states included candidates who openly denied the results of the 2020 presidential race, which Joe Biden won decisively and honestly. "Democracy Challenged" headlined the *New York Times* on September 19.[1] Among likely 2022 voters, 75 percent saw the United States heading in the wrong direction, a pessimistic outlook that continued in early 2023. "Threats to democracy" sometimes topped "cost of living" as the country's most critical issue. A polling record 58 percent believed the nation's best years have come and gone.[2] With inflation high and Joe Biden's approval low, a "red wave" election, guaranteeing Republican control of Congress, seemed sure.

Election Day results didn't go that way. By a slim margin, Republicans took the House of Representatives, but Democrats kept control of the Senate. Clinging to the Big Lie that the presidency had been stolen from Donald Trump in 2020, election-denying and abortion-restricting Republicans were defeated by voters who said democracy matters, fair and free elections are essential, and antidemocratic policies that take away fundamental rights are unacceptable. The margins of victory, however, were slim. In the nation's intensely partisan political struggles, the battle lines barely shifted.

1. Kahn, "Democracy Challenged."
2. Murray, "NBC News Poll."

Democracy was on the American ballot in the 2022 midterm elections. It won yet remains fragile and endangered. Americans stepped back from an antidemocratic abyss in 2022, but what awaits in 2024? Democracy reprieved is not democracy assured. As the astute analyst Peter Wehner wisely observed in the *Atlantic* after the 2022 election, "it's hard to overstate how radicalized and anarchic the base of the Republican Party remains . . . The Republican Party today has more, not fewer MAGA ["make America great again"] figures in it than in the past . . . more than 200 election deniers will take office at the national and state level in January."[3] If Republicans break with Trump, they are unlikely to do so for moral reasons but because he costs them power. As long as Trump was in power and seen by Republicans as a source of more power, Wehner adds, "everything else he did—the relentless assault on truth, the unlimited corruption, the cruelty and incitements to violence, the lawlessness, the sheer depravity—was tolerable and even celebrated." The 2022 election did not remove these threats. Emblematic of Republican extremism, corrosive grievance politics and election denialism—if "our" party or candidate didn't win, the election was unfair and illegitimate—remain rife in the United States. Trump and his "make America great again" (MAGA) Republicans took American democracy near the brink. On December 3, 2022, Trump even argued that election fraud and theft—all baseless claims without any merit whatsoever—justified suspension of the Constitution to put him back in the White House.[4] Widespread rebukes followed, but far from being out of the woods, which it never is, American democracy remains at risk. It could be trumped by conspiratorial, vengeance-driven, violence-prone, antidemocratic authoritarianism, an American version of fascism.[5]

As the campaigns intensify for the 2024 presidential election, Americans need to double down on the defense of democracy that many voters—but by no means all—mounted in 2022. That commitment cannot be made too soon. Already on Tuesday, November 15, 2022, Trump proclaimed, "In order to make America great and glorious again, I am tonight announcing my candidacy for president of the United States." His declaration is a way of seeking protection from criminal prosecution and advancing fundraising to enrich himself, but Trump wants power too, and he's likely to attempt "burning the house down" if denied it. Twice impeached, two-time loser of the popular vote for the presidency, and facing multiple criminal investigations, Trump and his "always Trump"

3. Wehner, "More MAGA Than Ever." See also Wehner, "Trump Abandonment."

4. Demirjian and Olorunnipa, "White House Rebukes."

5. On these points, see Stanley, *How Fascism Works.*

followers have not yet been sidelined.[6] Speaking to the conservative radio host Hugh Hewitt on September 15, 2022, for example, Trump issued a less-than-veiled threat of violence if he is criminally indicted. "I don't think the people of the United States would stand for it," said Trump. His indictment, Trump advised, would produce "problems in this country the likes of which perhaps we've never seen before."[7]

A disgusting warning about such "problems" took place on Friday morning, October 28, 2022, when a politically motivated intruder used a hammer to bash the skull of Paul Pelosi, the eighty-two-year-old spouse of House Speaker Nancy Pelosi, in their San Francisco home. Nevertheless, as investigations and court proceedings continued in Washington, DC, Georgia, and New York, Trump's legal jeopardy grew in early 2023, prompting Norman L. Eisen, E. Danya Perry, and Amy Lee Copeland to write as follows in the *New York Times* on February 17, 2023: "We need to prepare for a first in our 246-year history as a nation: The possible criminal prosecution of a former president. If Mr. Trump is charged, it will be difficult and at times even perilous for American democracy—but it is necessary to deter him and others from future attempted coups."[8] Ever defiant, Trump told the Conservative Political Action Conference (CPAC) on March 4, 2023, that he would stay a presidential candidate in 2024 even if he is criminally indicted, underscoring for his loyalists that "in 2016, I declared I am your voice. Today, I add: I am your warrior. I am your justice. And for those who have been wronged and betrayed: I am your retribution."[9] When CPAC adjourned, the Republican presidential nomination remained Trump's to lose.

As 2023 unfolded, the winter's breaking news included at least four more fact-clusters that keep the future of American democracy in suspense.

1. Concluding that the January 6, 2021, insurrection was centrally caused by "one man, former President Donald Trump, whom many others followed" and that "none of the events of January 6, would have happened without him," the United States House Select Committee on the January 6 Attack referred Trump to the Department of Justice for violating four statutes: obstructing an official proceeding, making false statements, defrauding the US, and inciting an insurrection.[10] The report showed how narrowly the United States escaped

6. Baker, "Story So Far."

7. See Paybarah, "Trump Warns."

8. Eisen et al., "It's Time to Prepare."

9. See Kornfield, "Trump Takes Victory Lap."

10. United States Congress, Select Committee, *January 6 Report*, 8. See also the critical analysis of this report in Lepore, "January 6th Report."

democracy's undoing. Blocking Trumpism's temptation to steal power by overriding fair and free elections cannot take place without indictment and conviction of Trump and his chief accomplices for crimes they have committed, but those outcomes are pending and may not arrive soon enough if at all.

2. MAGA Republican control of the US House of Representatives bodes ill for American democracy because the Republican Party, engulfed in failures of moral courage, continues to be an election-denying, insurrectionist-welcoming party of lies. Still in thrall to Trump, whose political violence-spawning Big Lie was accompanied by more than thirty thousand documented falsehoods during his presidency,[11] the GOP follows the classic authoritarian playbook: the aim is not only that people should accept lies as truths but also that they should be numbed by lie-driven chaos, engulfed in muddied waters, so that they stop trying to figure out and defend what's right and reject what's not. As the 2024 elections approach, the Republican Party has enough power, enough followers, and definitely enough lying and duplicity to diminish if not destroy American democracy.

3. No bastion of strength, the Democratic Party defends democracy but can scarcely be assured victory in 2024. The eightysomething Joe Biden has had notable accomplishments in his first presidential term. He is running for a second term, and he could prevail against Trump as he did in 2020, but how the aging Biden's health and his appeal against a different Republican nominee may fare in 2024 are fraught with uncertainty.

   MAGA Republicans sought to weaken Biden and vindicate Trump when it became known in early 2023 that Biden possessed a small number of classified documents, apparently inadvertently retained after he left the vice presidency in Barack Obama's administration. Republicans launched a cavalcade of whataboutism and "everybody-does-it" justifications to distract from Trump's felonious theft of such documents as he left the presidency in 2020 and to tar Biden with a criminal brush. The situation caused attorney general Merrick Garland to name Robert Hur, a Trump appointee, as special counsel to investigate whether Biden improperly handled classified material. The two cases are vastly different.[12] Biden made a mistake; Trump committed crimes. Matters were complicated further, however, when former vice president Mike Pence acknowledged that classified

11. Kessler, "Trump Made 30,573 False or Misleading Claims."

12. See Feldman, "Difference."

documents had been found at his Indiana home in mid-January 2023. As in Biden's case, the Pence misstep was inadvertent, not criminal. Nevertheless, these troublesome events added to the current president's vulnerabilities, and a compelling substitute for Biden in the 2024 presidential contest may not emerge.

Meanwhile, needing to defend twenty-three of the thirty-three seats up for election, Democrats have a steep 2024 climb to retain their narrow margin in the Senate. Republican-gerrymandered congressional districts ensure that Democrats also face daunting challenges to regain control of the House of Representatives. The Democrats may not have enough appeal and power to defend democracy sufficiently in the United States. The tangled web of politics and law shows that American democracy remains endangered as the 2020s continue to unfold.

4. The United States had a momentous day on Tuesday, April 4, 2023. It was the fifty-fifth anniversary of the assassination of Martin Luther King Jr., whose dream of an inclusive, pluralistic American democracy lives on too precariously. Vladimir Putin suffered a strategic defeat when Finland became the thirty-first member of NATO,[13] but the future of Ukraine and its democracy remains uncertain. In a high-stakes state supreme court contest, Wisconsin voters decisively elected Janet Protasiewicz, creating a liberal majority in that court for the first time in fifteen years. In addition to determining whether abortion will be legal in Wisconsin, Protasiewicz's election affects whether the Republican-gerrymandered political map prevails in a key midwestern swing state, an issue with national implications for the 2024 elections.[14]

On April 4, 2023, American attention riveted even more on the first-ever criminal indictment of a former or sitting president. It took place that Tuesday afternoon in a Manhattan courtroom, where Donald Trump pleaded not guilty to thirty-four felony counts of falsifying business records involving hush money payments to porn film star Stephanie Clifford (aka Stormy Daniels) during the 2016 presidential campaign.[15] Reactions from the legal community questioned the strength of district attorney Alvin Bragg's case, but Trump's lawyers will have to defend him against charges that he orchestrated an illegal conspiracy to win the presidency. Before and after the indictment, Trump viciously attacked Bragg, Judge Juan Merchan, and the

13. North Atlantic Treaty Organization (NATO), "Finland Joins NATO."

14. Epstein, "Liberal Wins Wisconsin Court Race."

15. Bromwich et al. "From President to Defendant."

legal system itself.[16] Despite claims that freedom of speech is at play, Trump may cross enough lines, including incitement of violence, that the court steps in and sanctions him.

Although trial in the Manhattan case is months away, that prospect is only one of Trump's legal woes. Atlanta district attorney Fani Willis may indict Trump for election subversion in Georgia. Special counsel Jack Smith may charge Trump with mishandling federal government documents and obstructing justice in the process. Most important of all, Trump could face federal indictment for attempting to subvert the 2020 presidential election, overturn that election's results, and incite insurrection against the United States.[17] None of these actions, however, could prevent Trump from running and even winning the 2024 election. Indeed, in the immediate aftermath of his April 4, 2023, indictment, Trump's fundraising soared and so did support from his MAGA Republican allies. As long as that enthusiasm lasts, American democracy will be endangered.

Focusing on portents about the 2024 American elections and beyond, we started writing this book in January 2022. That January 6, the one-year anniversary of the violent and seditious insurrection that Donald Trump unleashed on the nation's Capitol, the former president doubled down on the Big Lie that voter fraud stole the 2020 presidential election from him. A few days earlier, on January 3, Trump showed his fascist colors by endorsing the reelection of Viktor Orbán, the Hungarian dictator. With his Republican acolytes eagerly bending their knees to Trump's whims and wishes, antidemocratic authoritarianism was in full cry in the United States. We heard echoes of 1930s Germany and the widespread support that Adolf Hitler and his antisemitic Nazism enjoyed in the United States during that decade, a cautionary tale well-told in Rachel Maddow's 2022 *Ultra* podcast and by historians such as Bradley Hart.[18]

The investigative work of the Select Committee was underway as 2022 began. Its summer hearings showed how close the overthrow of the 2020 election had been, and how deeply Trump and his followers are implicated in disregard for the rule of law and disrespect for democracy itself. By then, Vladimir Putin's brazen invasion of Ukraine on February 24, 2022, added to democracy's peril. In early 2023 the battle lines in Ukraine resembled the trench warfare of World War I. The war in Ukraine, the worst on European soil since World War II, will not end anytime soon. As

16. Arnsdorf and Dawsey, "Trump Goes Silent, Then Seethes."

17. Graham, "Cases against Trump."

18. See Maddow, *Ultra*; Hart, *Hitler's American Friends.*

the 2024 elections approach, issues about American resolve against Russia and support for Ukraine will be on the ballot.

When the war began, Putin euphemistically termed his brutal invasion "a special military operation." It took him ten months to call it *war*. His brutal aggression—far exceeding what Republican presidential hopeful Ron DeSantis misguidedly called a "territorial dispute"[19]—is reminiscent of Adolf Hitler's ruthless invasion of Poland on September 1, 1939, which started World War II and the mass murder of Jews in eastern Europe. Nazi Germany murdered an estimated 1.5 million Ukrainian Jews, including thirty-four thousand in the shooting massacre at the Babyn Yar ravine near Kyiv on September 29 and 30, 1941. Before that, in 1932 and 1933, Joseph Stalin's reign of terror induced genocidal famine—the Holodomor (death by hunger), as Ukrainians call it—that starved about four million Ukrainians to death.[20] Using Hitler's and Stalin's playbook, by invading Ukraine the treacherous Putin embraces two of the most antidemocratic principles imaginable: might makes right, and let the strong take advantage of the weak. If Trump's and Putin's ways are allowed to prevail, the global post–Cold War security order will be upended. Democracy everywhere will be threatened.

Now in our eighties, we live a continent apart—Lenny in the suburbs of New York City, John on the eastern slope of the Cascade Mountains in rural Washington State. We do not meet in person as much as we used to, but deep friendship goes beyond that limitation. Zoom conversation and essay writing advance the inquiry we share. This book puts our dialogues together as written exchanges. We write in silence, but each hears the other's voice. What will Lenny think about John's reflections? What will John say about Lenny's? Present even when absent, we nudge each another.

The Auschwitz survivor Elie Wiesel wrote an essay called "My Teachers."[21] Nearly all of them were murdered in the Holocaust. Wiesel imagines one, the "Selishter Rebbe," peering over his student's shoulder to read what's being written. Does the writing enrich the world or impoverish it? That's what Wiesel hears his teacher asking him. Will the writing help to defend American democracy? With the Holocaust's warnings holding us accountable, that's the test that Lenny and John set for each other. That test includes a question that requires attention straightaway because it focuses on key words: What do we take the term *democracy* and the pronoun *we* to mean? Both words appear early and often; both are pivotal in our book's warnings.

19. Kinnard, "DeSantis Walks Back."

20. Ruane, "Cut Off from Food."

21. The essay appears in Wiesel, *Legends of Our Time*, 8–15.

As a form of national government, democracy requires institutions and procedures—for example, legislatures and courts, elections and laws—grounded in a country's people and the officials who represent them. The chapters that follow have much to say about the institutions and procedures of American democracy. That discussion entails two points—both elaborated in what's ahead—that are decisive for confronting the perils democracy faces in 2020s America. First, the institutions and procedures of democracy guarantee neither its health nor its survival. Long ago, Plato and Aristotle saw that democracy can degenerate into despotism and pave the way for tyranny. In what is called illiberal democracy or electoral authoritarianism, "freedom" is touted and traces of democracy remain, but not genuine liberty or democracy.[22] In illiberal democracies such as Putin's and Orbán's, parliaments exist but true political opposition does not. Elections are held but not with their outcomes contested and in doubt before the votes are cast and counted. Courts of law convene but without justice being done. Pluralism is excluded. Instead hostility to immigrants and LGBTQ+ rights combines with ethnic nationalism, closed borders, and privileged Christianity to produce an illiberal or nonliberal state.

Liberal democracy—that's what this book means by democracy—resists such perversions, but we don't overidealize it. Even where liberal democracy exists, wrongdoing intrudes and harm's way remains. Liberal democracy has to keep democratizing itself lest it lose vitality and direction. Liberal democracy's life depends on how well it protects liberty, honors the rule of law, insists on election integrity, and promotes inclusive pluralism, the ideal that community at its best supports and depends upon mutually respected expressions of life's variety—cultural, religious, political, and individual. No American writers captured the central importance of that pluralism better than the nineteenth-century poet Walt Whitman, whose "Song of Myself" had American democracy in mind when he said, "I resist anything better than my own diversity,"[23] and the Black novelist Ralph Ellison, whose eloquent epilogue to his prodigious novel *Invisible Man* (1952) sets the tone that defense of American democracy needs.

> Whence all this passion toward conformity anyway?—diversity is the word. Let man keep his many parts and you'll have no tyrant states . . . America is woven of many strands; I would recognize them and let it so remain. Its 'winner take nothing' that is the great truth of our country or of any country. Life is to be lived, not controlled; and humanity is won by continuing to

22. See Main, *Rise of Illiberalism*.

23. Whitman, "Song of Myself," 108.

> play in the face of certain defeat. Our fate is to become one, and yet many—This is not prophecy, but description.[24]

Success for the needed work requires being alert and prepared to cope with a persistent paradox: Democracy's existence invites its demise.[25] That's because popularly elected legislatures can enact laws that restrict and destroy human rights. That's because a democracy's courts can interpret the law in ways that undercut justice and trump the fundamental principle that no person is above the law. Democracy's paradox does not necessarily lead to democracy's destruction, but it does mean that democracy is vulnerable to antidemocratic power. Americans still have liberal democracy, flawed though it is. We, Lenny and John, defend such democracy because the United States could lose it, especially if we Americans take for granted that we won't. The threat intensifies because liberal democracy's prospects hinge on much more than institutions and procedures. Such awareness leads to the second point that is especially relevant for confronting endangered American democracy.

The institutions and procedures of democracy are only as good as the people who create, inhabit, use, and change them. Character counts. Ethics matters. For American democracy to succeed and flourish, people have to respect one another. They need to seek and tell the truth. They need to listen and learn from each other. They need to reject exclusion—racism, antisemitism, persecution of LGBTQ+ persons (more than three hundred anti-LGBTQ+ bills were introduced in our state legislatures in 2022 alone[26]), every form of supremacy—and embrace inclusive pluralism instead. They have to be courageous and just, as far as that is humanly possible. These insights mean understanding that key conditions necessary for democracy cannot be codified into laws and rules, at least not completely.

American democracy depends upon—indeed it is—a culture that fosters and is informed by good habits of conduct in our personal and communal lives, by sound social norms—be truthful, for example, and respectful toward others—that are not necessarily laws but important normative standards that govern how people should act. As the perceptive scholar-diplomat Richard Haass persuasively argues, healthy American democracy depends not only on defense of rights but also on responsibly meeting the obligations of citizenship and trying our best to live as

24. Ellison, *Invisible Man*, 577.

25. See Gershberg and Illing, *Paradox of Democracy*. See also Klein's podcast interview with Illing, "How We Communicate Will Decide Whether Democracy Lives or Dies."

26. Movement Advancement Project, *Under Fire*, 2.

good citizens ought to do. That work, he affirms, requires the cultivation of trustworthy habits: be well informed, for instance, promote the common good by caring about one's neighbors and fellow citizens, take an active part in our democracy, which means voting and then respecting the results of fair and free elections.[27] When such qualities grow, democracy changes for the better. When such qualities wither, democracy changes for the worse. Advancing liberal democracy takes determination because it is never fixed and secure. Democracy does not exist apart from change, but how it changes is the difference between its life and death. We Americans are the ones who determine how the process of democracy unfolds and where it ought to be going in the United States.

We are the ones—there's that fraught and fickle pronoun. American democracy's *we* is "we the people," who number 333 million, about 4.25 percent of the world's eight billion people. That American *we* includes every citizen of the United States. It confers responsibility, especially on those of voting age, to care about and look after the good of all Americans. Too often and for too long, however, American democracy's "we the people" have been antidemocratically exclusive. *We* entails *us*. Liberal democracy insists that the American *we* and *us* must be inclusive. "We the people" must commit to resisting threats that divide Americans into *we* and *they*, *us* and *them*. Liberal democracy's future depends on that commitment.

On March 4, 1861, with the eruption of the Civil War just a month away, Abraham Lincoln delivered his first inaugural address. It ended with these memorable lines, which are as timely now as they were then.

> We are not enemies, but friends. We must not be enemies. Though passion may have strained it must not break our bonds of affection. The mystic chords of memory, stretching from every battlefield and patriot grave to every living heart and hearthstone all over this broad land, will yet swell the chorus of the Union, when again touched, as surely they will be, by the better angels of our nature.[28]

Lincoln's eloquence could not prevent civil war. Americans were enemies then, and we dangerously see one another that way now. The better angels of our nature went missing in the 1860s. Where are they in the 2020s? Do mystic chords of memory exist and move us? What if they don't? Such questions are as unsettling as they are unsettled. We the people—we Americans now—have to decide whether we can be better than we have been, better than we have been thus far in the 2020s. This book argues for a changing,

27. See Haass, *Bill of Obligations*.

28. Lincoln, First Inaugural Address.

growing, pluralistic understanding and appreciation of *we* and *us*. It warns that American democracy is threatened to the extent that the people of the United States fail to move toward such an understanding.

As we, Lenny and John, reflect on these pivotal matters, Irish music enriches our friendship. We have traveled Ireland together to hear and feel it. That pursuit put us in contact with the legendary Irish musician Tommy Sands. For decades he has shown that fragile and seemingly powerless realities—his guitar, for example, and his voice singing songs that he recalls from the past or writes for the present and future—can be resilient sources of strength, inspiring commitment to deepen understanding, cultivate respect, and heal discord. Two hallmarks of his music, which played important parts in the 1990s peace process that calmed the violent Troubles long separating Protestants and Catholics in Northern Ireland, are persistence and inclusion.

Carry on, don't give up—that's one of Sands's refrains, as he sings for justice and peace.[29] Traditional Irish music, and Sands's versions of it are no exception, is scarcely triumphal. It assumes no guarantees that what is right and good will prevail. Lamenting the wounding and loss of life, yearning for conditions that preserve and sustain the good that people share, this music carries on by summoning resistance against the joy-robbing afflictions produced by disrespect for truth and justice and by exclusion that defaces respect and wrecks pluralism. Absent persistence that resists injustice and heals suffering, what Sands calls "the lonely years of sorrow" are likely to go on and on, leaving immense waste and no peace in their wake.[30]

Sands suggests that pluralism involves sharing stories—new and old.[31] Every American has stories to share. This book is full of them. Not all the stories, however, are good. The ones we need are those that affirm Sands's insight, which shows why democracy is as precious as it is necessary: "In the main," says Sands, "people are the same everywhere." They are "in search of love, friendship, laughter, intrigue and a rightful place in the Family of Man."[32] This book's understanding and defense of democracy head in those directions.

29. For more detail on Sands, see Sands, *Songman*, his autobiography. For Sands's commentary on his "carry on" lyric, see Sands, *Songman*, 252–57.

30. Sands, *Songman*, 256.

31. Sands, *Songman*, 256.

32. See the comments by Sands that accompany his album *Let the Circle Be Wide*.

1

The Eleventh Hour

ON THE EVENING OF Thursday, October 21, 2021, MSNBC's Brian Williams interviewed the novelist and political activist Don Winslow. "If you can picture the face of a clock," said Williams to Winslow, "and if midnight is the end of our democracy . . . what time is it right now?" Winslow responded: "11."[1]

Americans love democracy—except when we don't. The 2020s bring to mind the 1930s in Germany. Today democracy is under siege, just as it was then. In the 1930s, Nazis destroyed democracy in Germany. In the 2020s, democracy in America is tested more severely than it has been since the Civil War in the 1860s. Vladimir Putin's invasion of Ukraine in late February 2022 compounds the difficulties.

A January 3, 2022, poll of Americans conducted by National Public Radio and Ipsos found that "overall, 64% agree that American democracy is in crisis and at risk of failing. Even more, 70%, feel the same about America itself."[2] Some analysts think a new American civil war is coming, not like the one fought in the nineteenth century, but a twenty-first-century version akin to the Troubles that plagued Northern Ireland for thirty years in the late twentieth century.[3] Whether civil war happens or not, democracy will be on the ballot in the 2024 elections.

No American president's words are better known than Abraham Lincoln's Gettysburg Address, which he delivered on November 19, 1863. About four months earlier, in the stifling heat of July 1–3, thousands of Americans maimed and killed one another in the largest battle of the American Civil War. Lincoln's brief but memorable address began by remembering and idealizing the eighteenth-century founding of "a new nation, conceived in liberty,

1. See Williams et al., "Transcript."

2. NPR/Ipsos, "Seven in Ten Americans Say the Country Is in Crisis."

3. On these points, see, for example, Levitsky and Ziblatt, *How Democracies Die*; Marche, *Next Civil War*; Suri, *Civil War by Other Means*; Walter, *How Civil Wars Start.*

and dedicated to the proposition that all men are created equal."[4] The Battle of Gettysburg turned the tide against Confederate rebels, insurrectionists who denied that fundamental proposition and defended slavery instead, but Lincoln's tone on that November day in 1863 was scarcely triumphal. Serious and somber, Lincoln wondered whether "that nation, or any nation so conceived and so dedicated, can long endure." As he honored those who had given their lives to save the Union, not to fracture and destroy it, Lincoln urged commitment for Americans to do their best to ensure that the United States would have "a new birth of freedom, and that government of the people, by the people, for the people, shall not perish from the earth."

Lincoln's well-known cadence—of the people, by the people, for the people—sums up core meanings of democracy. In American democracy, those meanings prioritize fundamental equality of persons, which excludes discrimination based on race or ethnicity, religion or gender, economic class or sexual orientation. Moreover, democracy in America entails the right of citizens to vote in free and fair elections; voter suppression and fraud, including fraudulent claims that elections have been "rigged" or "stolen," should have no place in our system. In addition, democracy requires respect for the rule of law, conviction that no one is above the law, and rejection of minority or authoritarian control.

Work in Progress

Democracy in America has been and will remain a work (hopefully) in progress. The US Constitution was ratified in 1788, but it required amendments, ten of them—the Bill of Rights—in 1791. Slavery was not abolished until the 13th Amendment said so in 1865. Black Americans were denied citizenship until the Fourteenth Amendment removed that ban. Senators were not directly elected by the people in the state they represent until the Seventeenth Amendment established that requirement in 1913. American women did not get the right to vote until the Twentieth Amendment affirmed it in 1920. These changes did not come easily. "It's always been hard to amend the Constitution," says the historian Jill Lepore, because amending it "requires a double supermajority: an amendment introduced in Congress has to pass both houses by a two-thirds vote, and then must be approved by the legislatures of three-quarters of the states."[5] American constitutional democracy is further complicated as politics in the 2020s and beyond arguably renders the Constitution unamendable but not unchangeable. "Its meaning,"

4. Lincoln, Gettysburg Address.
5. Lepore, "Unamendable Constitution."

continues Lepore, "can be altered by the nine people who serve on the Supreme Court," the least democratic of our three branches of government. "They can't *rewrite* [the Constitution], but they can *reread* it."[6]

Debate and struggle about the future of liberal democracy in the United States intensify because the Constitution also enshrines both majority rule and minority rights. Tension results because majority rule can be unjust and oppressive. Constitutional provisions for freedom of speech and freedom of the press, for instance, guard against majority overreach and ensure that minority viewpoints can be expressed. A healthy liberal democracy tempers majority rule with respect for minority rights; it welcomes debate that seeks a trustworthy balance between these essential but often competing concerns and clashing interests. Such balance, moreover, does not confuse minority rights with minority rule, which can undercut democracy no less than tyranny of the majority.

Such insight reinforces recognition that at least five internal obstacles presently hinder the advancement of American democracy. The fact that their complete removal is unlikely, if not impossible, reveals that the founding of American democracy set up structures that were not democratic or friendly toward democracy's expansion.[7] Therefore, the work to democratize American democracy is never-ending.

The first obstacle is an archaic Electoral College system. It dishonors a fundamental principle of democracy—one person, one vote—permitting the American president to be elected by a minority of American voters. According to the constitutional requirements, Donald J. Trump, for example, was duly elected president in 2016 because he received 304 Electoral College votes cast by state electors to Hillary Clinton's 227. But the actual vote of the American people favored Clinton, who beat Trump by 2.9 million votes. If democracy is to advance in the United States, then American people, not an antiquated Electoral College system, should decide who serves as president. Liberal democracy means that the candidate with the most votes nationwide should be the presidential winner.

A second example shows further how the US Constitution problematically supports minority rather than majority rule. Each American state elects two senators. In 1787, James Madison argued that Senate representation should be based on population. Not only did he lose that debate, but also Article V of the Constitution meant that the rule—two senators for each state—was not subject to amendment: "no State, without its Consent,

6. Lepore, "United States' Unamendable Constitution" (italics original)

7. On this point, see Leonhardt, "Crisis Coming"; Menand, "American Democracy."

shall be deprived of its equal Suffrage in the Senate."[8] Those provisions favor land over people, because a senator from Vermont or Wyoming, for instance, represents about 623 thousand or 582 thousand persons, respectively, compared to one who represents California with a population of more than 39 million people or Texas with a population of more than 29 million. The combined population of North and South Dakota is less than 1.7 million. The city of Phoenix, Arizona, has more than that, but the Dakotas get four senators. Small-population states punch unfairly far above their weight when it comes to affecting policy.

Third, not for the first or last time the Supreme Court of the United States (SCOTUS) added to the tilt toward minority rule with its 5–4 decision in *Citizens United v. Federal Election Commission* (2010). It paved the way for massive spending by corporations and political action committees (PACs) to influence and corrupt election outcomes. Thanks to SCOTUS, "dark money," election-related spending from secret sources, has become the problematically legal coin of a realm that subverts democracy by skewing the election system to favor wealthy donors.

Fourth, the Senate's filibuster, long used to support racial segregation and inequality, requires a sixty-vote majority to end debate and move to a vote on legislation, which means that a small minority of senators can stop legislation from passing even if it has majority support. Fifth, minority rule also benefits from partisan gerrymandering of voting districts, a profoundly antidemocratic practice because it lets politicians choose their voters rather than voters choose their representatives.

Definitely not eternal, democracy in America has not been achieved, at least not enough. Indeed, American democracy can be its own worst enemy. Far from our "institutions will save us," as some pundits hoped when Trump and his followers took one "unprecedented" step after another to corrupt those institutions, Americans who care about democracy are learning to our anguish and sorrow how vulnerable and fragile it is. Even the rule of law can be used to undermine the rule of law. Such realizations intensify with the insight that at least three social conditions are essential for democracy to work and sustain itself: (1) Citizens must be as well educated as possible. (2) They must treat one another with civility and respect, especially when they deliberate, debate, and disagree. (3) They must have—and trust one another accordingly—representatives and leaders who truly act in the best interests of the nation and for the common good, not primarily for a political party, cultural tribe, or personal power and wealth.

8. On these points see Rakove, "James Madison's Critique."

These social conditions are immensely difficult to create and maintain because democracy is prone to what James Madison called "the violence of faction."[9] In *The Federalist Papers*, No. 10 (1787), he identified a faction as a group "united and actuated by some common impulse of passion, or of interest, adversed to the rights of other citizens, or to the permanent and aggregate interests of the community." Madison argued that ratification of the proposed Constitution of the United States of America could control the effects of faction, though it could not control its causes. Madison's eighteenth-century Enlightenment philosophy was too optimistic. George Washington, the first American president, sensed as much in his 1796 Farewell Address, warning "in the most solemn manner against the baneful effects of the spirit of party generally."[10] His rhetoric from times long gone nevertheless rings with authenticity and insight for the 2020s.

Washington saw that the dangers of hyperpartisanship are found in their "greatest rankness" in democracies. Even more than foreign threats, factions can be democracy's undoing. That's because "the disorders and miseries" resulting from such divisiveness incline people to welcome despotism and "to seek security and repose in the absolute power of an individual; and sooner or later the chief of some prevailing faction, more able or more fortunate than his competitors, turns this disposition to the purposes of his own elevation, on the ruins of public liberty." If partisan divisiveness is not discouraged and restrained, Washington added,

> It serves always to distract the public councils and enfeeble the public administration. It agitates the community with ill-founded jealousies and false alarms; kindles the animosity of one part against another, foments occasionally riot and insurrection. It opens the door to foreign influence and corruption, which find a facilitated access to the government itself through channels of public passion.

Urgent in the 1790s, when the United States was young, Washington's warnings are arguably more dire in the 2020s, when the country, battered and bruised, no longer is, if it ever was, the exceptional "shining city upon a hill" that Ronald Reagan's "morning in America" mythology promoted.[11] That problematic history includes the fact that American democracy wobbles in the 2020s because antisemitism and racism, including their cousins Christian nationalism and White supremacy, are resurgent.[12] Cloaked as ensuring

9. Madison, *Federalist Papers*, No. 10.
10. Washington, Farewell Address.
11. Reagan, "Farewell Address."
12. While affirming that race and ethnicity are human constructs, we—two White

election integrity in response to the Big Lie that the 2020 election was stolen, voter suppression and nullification loom large as Republican-controlled state legislatures, textbook factions that they are, enact one antidemocratic strategy after another to secure the minority rule they covet.

The Question Will Be Asked

Elijah Cummings, the son of Black sharecroppers, served Maryland's seventh congressional district with distinction from 1996 until he died at sixty-eight on October 17, 2019. "When we're dancing with the angels," he liked to say, "the question will be asked, . . . what did we do to make sure we kept our democracy intact?"[13] On October 25, 2019, some four thousand people, including former presidents Barack Obama and Bill Clinton, filled Baltimore's New Psalmist Baptist Church to pay him homage at a four-hour, nationally televised funeral. Donald Trump, president of the United States at the time, did not attend.

As Cummings knew, keeping American democracy intact is arduous work that has no inevitable positive conclusion. Evidence supporting that awareness and commitment lives in the fact that Americans use the numerical abbreviation 9/11 to remind them of the carnage inflicted by al-Qaeda on September 11, 2001, when terrorists hijacked four commercial airliners, flew two into the twin towers of the World Trade Center in New York City, and hurtled a third into the Pentagon outside Washington, DC. Heroic passenger intervention caused the fourth plane to crash in a field near Shanksville, Pennsylvania, before its target, the nation's Capitol, could be reached. The

---

American men—want to advance the increasingly widespread practice of capitalizing *White* when the term refers to a person's or group's racial or ethnic identity. That step does not imply esteem or pride let alone superiority or supremacy. Rather it supports what the Black sociologist Eve L. Ewing rightly underscores when she argues that Whiteness is "a specific social category that confers identifiable and measurable social benefits." One of the benefits is that White people can usually "move through the world without ever considering the fact of their Whiteness . . . White people get to be only normal, neutral, or without any race at all, while the rest of us are saddled with this unpleasant business of being racialized . . . When we ignore the specificity and significance of Whiteness—the things that it is, the things that it does—we contribute to its seeming neutrality and thereby grant it power to maintain its invisibility." Destabilizing such neutrality, exposing such invisibility, capitalizing *White* is a small but significant step toward the honesty and truth, the awareness and accountability that the defense and expansion of American democracy require. See Ewing, "Here's Why I Capitalize 'White.'"

13. As chair of the US House of Representatives Oversight Committee, Cummings made this statement on February 27, 2019, in his closing remarks after Michael Cohen, personal attorney for Donald Trump, gave testimony.

deadliest terrorist attacks on American soil in US history killed almost three thousand persons and injured twenty-five thousand more.

Two decades later, Americans have come to use another numerical abbreviation, 1/6, to remind them of the carnage inflicted by a mob of lethally armed American terrorists—insurrectionist, seditious, and White Christian nationalists—who, replete with antisemitic neo-Nazi insignias and Confederate flags as well as Christian crosses and Jesus Saves banners, stormed, looted, and desecrated the US Capitol, the hallowed center of American democracy, on January 6, 2021. The shock and shame of the heinous crimes committed that ominous day were compounded because the twice-impeached Donald Trump, now the first criminally-indicted former president as well, incited the mob as part of the coup attempt he fomented to overturn the election of Joseph R. Biden Jr. At that very time the US Congress was in session to certify the election that Biden won and that Trump decisively lost.

More than a dozen extremist groups—the Proud Boys, Three Percenters, and Oath Keepers prominent among them—led the violent charge that ravaged the Capitol; attacked, wounded, and killed police; and threatened members of Congress. Howls—"Hang Mike Pence"—resounded because the scarcely heroic vice president declined to do Trump's bidding to overturn the results of the presidential election, which Pence had no lawful power to do. Moreover, as the Select Committee to Investigate the January 6th Attack on the United States Capitol has documented, the insurrection was no one-off riot. At the very least, a "soft coup" to ensure continuation of Trump's authoritarian rule almost succeeded. It becomes increasingly clear that this criminal action was incited, planned, and orchestrated by Trump and his associates. Americans who care about democracy can take little comfort from the failure of sedition. Successful overthrow of democratic government was too close for that. Nor is the threat over. Far from it, January 6 may have been a dress rehearsal for worse to come.[14]

On Friday, January 20, 2017, in a sixteen-minute inaugural address after taking the oath of office to "preserve, protect and defend the Constitution of the United States," something he utterly failed time and again to do, Trump's jaundiced description—"American carnage"—cast his dystopian shadow on the country that would be under his administration: "Mothers and children trapped in poverty in our inner cities; rusted-out factories scattered like tombstones across the landscape of our nation, an education system, flush with cash, but which leaves our young and beautiful students deprived of knowledge, and the crime, and the gangs and

14. Incisive analysis on this point is provided by the *Atlantic*, January–February 2022, a special issue on American democracy in crisis, which features Gellman, "January 6 Was Practice."

the drugs that have stolen too many lives and robbed our country of so much unrealized potential." Insisting that "this American carnage stops right here and stops right now," Trump promised to make America strong again, wealthy again, proud again, safe again, "and yes," he concluded, "We will make America great again."[15]

Trump appealed especially to his much-touted "base," which mainly includes White Americans who feel aggrieved and see themselves downgraded from deserved dominance. But as far as making America great, Trump did no such thing. With his more than thirty thousand documented lies fueling chaos day in and day out, this Lord of the Lies, as he has been called,[16] ungraciously exited the White House on January 20, 2021.[17] He left the US deeply divided and the nation's health wrecked by his indifference and incompetence in the face of a global pandemic so that the resulting COVID-19 death toll was greater than four hundred thousand in one year—more fatalities than in the nation's entire World War II combat. An economy in ruins, hungry and undereducated children, democracy degraded, the rule of law disregarded, truth denied and disrespected—these failures, not greatness, are the legacy that Trump and his leadership cadre (as blind and corrupt as they are self-centered, cunning, and zealous) left the American people, conditions that Americans must acknowledge and correct if the country is to get back on a promising track again. Trump did all he could to "stop the steal" that he falsely alleged—and all too successfully led his followers to believe—had deprived him of a winning election and a second presidential term. In fact, election theft was Trump's intent, which was aided and abetted by too many Americans who knew better. Carnage—far from stopping it, Trump and his followers unleashed and increased it and often reveled in doing so.

Responding to Trump's carnage and to Cummings's question—"what did we do to make sure we kept our democracy intact?"—this book backs American democracy by recalling the Holocaust, a catastrophe laden with warnings that echo and exceed those laid out by Madison, Washington, and Lincoln. Vladimir Putin's unwarranted invasion of Ukraine compels attention too because his attack on democracy echoes Hitler's. If our insights help others to find and live out their own helpful answers to Cummings's query, the book will fulfill our hopes for it.

15. Trump, "Full Text [Inaugural Address]."

16. See Egan, "Lord of the Lies."

17. On Trump's lies, including his often-repeated Big Lie that the 2020 presidential election was fraudulent and stolen from him, see Kessler, "Trump Made 30,573 False or Misleading Claims."

Inquiry That Goes Deep Down

Life could have unfolded so that we—Lenny and John—never met. For almost fifty years, we were strangers. Our personal histories do not explain, at least not completely, how strangers became friends. But such narratives help to show why we are compelled to write about the Holocaust, Ukraine, and endangered American democracy.

We first met at Lessons and Legacies, a conference sponsored by the Holocaust Educational Foundation, which took place at Dartmouth College in early November 1994. Two years later, John was on a Fulbright fellowship in Norway when he saw an announcement about a project organized by Lenny and the theologian Henry (Hank) Knight. John applied to participate in a symposium on the Holocaust, which would create a group—international, interdisciplinary, interfaith, and intergenerational—convening biennially at Fairleigh Dickinson University's Wroxton College campus in Oxfordshire, England. The symposium's work has continued ever since it began in 1996. It deepened our relationship, which in these pages follows Elie Wiesel's insight that "the Holocaust demands interrogation and calls everything into question."[18] That injunction makes us ask: What needs to be done to revive, protect, and, if possible, expand democracy in 2020s America?" Americans need to ask that big question repeatedly and insistently. Small answers will not do.

Sound responses to imperiled democracy compel inquiry that goes deep down. Along with the Holocaust, Vladimir Putin's brutal and genocidal invasion of Ukraine drives that point home. Its ominous portents include a possible Third World War and threats of nuclear carnage. Ezra Klein's April 12, 2022, podcast interview with the Ukrainian philosopher Volodymyr Yermolenko sticks with us.[19] When Klein asked Yermolenko what it's like in Kyiv, a city that war changed overnight, the philosopher's simple and profound response was that "the meaning of things has changed." A window is no longer a window, he said, light is no longer light. Looking out a window can bring death from shelling. Keeping light on in the dark creates Russian targets. Time, Yermolenko told Klein, is no longer a menu from which you can choose this or that. A wrong decision can be your last. Likewise with space—for Ukrainians, said Yermolenko, it now has but two dimensions: where you are safe and where you are not. The word *home* can no longer mean a place to return to, because bombs have turned home to rubble.

18. Wiesel foreword to Cargas, *Shadows of Auschwitz*, ix.

19. Yermolenko, "Ezra Klein Interviews Volodymyr Yermolenko."

Democracy and the values that support and sustain it, the Ukrainian philosopher emphasized, must not be taken for granted. They must be protected, defended, fought for. And then in a sobering and challenging proposition, one that should give us Americans pause, he said: If you take democracy and its values for granted, "you no longer believe in them," because you aren't taking them seriously enough. In taking good things for granted, Yermolenko implied, we not only fail to grasp how fragile and precarious they are but we also show indifference toward them.

Elie Wiesel despised indifference. So do we because Wiesel was right when he said that indifference is "the epitome of evil. The opposite of love is not hate, it's indifference. The opposite of art is not ugliness, it's indifference. The opposite of faith is not heresy, it's indifference. And the opposite of life is not death, its indifference. Because of indifference, one dies before one actually dies."[20] The opposite of democracy, Wiesel might have added, is not tyranny, it's indifference. Because of indifference, democracy can die before it actually dies. Curbing and reversing indifference, producing care for and commitment to democracy instead, are work that entails honesty and modesty but also persistence and boldness. Probing and prodding, we—Lenny and John—urge each other to search and write in that way. To do that well, and to show how our questioning unfolds and where it leads, we have to recall further how life makes us the persons we are.

Lenny's Journey

During my time as a single parent of two children in the early 1970s, I met and married my beloved Susan and entered into a blended family with her and her two children. We have eight grandchildren and one great-grandchild. The lives of these children, their prospects for the future, do much to explain why I feel urgency about the health of democracy in 2020s America. But my family's history, the past as well as the present and future, also profoundly affects my concern about American democracy and my conviction that warnings from the Holocaust and Ukraine are ignored at our peril.

I was born in Bridgeport, Connecticut, on February 18, 1939. Less than three weeks before my birth, on January 30, 1939, Nazi Germany celebrated the sixth anniversary of Adolf Hitler's appointment as Germany's chancellor. By then democracy in Germany was dead. His speech to the nation on that occasion criticized "the whole democratic world," slurred Jews as parasites "living on the body and the productive work of other nations," and ominously proclaimed:

20. Wiesel, "One Must Not Forget," 68.

> Today I will once more be a prophet: If the international Jewish financiers in and outside Europe should succeed in plunging the nations once more into a world war, then the result will not be the Bolshevization of the earth, and thus the victory of Jewry, but the annihilation of the Jewish race in Europe![21]

Hitler was a false prophet about Jews plunging the nations once more into a world war. He did that, not the Jews, when he ordered Nazi Germany's army to invade Poland on September 1, 1939. But when Hitler spoke about the annihilation of the European Jews, he meant it. When tyrants and dictators issue threats—Putin or Hitler—they should be believed. Failure to believe dictators is naïve and deadly.

My father, Bernard (Ben) Grob, the oldest son in a Jewish family of six children, was an immigrant. In 1921, at the age of seventeen, he arrived in the United States via Ellis Island from Stanisławów, a district capital in the Polish province of Eastern Galicia at the time. Now a city in Ukraine called Ivano-Frankivsk, it was attacked in Vladimir Putin's invasion in late February 2022. Jews had been in Stanisławów since the seventeenth century. At the time of my father's departure, about 15,800 Jews lived in Stanisławów, 30 percent of its population of fifty-one thousand.[22] The city was annexed to the Soviet Union in September 1939 after the Germans invaded western Poland and the Soviets advanced into eastern Poland, part of the deal brokered in the Molotov-Ribbentrop Pact (on August 23, 1939) that partitioned (dismembered) that country.

On June 22, 1941, Hitler's army launched Operation Barbarossa, the code name for a massive invasion of the USSR. By the end of that July, the Germans occupied Stanisławów, which meant that my father would be the sole member of his family to have escaped the Holocaust. His parents, five siblings, nephews, nieces, cousins were murdered there in early 1942. Stanisławów was liberated by Soviet troops on July 27, 1944. By that time, however, very few of the city's Jews were alive. Hitler's threat in 1939, a death sentence for members of my family and for millions of other Jews, was a dire consequence of the Nazi destruction of democracy in Germany.

My father met my mother in Bridgeport, when he made a delivery to the family's store where she was clerking. My mother, Lillian (Lilly), was also an immigrant, having arrived in the US from Vilna, Lithuania, at age two. I was the second child born to Ben and Lilly; my sister, Anita, had arrived seven years earlier. My family observed Jewish rituals, and I was

21. Hitler, "Speech to the Reichstag."

22. For more detail on Stanisławów, see the *Holocaust Encyclopedia* entry on the United States Holocaust Memorial Museum website.

exposed from an early age to synagogue and study of traditional Hebrew texts. Summers at a Hebrew-speaking camp and a year's grant to study in Israel at age nineteen followed. I thought about entering the rabbinate, but my study of philosophy at Yale College proved more compelling. I headed toward an academic career.

Pursuing existentialist thought, I earned my PhD at Pennsylvania State University and began forty years of teaching at Fairleigh Dickinson University (FDU) in New Jersey. There I served for extended periods as chairperson of the philosophy department and as director of FDU's interdisciplinary Humanities Core Program. I became passionate about the work of two twentieth-century Jewish existentialist thinkers, Martin Buber and Emmanuel Levinas, both of whom emphasized the importance of a life of dialogue. I published numerous articles on their philosophies, several dealing with nonviolence and education for peace.

In 1989, I took a "roots journey" to Eastern Europe to see for myself the sites of the destruction of my father's family, all shot in one day on the streets of Stanisławów. I recalled Ben Grob's oft-repeated wish to return to the city and weep on the soil where his family was murdered. My father never got the opportunity to return to Ukraine; I went there to realize his dream. Having located the home where Ben grew up, I wrote the names of family members on a piece of paper and tied the note around stems of flowers that I then placed on a windowsill of the home. There had been no funeral for these murdered ones; I had come to name the dead.

That experience took me into the field of Holocaust studies. My Holocaust-related writing, including three books coedited with John, focuses on ethics and education. My reflection underscores the Holocaust's implications for life today, including their significance for democracy. Many of the most meaningful contributions I have made to Holocaust education resulted from cofounding the Holocaust Symposium at Fairleigh Dickinson's Wroxton College, Oxfordshire, UK, where, for more than twenty-five years, thirty-six scholars from eight countries have met biennially, often collaborating on projects during the months between symposia.

Symposium sessions emphasize democratic pedagogies that feature dialogue in small group settings. Cofounder Henry Knight and I endeavored from the outset to create a community of scholars committed to return to Wroxton College every two years and to use the gatherings to generate projects for long-term collegial work. Eleven books have been published by our members thus far, most of them edited volumes in which five to twelve scholars have participated. Members continue to visit one another's universities either in person or virtually in the periods between symposia. Most important, our aim from the start has been to explore how we students of the Holocaust could realize lessons of the Holocaust leading us to work for *tikkun olam*, healing the world. Safeguarding our currently imperiled democracy is most certainly a key part of the healing process.

In the early 1990s, I was introduced to the work of an Israeli scholar-activist who used Buber's philosophy to advance a dialogue project involving Israeli Jewish and Israeli Arab high school students. Participating in that project deeply moved me. The experience led to devoting much of my scholarly work to ideas and projects aimed at resolution of the Israeli-Palestinian conflict. My Holocaust studies have provided necessary background for key aspects of this work; memory of the genocide of the Jews strongly informs Israeli political thought. Although yearning to return to historic Palestine has millennia-old roots in the ethos of the Jewish people, the State of Israel was born, in some substantial sense, of the destruction of two-thirds of European Jewry. In several of my publications, I ask how lessons of the Holocaust have helped shape Israel's dominant narrative, but also how those lessons can help Jews and Palestinians forge a peace that realizes self-determination for two peoples in a land both call home.

My writings in this area include *Teen Voices from the Holy Land: Who Am I To You?*, coauthored with a Palestinian American colleague. Mahmoud Watad and I interviewed thirty-four Israeli and Palestinian teens, asking them about relationships with parents, friends, school, sports, music—all elements of their daily lives. As we expected, commonalities unfolded. We helped put a human face on the other—in this case the other-as-enemy. Humanizing the other, however different from oneself, is a key element and aspiration for a democratic society.

For more than fifteen years I have served as assistant director of the Peace Consultancy (https://www.peaceconsultancy.org/), an NGO devoted to resolution of the Israeli-Palestinian conflict. In particular, my work brings peace proposals to the attention of United Nations ambassadors and their deputies. Peace Consultancy director Jerome Segal and I have found a welcoming of ideas that bridge formidable gaps in the positions of the two parties. Meeting with hundreds of diplomats through the years, I am committed to sowing seeds of hope in this seemingly intractable conflict.

All of this work involves dialogue, free and open exchanges, explorations of disagreements, and searches for common ground and communal good. Those qualities are essential for democracy. Wherever they are in short supply, as they were in Nazi Germany in the 1930s, as they are in Putin's Russia and now in the United States in the 2020s, democracy cannot thrive. When it doesn't, the consequences, as my family's history shows, are lethal.

John's Story

Like Lenny's father, my ancestors came to the United States from Europe. But the differences in those stories are more striking than the similarities. My Christian forebears—Scots-Irish Quakers and German pietist pacifists from Alsace-Lorraine—crossed the Atlantic in the mid-nineteenth century. My family tree contains no Holocaust victims or survivors, but family historians think that it may include Jewish branches.

I was born in Grand Haven, Michigan, on September 3, 1940. My father, Josiah, was a Presbyterian minister. My mother, Doris, and older sister, Muriel, were accomplished musicians. On my birthday, a Tuesday, the *New York Times* headlined two events. First, large formations of Nazi planes continued to bomb England as air raid sirens wailed in London during the Blitz, part of the Battle of Britain. By that time in 1940, Nazi Germany had not occupied Stanisławów, but most of the western European continent was under the swastika, and Hitler aimed to dominate the United Kingdom as well. The United States helped British resistance to the Nazi onslaught but did not enter the war completely until the Japanese attacked Pearl Harbor on December 7, 1941.

The second story the *Times* featured on September 3, 1940, focused on the speech that Franklin D. Roosevelt, the American president, had delivered the day before at the Labor Day dedication of the Great Smoky Mountains National Park.[23] Speaking at Newfound Gap, the main crest of the mountains that serves as a boundary between Tennessee and North Carolina, FDR called for national unity against Nazism, which had mounted, he said, "the greatest attack that has ever been launched against freedom of the individual." He also warned about an "enemy at home." He condemned "the mean and petty spirit that mocks at ideals, sneers at sacrifice and pretends that the American people can live by bread alone." Defense of democracy was on Roosevelt's mind as his speech echoed the oath that all Americans need to take and fulfill: namely, to "support and defend the Constitution of the United States against all enemies, foreign and domestic."

Born in the late Michigan summer of 1940, I have few firsthand recollections of World War II and none of the Holocaust. I can remember the ration books that my musical mother needed to buy sugar and shoes. My father grew vegetables in a "victory garden." I can recall that the family car had the windshield sticker required for regulated gasoline purchases. My mind's eye retains dim visions of strangely clothed men working in the countryside. My father told me they were German prisoners of war. A

23. Roosevelt, "Address at Dedication."

radio broadcast in August 1945 stands out because my parents listened to it so intently. It announced the August 6 dropping of the atomic bomb on Hiroshima, Japan.

At the age of five, I knew no living Jews, but biblical people—Abraham and Moses, Rachel and Ruth, David and Jonathan, Joseph and Mary, Jesus and his followers—were vivid in the Bible stories that my parents read to me each wartime night before I fell asleep. I knew about the Ten Commandments and the idea that we should love our neighbors as ourselves long before I had heard of Treblinka or Auschwitz, Ukraine, crimes against humanity, and genocide. Those biblical narratives—the people and teachings they contain—made deep and lasting impressions upon me.

Educated in public schools in Michigan, Indiana, and California, I graduated from Pomona College in 1962, and then spent a year at Yale Divinity School, where I considered following in my father's footsteps by entering the ministry. But just as Lenny considered the rabbinate only to be lured into an academic career in philosophy, I too loved that discipline, and after taking my PhD in philosophy at Yale University in 1966, I taught philosophy at Claremont McKenna College for more than forty years.

When I was a young professor, my philosophical work was deeply influenced by American thinkers such as Josiah Royce, John Dewey, and especially William James, whose lifelong conviction held that "philosophical study means the habit of always seeing an alternative, of not taking the usual for granted, of making conventionalities fluid again, of imagining foreign states of mind."[24] I share that outlook. Its insight serves democracy; its challenges keep me going.

Those challenges led me to teach an annual Claremont McKenna course called Perspectives on the American Dream. Black voices nudged me in that work, especially what I heard in the poetry of Langston Hughes, who sounded themes Americans always need to hear and heed. In his 1938 poem "Let America Be America Again," Hughes indicated that America never was America to him.[25] But the poem swears that America will be. The dream of America, Hughes affirms, lies deep in his heart.

Infused with the hopes and challenges of democracy, the American Dream is nowhere envisioned better and inspired more compactly and indispensably than in the preamble to the American Constitution:

> We the People of the United States, in Order to form a more perfect Union, establish Justice, insure domestic Tranquility, provide for the common defense, promote the general Welfare,

24. James, "Teaching of Philosophy," 178.
25. Hughes, "Let America Be America Again," 348–50.

> and secure the Blessings of Liberty to ourselves and our Posterity, do ordain and establish this Constitution for the United States of America.[26]

When Hughes said that America's dream lies deep in his heart, it lived in him with persistence and resistance, because the dream also kept lying there—not telling the truth, often intending not to do so, or at least not succeeding soon enough, faithfully enough, to make good on its promise. So, Hughes rightly implied, Americans have to remake America by redeeming, defending, and expanding democracy.

Early on, the Holocaust had affected me through the writings of Richard Rubenstein, especially his *After Auschwitz*, which I read shortly after its publication in 1966. Not until I read Elie Wiesel, however, did my life take the Holocaust turn that changed me personally and professionally. The change began in earnest during the summer of 1972 when I followed the suggestion of the late Frederick Sontag, my Pomona College philosophy teacher and ever since my special friend and colleague. Sontag thought I would find it worthwhile to read Wiesel's writings. Without knowing what awaited me, I bought some of Wiesel's books, and started to read them a few days after my second child, Sarah, was born on the Fourth of July, American Independence Day, which celebrates democracy. Circumstances, emotions, and words conspired to make that reading experience the most intense of my life. In two weeks, I read all of Wiesel's books that had thus far been published in English. The collision I experienced then between my good fortune—fatherhood, living my version of the American Dream, a promising academic career in a country where democracy is taken too much for granted—and the destruction of family, opportunity, justice, and hope explored in Wiesel's Holocaust reflections left lasting marks upon me.

Writing is important to me. One reason is that neither the Holocaust nor the war in Ukraine started with shooting, gassing, or missile strikes. Those onslaughts began with words—lying, antisemitic, antidemocratic words. Elie Wiesel warned, "Be careful with words."[27] Words can be dangerous; they can lead to human rights abuses and to indifference. Words can incite violence and insurrection. Words can kill, and their victims can include democracy. Conspiracy theories, arrogant boasts, lies big and small—they could scarcely exist without words, without speeches and rallies, writings and media that promote and spread them. Speaking and writing, our uses of words, are choices with responsibilities; they are ethical acts and too often immoral deeds. Do our words deceive, betray, rewrite history falsely, incite

26. Constitution of the United States.

27. See, for example, Wiesel, "My Teachers," 14.

ruinous insurrection, and undermine trust, or do they respect and communicate what is true, just, good, and right? Anyone who loves democracy does well to remember and heed the counsel of the biblical psalmist: "Let the words of my mouth and the meditation of my heart be acceptable to you, O Lord, my rock and my redeemer" (Ps 19:14). The lies of Hitler and Putin, the falsehoods of Trump and his acolytes disrespect those words and mock God. But it is up to truly democracy-loving Americans to vow that Saint Paul was right when he wrote, "Do not be deceived; God is not mocked, for you reap whatever you sow . . . So let us not grow weary in doing what is right, for we will reap at harvest-time, if we do not give up" (Gal 6:7, 9).

Among the many books I have written or edited, a recent one is called *Sources of Holocaust Insight*. It recognizes people who have profoundly influenced the learning and teaching about the Holocaust that I have been doing for more than fifty years. My parents, Doris and Josiah, top that list. Dedicated to them, *Sources of Holocaust Insight* is also for my students, who have taught me in irreplaceable ways. Support, inspiration, love—those gifts, sources of deep insight, have been abundantly bestowed upon me, day in and day out, by my wife, Lyn, my children, Andy and Sarah, and their spouses, Liz and Erik, and by a most special person, my granddaughter, Keeley Brooks. The nourishing presence of all of these people in my life is inseparable from American democracy. My love for all of them requires me to care about democracy too. The older I get, the more I do.

What's Next in the Eleventh Hour?

On Thursday, December 9, 2021, seven weeks after his interview with Don Winslow, Brian Williams concluded his twenty-eight-year career at NBC News with a final newscast on the nightly program aptly titled *The 11th Hour*. Williams's three-minute farewell echoed the theme that the United States is indeed in the eleventh hour of a severely threatened democracy whose flourishing cannot be taken for granted. Setting off, as he said, "into the great unknown, . . . for the first time in my sixty-two years, my biggest worry is for my country." Williams continued:

> The truth is I am not a liberal or a conservative. I am an institutionalist. I believe in this place, and in my love of country I yield to no one. But the darkness on the edge of town has spread to the main roads and highways and neighborhoods. It is now at the local bar and the bowling alley, at the school board and the grocery store. And it must be acknowledged and answered for. Grown men and women, who swore an oath to our Constitution—elected by their

> constituents, possessing the kind of college degrees I could only dream of—have decided to join the mob . . . while hoping we somehow forget who they were. They've decided to burn it all down with us inside. That should scare you to no end . . . I will wake up tomorrow in the America of the year 2021—a nation unrecognizable to those who came before us and fought to protect it, which is what you must do now.[28]

The year 2021 has come and gone. So have the 2022 midterm elections. But as the 2024 American elections come close, too little about our democracy has changed for the better. Ticktock—still in the eleventh hour, but with its minutes fleeting, we are close to midnight.

We Americans may assume that democracy is our heritage and birthright. But good things should never be taken for granted. Too many of us are bystanders if not sleepwalkers while democracy is in peril. We—Lenny and John—ask each other: How can we help to arouse our country in time? Maybe it's too late, but if not, could our writing, our dialogical exchanges still try to break through amid lying, disinformation, and disrespect for evidence that let chaos and carnage have their way? How well writers respond to that challenge affects democracy and the human future. Even aging philosophers in their personal eleventh hours must do their part to meet it.

President Joe Biden likes to say, "We are the United States of America. And there's nothing we can't do if we do it together." That optimism promises too much. But if we Americans get together enough, and stand firm with our allies, we can save and repair our democracy and perhaps the world's as well. So let's see what's next.

28. See Schwartz, "Brian Williams Channels Frank Sinatra."

2
Philosophy

No one did more than Socrates to create the discipline of philosophy. In Plato's *Republic*, for example, Socrates argued that it's bad, even evil, to be deceived or to deceive others about truth. Just the opposite, it's good and right to know and defend what is true. Knowing the truth, he added, means knowing things as they really are. Socrates set exacting standards. He believed that the quality and future of human life depend on commitment to meet them. Friendship grew among those who joined that journey with him. We, Lenny and John, are evidence of that, for philosophy, the search for truth and the love of wisdom, started and sustains our friendship.

Socrates showed that sound inquiry—and good friendship too—depends on dialogue. He added that dialogue requires what he called *dialectic*. The core of the "Socratic method," dialectic is the disciplined and sustained use of questioning, responding, and questioning some more. It reveals the difference between insight and blindness, discernment and dogmatism, intelligence and stupidity. Dialectic's rhythm is philosophy's heartbeat. Such inquiry weighs the strengths and weaknesses of different views. It aims at a more balanced and complete perspective than one's starting points or initial assumptions provide. One can practice the Socratic method in dialogue with others or oneself. Either way, such inquiry pursues truth but stays humble about possessing it. Errors and mistakes are common; there's always more to find out. Disagreements arise, but the Socratic counsel says, Keep as calm and cool as possible. Let the debate unfold. Keep testing what is said. Follow where questioning and evidence lead. Don't give up.[1]

Insistence on inquiry aimed at advancing awareness about what is true and what is not takes courage because it's not easy to admit that one is wrong or to show that others are mistaken. But seeking and loving truth often requires doing just that. Seeking and loving truth can be as dangerous as it is difficult. Socrates challenged assumptions and beliefs

1. Helpful reflection on these themes is found in Farnsworth, *Socratic Method*.

that powerful authorities preferred to leave uncriticized. He unmasked pretense, uncovered confusion, undermined dogmatism, undid false certitude, and, in general, left little unexamined. That work cost Socrates his life. Philosophers like us do not face trial and execution as Socrates did, but our post-Holocaust work isn't likely to be comforting because it questions fond hopes, criticizes cherished assumptions, and intensifies calls for human responsibility and accountability. If such probing isn't popular, that's all the more reason it can't be ignored with impunity.

In 2017, the insightful Russian American journalist and scholar Masha Gessen published an important book about the resurgence of totalitarianism in post–Cold War Russia. Gessen called it *The Future Is History*. That paradoxical title is both arresting and ominous. The phrase could suggest that the future is bleak if it can be said to exist at all. When we say that something, including the future, is history, that's often what is meant. But the idea that the future is history could also mean that the future isn't future at all because it has already happened. We've seen this movie before, as the saying goes. It's not that history repeats but that its basic narrative, its patterns and pitfalls recur in discouraging ways. In either or both of those senses, what if democracy's future is history?

Ours is a post-Holocaust future. It is inseparable from that genocidal catastrophe and its ongoing reverberations. Ours is an American future. It is inseparable from Trumpism's antidemocratic and seditious threats. Ours is also a Ukrainian future. It is inseparable from Vladimir Putin's corrupt and corrupting power, which cannot be assumed to stop short of unleashing chemical-biological or nuclear war. If Ukraine falls, Putin's autocracy gains, democracy loses, and the world's safety declines.

Once 1984 was in the future, and George Orwell's *1984* could be read that way. But his dystopian cautionary tale has an image that shows what could happen if the future is history. Winston Smith, the novel's protagonist, thought that a man named O'Brien was his friend, but that trust shattered when the "friend" revealed himself to be a cunning agent of the Thought Police. Specializing in betrayal and domination, O'Brien rebutted Winston's hope that "the spirit of Man" will prevail. "If you want a picture of the future," O'Brien told Winston, "imagine a boot stamping on a human face—forever."[2]

In Orwell's fictional land of Oceania, no aim of the regime is more important than stopping people from thinking, which entails suppression of questioning. So the Ministry of Truth asserts mind-numbing slogans

2. Orwell, *1984*, 220.

that dictate the truths that must be embraced: War Is Peace. Freedom Is Slavery. Ignorance Is Strength.[3]

In the 2020s, it's worth recalling some of the mind-numbing propositions, akin to those advanced by Oceania's Ministry of Truth, that have jeopardized democracy. Adolf Hitler (in his June 22, 1941, announcement of Nazi Germany's "Operation Barbarossa" invasion of the Soviet Union): "The purpose of this front is no longer the protection of the individual nations, but rather the safety of Europe, and therefore the salvation of everyone."[4] Donald Trump (on December 2, 2020): "This election [2020] was rigged. Everybody knows it."[5] Trump again (on February 22, 2022): "I went in yesterday and there was a television screen, and I said, 'This is genius.' Putin declares a big portion of the Ukraine—of Ukraine—Putin declares it as independent. Oh, that's wonderful. He used the word 'independent' and 'we're gonna go out and we're gonna go in and we're gonna help keep peace.' You gotta say that's pretty savvy."[6] Vladimir Putin (on February 21, 2022): "A stable statehood has never developed in Ukraine . . . Russia has always advocated the resolution of the most complicated problems by political and diplomatic means, at the negotiating table."[7] Three days later Russia invaded Ukraine, the action called "a special military action" but not a war. At that time in Russia, calling Putin's war on Ukraine a war was to risk a long prison term.

If the future is to be more than history, if the future is to include hopeful possibility and resilient democracy, philosophy and philosophers have work to do. That work includes fact-checking to show how statements like the ones above from Hitler, Trump, and Putin are at odds with reality. At least for American philosophers, it also should include remembering that Donald Trump became president of the United States partly because Vladimir Putin launched cyberwar to help Trump win and thereby to advance Russian intentions to destroy our democracy and our country, goals that became Trump's as well.[8] So American philosophers should also boldly express thanks that Donald Trump is not president of the United States, affirming that he must never be again, as his friend Putin seeks to bring Ukraine and democracy to their knees. But the work goes deeper and further than that. Philosophy needs to show what it means, what is lost, if the

3. Orwell, *1984*, 7.
4. Hitler, "Führer to the German People."
5. Rucker, "Trump Escalates Baseless Attacks."
6. Bump, "'Genius,' 'Savvy.'"
7. Putin, "Address by the President of the Russian Federation."
8. See Jamieson, *Cyberwar*; Mayer, "How Russia Helped."

words above from Hitler, Trump, and Putin are acceptable and accepted. It needs to show what must change and be different if lies, disinformation, and untruth are to be curbed, and if honesty, lucidity, and truthfulness are to have the respect they deserve. Philosophy needs to show what the future can be if people reject historical inevitability and its illusions about automatic progress and national exceptionalism and instead embrace the truth that John Lewis, the American civil rights leader, saw when he said that "democracy is not a state. It is an act."[9] That responsibility's weight may be more than philosophy can bear. But true philosophers never give up, and that's what our friendship helps us to do.

Lenny's Reflections

In the fall of 1994, I attended a conference of Holocaust scholars at Dartmouth University. John Roth, a fellow philosopher studying the Holocaust, was one of the speakers. Having read some of his works but never having met him face-to-face, I was eager to hear him. In the course of his presentation. John spoke words that addressed me directly: "I am a better philosopher for being a Holocaust scholar."[10] I had experienced the same sentiment after entering the field of Holocaust studies. At the close of John's talk, I told him exactly that. Collaboration, up to and including our coauthoring this book, soon began.

Not only am I a better philosopher for being a Holocaust scholar, but the converse is also true: I am a better Holocaust scholar for being a philosopher. I will try to elucidate these claims and argue that post-Holocaust philosophical thinking can help preserve democracy in the face of the attacks leveled against it in the 2020s.

The relative silence of academic philosophers in the face of the Holocaust is deafening. Allegedly committed to the Socratic imperative to lead an examined life, philosophers have too often gone about their business as if the genocidal events that bloodied the twentieth century, and still loom large in the twenty-first, had never occurred. This is not to say that no philosophers have addressed the evil of the Holocaust. Emil Fackenheim, for example, argued that the Holocaust calls on the discipline to reexamine itself. The

9. Lewis, "Together, You Can Redeem the Soul of Our Nation." Lewis wrote this posthumously published essay shortly before he died on July 17, 2020.

10. Roth made this comment in the discussion following presentations during the Lessons and Legacies panel on Disciplinary Reflections. For Roth's presentation, see Roth, "Holocaust and Philosophy."

Holocaust, he said, is "the rupture that ruptures philosophy."[11] With regard to ethics, the philosopher-theologian Irving Greenberg echoes Fackenheim's thinking: "Neither faith nor morality can function . . . unless they are illuminated by the fires of Auschwitz and Treblinka."[12]

Some other contemporary philosophers have taken their discipline to task for its silence about the Holocaust. Wendy C. Hamblet, executive director of Philosophers Concerned for Peace, summons her fellow philosophers to radically rethink their discipline. She asks a seminal question: "How is it that the philosopher, physician of the soul, has . . . proven impotent in healing the misery, brutality and decadence that characterizes human existence?"[13] In other words, traditional philosophy has not adequately addressed evil in general or, in particular, evil writ large in the Holocaust.

Post-Holocaust philosophers have often neglected to examine how traditional ethics failed to prevent Germany, deemed a beacon of Enlightenment values, from becoming the nation that perpetrated the Holocaust. And America is not impervious to threats to democracy that have often become a prelude to genocide. Many in the United States too easily assume that the underpinnings of democracy provided by the country's founders are a sufficient bulwark against democracy's dismantling. Trumpist attacks not only on Democratic rivals *but on truth itself* show how naïve and unthinking were those of us who assumed that our founders' democratic principles would be forever safe and sound.

The philosopher Emmanuel Levinas, a Jew who did forced labor under the Nazis as a French prisoner of war, and whose Lithuanian family—almost all—were murdered during the Holocaust, has been unsparing in taking the measure of his discipline in light of its virtual silence about the Holocaust. Levinas takes the traditional translation of the Greek *philosophia*, "the love of wisdom," and turns it around: he says that philosophy, at root, is "the wisdom of love."[14] Instead of agreeing that the traditional belief that metaphysics—the quest for theory that explains all that exists—is the core of philosophy, Levinas argues that ethics must take its place as "first philosophy." Philosophy, in his view and in my own, stresses inquiry about how we can live well with one another. With its fundamental emphasis on dialogue, philosophy can guide us toward peacemaking, supplying a model for resolving the conflicts that arise among individuals and communities. Egoist

11. Fackenheim, *To Mend the World*, 266. For further discussion about philosophy and the Holocaust, see Roth, "Ethics"; and Roth, ed., *Genocide and Human Rights*.

12. Greenberg, "Cloud of Smoke, Pillar of Fire," 22.

13. Hamblet, "Pathological Goodness," 172–73.

14. Levinas, *Otherwise Than Being*, 162.

inclinations—common to us all—need correction by philosophy's call for humility, summoning us to honor the personhood of one another in the face of today's rampant racism and the "othering" championed by Trumpism. The Holocaust warns us what can happen when dialogue is abandoned and antidemocratic power rejects and replaces it. Absent dialogical thinking, the odds favor autocracy's assault on democracy. Trumpism, even without Trump, signals authoritarian rule.

My life as a philosopher has been heavily influenced by Levinas's endeavor to transform the ethical sensibilities of his readers. That work, he says, "is dominated by the presentiment and memory of the Nazi horror."[15] In his view, traditional philosophy-as-metaphysics has not only failed to address the Holocaust; it may have fostered a mode of thinking that aids domineering and even genocidal modes of thought. This dramatic assertion rests on the claim that from Aristotle to Hegel and beyond, Western philosophy has tried to comprehend *all that exists* within its conceptual structures. In other words, traditional philosophers have most often tried to understand *everything*—the totality of existence. But this totalizing aim of philosophy can make philosophers perversely godlike in their ambition to grasp all that is. Totalizing can sometimes turn into totalitarianism. We are familiar with overarching ideological schemas in which others are subsumed under categories of thought such as "the enemy." After that, it's a short step to denigrate these others as less than human—as "vermin," for example, or as "viruses," and "lives unworthy of living" Such Nazi designations mattered; they led to genocide. Levinas reminds us that philosophy has to rethink itself. It has to become post-Holocaust philosophy that insists on the inviolable personhood of others.

I am a better philosopher not simply because I have chosen to study ethics, but because I keep listening to the voices of Holocaust victims. They summon me to examine my own conduct as well as society's. Philosophy that summons in this way can help us to address the current evils besetting America. As a teacher of philosophy and a scholar writing articles and books, I can help my students and readers to discern current threats to democracy. As a philosopher committed to "ethics as first philosophy," I am inspired by the voices of Holocaust victims to keep embracing and practicing dialogue. Thus inspired, I can try my best to embody and model the values of a democratic society so imperiled in present-day America.

15. Levinas, *Difficult Freedom*, 291.

John's Questions

We philosophers often have high estimates of ourselves. Philosophy—understood either as the love of wisdom or, as Emmanuel Levinas suggests, the wisdom of love—depicts itself as occupying high moral ground. Philosophers tend to see themselves—I include myself in these judgments—as extending a tradition that serves free inquiry and honors truth, goodness, beauty, justice, and democracy. But as you rightly underscore, philosophy has darker dimensions, and philosophers have been less than forthcoming about them. Philosophy and philosophers, the Holocaust and Vladimir Putin's unwarranted, brutal, and nuclear-war-threatening invasion of Ukraine, Trumpism and diminished American democracy—these realities coexist. But philosophy and philosophers do not always oppose, at least not sufficiently, power that corrupts and kills. That indictment and the challenge it puts before philosophers and philosophy in the 2020s lead to three threads that I hope you will follow with me.

First, we agree that studying the Holocaust makes us better philosophers, and we also think that we are better scholars and teachers about that catastrophe and others because we are philosophers. You think that attention to the Holocaust warns you against the temptation to think that everything—the totality of existence—can be understood. How and why does the Holocaust do that? Would you say the same about attention to the war in Ukraine or about attention to the coup against American democracy attempted by Donald Trump and his henchmen? Absent the humility produced by the warning you advance, a totalizing aim can infect philosophy, and, you add, "totalizing can sometimes turn into totalitarianism." Such impulses drove Hitler and Nazism to privilege their version of German nationalism, which was so threatened by Jews that they had to be destroyed root and branch. Do you see related totalizing impulses in Donald Trump and Trumpism and in Vladimir Putin and what many are calling Putinism? What, if anything, can philosophy do to combat such impulses? That question takes me back to a point you make about truth. Hitler, Trump, and Putin share at least one lethal flaw: they have been unrelenting and unrepentant liars, disregarding and disrespecting truth at every turn. How should philosophy respond to that fact? How can philosophers best defend truth? Are the defense of truth and the defense of democracy inseparable?

Second, philosophy and philosophers were not effective in stopping Hitler and Nazism before they engulfed the world in war and committed genocide against the European Jews. If the defense of democracy in the United States or Ukraine depended on philosophy and philosophers, the cause would be forlorn if not lost. Following Levinas, you want philosophy to put ethics first, which entails respect for persons and dialogue about how we are to live well together. But ethics, respect, and dialogue so often seem to come too late, if they arrive at all. What, if anything, can be done about that?

Third, in the beleaguered 2020s, what do philosophers and philosophy most need to be and do if they are to help save democracy? A key hint in your essay may found when you recall listening to "the voices of Holocaust victims." How could such listening guide what you and I should say and do, especially if we add listening to suffering Ukrainians and to Americans anguished by threats to democracy at home and abroad?

Lenny's Response

You note my claim that study of the Holocaust warns me against the temptation to think that all that exists can be comprehended—a temptation that traditional philosophy often failed to resist. Researching the Holocaust brings home the dangers of seeing my neighbor not as the unique individual she or he is, but as someone who is merely an element in an overarching whole. In war, the other person is objectified as *enemy*. That totalizing designation is dehumanizing too. Genocidal threats increase when an *entire* people is designated as hostile and threatening. Jews were not seen as individuals during the Holocaust. They were catalogued as representatives of a class of "subhumans" who would destroy Aryan racial purity.

Studying the Holocaust has alerted me to the dangers of such categorization in my own time. In thinking as lethal as it is bizarre, Putin has labeled Ukrainians "Nazis" to legitimate his genocidal warfare. Trumpism is not as ideological as Nazism or Putinism, but totalizing others infects the MAGA thinking of Trump and his followers. Opponents of Trump and his MAGA followers—especially journalists—are deemed "enemies of the people." Trumpists see people of color and certain ethnic groups as the aggregate of those who reject the rightful hegemony of White Americans. People who deny the need for a strongman to take the reins of government merely represent a class of "losers," the weak, exemplified for Trumpists by a Joe Biden whose impotence, it has been falsely claimed, allowed the Russians to invade Ukraine.

Totalizing harbors totalitarianism. Putin sees Ukrainians and Russians as one people. Refusing to acknowledge their "proper" role in Russia's presumed historical destiny, Ukrainians who resist as citizens of a sovereign state of their own are labeled "Nazis," a status that targets them for destruction by Putin's Russia. As the editorial board of the *New York Times* rightly said, Putin's attack on Ukraine "is not primarily about NATO or security. It's all about his xenophobic, imperial and misguided notion that Ukraine was inherently an appendage of Russia, its independence a historical fluke."[16] Ukrainians are totalized as usurpers. According to Putin, the invasion and conquest of Ukraine are justified.

Rejecting a tradition that has so often embraced overarching conceptual structures, some contemporary philosophers resist the temptation to totalize. Philosophy at its best is always growing, always questioning inherited traditions, always aspiring to rethink itself. I have written that such philosophy can guide us toward respect for the personhood of others, an essential ingredient of the democracy so imperiled in today's America. Philosophy did not stop Hitler's genocide of the Jews, nor has it prevented Putin's and Trump's attacks on democracy. In that sense, my emphasis on philosophy's enabling us to live well with one another seems naïve. But philosophy, true to its Socratic roots, has an impact on politics from the ground up; philosophy's impact on politics is indeed a paradox for many who see philosophy as the height of intellectual exercise. At its best, philosophy disturbs all of us, calls on us to probe our "givens," our most basic assumptions, the often-unexamined societal norms according to which we live. Plato identified philosophy as therapy for the soul. Yes, philosophy-as-ethics did not prevent the rise of Nazism in the 1930s and has not halted the threats to destroy democracy today. It is no short-term endeavor to help move us toward greater regard for others. Philosophy's incremental influence on politics is subtle, indirect—not easily discernible, but potentially effective.

What does it mean to assert that philosophy can be effective in the political realm? Among the many assumptions that philosophy summons us to examine is the claim, prevalent in both philosophical and ordinary discourse, that self-interest is the central, even sole determinant of human conduct. In other words, we humans are defined as fundamentally solitary egos seeking to fulfill our needs. Some contemporary philosophers contest this view. In the endeavor to probe who we are as human persons, Martin Buber, for example, invokes a biblical theme when he says that "in the beginning is relation."[17] What exists *between* individuals—the quality of our relationships—shows fundamentally who we are. Dialogue is the name given to those encounters in which partners view one another not in the mode of subject-to-object, but as subject-to-subject. According to Buber, "in a genuine dialogue each of the partners, even when he stands in opposition to the other, heeds, affirms, and confirms his opponent."[18] On the other hand, in monologue or

16. Editorial Board, "No Justification for a Brazen Invasion."

17. Buber, *I and Thou*, 18.

18. Buber, *Pointing the Way*, 227.

even in "negotiation," real listening is subordinated to arguments and claims that each wants the other to accept. If self-interest rules encounters between beings, including nations, such encounters deepen divisions and become conflicts. Such hostility can wreck democracy. At its core, philosophy-as-dialogue is peacemaking. It provides a model for a truly democratic politics, one in which self-interest takes a back seat to striving for mutual understanding and cooperation. Philosophy has not prevented genocide or unjustified war against Ukraine and attacks on democracy. What it can do is model a form of human interaction that can ever-so-gradually, but insistently, aid efforts to revive and sustain democratic values.

But can democracy continue to exist amid Trumpist attacks on truth? Democracy is rooted in truth, even if—or, better, *due to the fact* that—no one individual or group of individuals is authorized to define it. The search for truth is in the hands of the people, rather than decreed in a play of power. Philosophy reinforces the notion that in a democracy truth is more verb than noun. Inquiry leads us to discern it and to correct mistakes and errors about it. Truth is always in the process of being rethought, yet durable enough to provide a foundation of agreed-upon facts and shared norms that allows a society to cohere. Democracy bears witness to a creative tension between truth as stable and truth as ever-evolving. Although there have always been disputes about how we come to know what is true, we are currently faced by the Trumpist celebration of the lie, of mis- and disinformation, and of conspiracy theories. Some warn that should this assault on truth continue, we might enter a "post-truth" era. Social media and the internet more broadly accelerate the threat because anything and everything can be asserted or denied without verifiable evidence. Yet there has been enough creative pushback to give us hope. Freedom of expression and an independent press—both essential for robust democracy—remain strong. Putin's repression of information and dissent in Russia shows how much tyrants fear truth's power. Critics of current MAGA Republican submission to Trumpism speak in increasingly forceful tones. Fact-checking intensifies. Evidence produced by thoughtful inquiry shows the truth: Donald Trump committed crimes and betrayed the nation's security. If it is true in America that no person is above the law, his indictment and conviction will follow. Although lies and conspiracy theories continue to thrive, our core institutions—ones we *now* know are *not* impervious to destructive forces—remain resilient and must be bolstered.

Your questions about the role that philosophy can play in preserving and advancing democracy make me elaborate on the crucial need to listen to the victims of the Holocaust and other atrocities and injustices. Listening to the dead, the wounded, the displaced—all those who have suffered or continue to suffer—is essential if philosophers are to speak *with integrity* about righting wrongs. Philosophers face an occupational hazard. We have to take extra care not to speak abstractly, not to speak from a lofty perch—and especially not to speak as if we somehow "know" the suffering about which we talk. We have to take our cues from the voices of those who have suffered. Only then can we respond responsibly. A crucial part of what I hear from the victims is the injunction to remember. The kind of remembering called for, however, is not primarily an exercise of the mind. As a scholar of the Holocaust and as a philosopher, I can take what I hear and respond by working to defend democracy under threat in my own nation. As an academic who teaches and writes, I can respond to victims with words, yes, but with words substantiated by the ways I *live* democracy alongside students, family, and friends—and how I raise my voice in public settings of protest. May I continue to listen well.

John's Reflections

My digital subscription to the *Washington Post* delivers a daily posting called "The 7." It provides quick "get caught up" headlines about key events. One day's top three: The humanitarian crisis in Ukraine is getting worse; the average gas prices in the United States hit record highs; more than six million people have died of COVID-19 worldwide.

Such predicaments challenge democracy. Vladimir Putin's hostility to a democratic Ukraine not only created the worst refugee and humanitarian crisis since World War II but also reinforces nuclear threats that could destroy civilization. Worrisome gas prices are a by-product of that crisis and threat. The American death toll from COVID-19 skyrocketed during the inept administration of the antidemocratic Donald Trump.

Decades before Trump was elected president of the United States in 2016 and Putin invaded Ukraine in 2022, the Holocaust erupted in the 1940s. During the eighty-plus years of my life, corrupt political power and immense ethical and religious failure have combined to unleash massive injustice and needless suffering. None of that destruction had to happen. No historical inevitability fated it. The carnage resulted from human choices and decisions. Nothing human, natural, or divine guarantees respect for democracy, but in the 2020s the commitment to protect and honor democracy is as fundamental as it is fragile, as precious as it is at risk. Those realities and challenges make me wonder.

Wonder made me a philosopher. That's fitting because Plato and Aristotle, who did so much to establish the philosopher's discipline, believed that philosophy begins in wonder. Life makes us wonder how events happen and why they happen as they do. Wonder makes us aware of how little we know and how much we need to find out. Wonder produces questions and makes us consider what we ought to do.

On January 4, 1941, I was an infant when an eighty-year-old philosopher—about my age now—died in Paris. A well-known French thinker, Henri Bergson, who won the 1927 Nobel Prize for Literature, was born Jewish but was not a practicing Jew. During World War II, after France capitulated to Nazi Germany in June 1940, the puppet Vichy regime installed by the Germans offered to excuse the famous philosopher from its anti-Jewish laws. Bergson refused the exemption. Instead, he stood in solidarity with the Jewish community. His long winter-cold wait outdoors to register as a Jew quickened the illness that took his life.

Twenty years before Bergson died, he published a collection of lectures and essays under the title *Mind-Energy*. In one of the lectures, "The Soul and the Body," originally delivered in Paris on April 28, 1912, Bergson suggested that three wondering questions define philosophy: Where do we come from? What are we doing here? Where are we going? If philosophy can offer no insight in response to those fundamental questions, Bergson added, it's "not worth an hour's trouble."[19]

Bergson clearly thought that philosophy was worth much more than that. I do too. His three questions, moreover, go far toward defining philosophy, whose importance pivots around its insistent inquiry and persistent dialogue about what it means to be human, what values and virtues are most important as history unfolds, and what directions and destinations should be ours. Philosophy's virtues are persistent questioning, critical argumentation, ongoing dialogue, boldly reasoned asserting and testing of hypotheses, and a deep commitment to discerning what is true, good, and right as far as human minds are capable of doing so.

The American philosopher William James held that philosophy could give people courage. That's because philosophical inquiry at its best—the qualification is crucial—does not flinch. It goes where facts and evidence lead. It pursues justice and defends democracy. It makes me hold that democracy and philosophy are interdependent. Democracy cannot flourish without responsible freedom of inquiry, speech, and action. Nor can philosophy flourish unless philosophers uphold and advance democracy.

I am a philosopher tripped up by history and especially by the Holocaust and its reverberations. More than fifty years ago, I was deeply moved by my reading of Elie Wiesel's *Night*, his classic memoir about his

19. Bergson, *Mind-Energy*, 58.

experience in Auschwitz. As I learned increasingly about that catastrophe through the writings of other survivors—Primo Levi, Charlotte Delbo, Jean Améry, Sarah Kofman—I realized that my philosophical work needed to be governed by Wiesel's imperative: "Traditional ideas and acquired values, philosophical systems and social theories—all must be revised in the shadow of Birkenau."[20] The gassing and killing center at Auschwitz, Birkenau was the epicenter of the Nazis' "Final Solution." A key insight I took from Wiesel is that nothing exceeds the Holocaust's power to evoke and intensify the question *why?* That authority puts everything else to the test. Whatever the traditional ideas and acquired values that have existed, whatever the philosophical systems and social theories that human minds have produced, they were either inadequate to prevent Auschwitz or, worse, they helped pave the way to that place. The Holocaust insists, therefore, that how one thinks and acts needs revision in the face of those facts, unless one wishes to aid and abet the same blindness and corruption that produced the darkness of *Night*. The needed revisions, of course, do not guarantee a better outcome. And yet failure to use the Holocaust to call ourselves and each other into question diminishes chances to mend the world.

I agree with Michael Berenbaum that the Holocaust has become and must remain a "negative absolute."[21] Even if people remain skeptical that rational agreement can be obtained about what is right, just, and good, the Holocaust convinces me that what happened at Auschwitz and Treblinka was wrong, unjust, and evil—period, full stop. That disaster can be a compass that orients us toward its opposite, toward what is right, just, and good. I also agree with the British philosopher Geoffrey J. Warnock, who said, "That it is a bad thing to be tortured or starved, humiliated or hurt, is not an opinion; it is a fact. That it is better for people to be loved and attended to, rather than hated or neglected, is again a plain fact, not a matter of opinion."[22] No one, Warnock added, should be permitted to bully that truth away. In our world, however, such bullying and worse abound. But why? A question seems too fragile to resist the danger all around us, but unless questions are raised repeatedly and resolutely, the defense of truth, justice, and goodness becomes more forlorn and more bereft than ever.

Asking questions (who, what, where, when, how, and above all, *why*?) is one of the most crucial features of human life. If we could not ask questions, if we do not pursue what Wiesel called the right and real questions and follow where they lead, life would be and will be diminished, indeed

20. Wiesel, foreword to Cargas, *Shadows of Auschwitz*.

21. Berenbaum, "Who Owns the Holocaust?" 60.

22. Warnock, *Contemporary Moral Philosophy*, 60.

impoverished. Without the capacity to question, curiosity and inquiry will be stunted and may be absent altogether. Learning will be hampered, if it takes place at all. Critical thinking will be unthinkable; creativity will diminish. Error, lying, dogmatism, tyranny, hate, injustice, and violence will gain traction they do not deserve.

Who are we? What is right and what is not? What is good and what is most important? Are we doing the best we can? What about God, or is that question absurd? How can we curb hate, resist injustice, and forestall despair? Where are we going, or where should we be going? What are we, what should we be, doing? What must change in order to curb and heal the wasting of the world? Are our judgments true? Can our responses to such questions stand scrutiny, or do they require further inquiry and evidence to support them? No event exceeds the Holocaust's power to raise such right and real questions and to beckon us to reckon with them. Wrestling with those questions will not be sufficient to resist further disasters, but that struggle may be a necessary condition for doing so.

Asking questions is more important than getting what might be thought of as answers, because so often the answers we get are incomplete, short-sighted, limited and limiting, mistaken, partisan, foolish and false, life-threatening and life-destroying. On the other hand, insistently asking questions keeps inquiry going, helps us to look further and better, urges us to think twice rather than to plunge ahead recklessly, murderously. Persistently asking questions seeks evidence to support or correct judgments, makes us wonder if we might be mistaken, and tests what we think and believe. Asking key questions can help us to make good choices, or at least to avoid bad ones. Resistently asking questions can help us to avoid taking good things for granted.

To a large degree, the Holocaust, Putin's war against Ukraine, and the deterioration of American democracy resulted because too many people failed to ask the right and real questions long or well enough. Philosophy is needed to give people courage to wonder *why*, to keep questioning, and in that way to sound warnings and sharpen insights that may keep contemporary threats at bay. Trying to be a philosopher who contributes to democracy in those ways remains my calling.

Lenny's Questions

I share your understanding of philosophy as born in wonder and rooted in awareness that we lack much that we need to know and must inquire to close the gap. I also stand with you in valuing philosophy's "commitment to discerning what is true, good, and right." As a philosopher, I too embrace dialogue and the spirit of inquiry regarding the meaning of the human condition We hold much in common. We agree that the Holocaust is a test for philosophers. We must do more than theorize; philosophers must ask, concretely, how we might heal, in thought and action, the "wasting of the world." Philosophy must rethink its vocation in light of the Holocaust's radical evil. What has happened in Ukraine urges and motivates us to practice, in word and deed, the kind of philosophy we both embrace.

In Plato's dialogues, Socrates emphasizes that the unexamined life is not worth living. I stand by that maxim. But I have also been influenced by my teacher, Alphonso Lingis, who asserts, conversely, that the "unlived life is not worth examining." The "unlived life" can be understood as a life devoid of vitality, passion, joy, enchantment, mystery. Might the life of examining, of calling everything into question, be so faithful to one dimension of our existence that it fails to touch others—in particular, elements of the heart? Is even ethics susceptible to a narrowing of focus that would prevent us from realizing we are head, heart, spirit—all as one? Western philosophers through the ages have often celebrated reason as the bar before which ideas are to be brought. But might this focus on reason impede us from embarking on a quest for what may transcend it? Can philosophy, as you view it, touch transcendence? Is striving to do so part of your understanding of the philosopher's mission?

More questions: Do we philosophers stand in danger of forgetting that we are *embodied* beings? How do we incorporate our bodily existence into our vocation? How do we "embody" our philosophical insights in general, and how, in particular, do we do so in the face of both the current horrors of war in Ukraine and the attacks on democracy at home? How do we "live" philosophy?

John's Response

On March 16, 2022, Ukraine's president, Volodymyr Zelenskyy, his country invaded by Vladimir Putin three weeks earlier, addressed the US Congress from Kyiv, Ukraine's capital, which the Russians have besieged with air and missile strikes.[23] His speech provided insightful points of departure for my response to your questions. They ask me to amplify my views about philosophy's importance by considering four factors: reason, embodiment, transcendence, and what you sensitively call "elements of the heart."

23. Zelenskyy, "Text of President Zelensky's Virtual Address to Congress."

In words that were lucid and charged with emotion, Zelenskyy said that "the Ukrainian people are defending not only Ukraine, we are fighting for the values of Europe and the world, sacrificing our lives in the name of the future. That's why today the American people are helping not just Ukraine, but Europe and the world to keep the planet alive, to keep justice in history." Such work is not likely to be successful unless clear and careful thinking governs it. Reason is an important and indispensable ally of what is good and right. But reason alone is not enough to defend and advance those values and realities. It must encourage and be augmented by force of will, assertion, and commitment. Reason, in turn, is needed to curb and correct the excesses and extremes to which passion and power are prone.

Finding the vital balance is a process that needs a compass to guide it. At least in part, that compass may be found by understanding that human life and thought are always embodied. As his speech to Congress drew to a close, Zelenskyy said that he was almost forty-five years old, but "today my age stopped when the hearts of more than one hundred children stopped beating. I see no sense in life," Zelenskyy continued, "if it cannot stop death. And this is my main mission as the Leader of my people—great Ukrainians." Zelenskyy saw that ideas and philosophies matter because they can be embodied in acts of war that murder children. Their tragically lost lives cannot be revived and recovered, but if anything approaching justice in history is to be found, philosophy of a vastly different kind than Putin's—or Hitler's or Trump's—must become embodied, which means that philosophers are accountable for helping or hindering that process.

For persons and ideas, embodiment means that actions and reactions take place. It takes embodiment to keep the planet alive and to keep justice in history. But that fact also entails that philosophers and philosophy have to consider and advance awareness of transcendence. The American theologian Reinhold Niebuhr offered insight about what that awareness involves. "Nothing that is worth doing," said Niebuhr, "can be achieved in our lifetime."[24] Niebuhr had in mind the things that matter most. Defending democracy, pursuing justice, relieving suffering, loving our children, making peace instead of war, helping one another—all of those aims fit his point and understanding. We cannot complete those tasks. Nor can we do by ourselves alone all that is needed. The things that matter most always give us more to do, and our embodied lives, finite and fragile, will end before the work is done. Awareness that we can neither understand nor do everything liberates us to discern and do the best we can. Thus, the work of philosophy and philosophers has to include keeping hope, faith, and love alive.

24. Niebuhr, *Irony of American History*, 63.

Zelenskyy urged his American audience to remember. I think that what you call "elements of the heart" are found in memory and memories. Remember Pearl Harbor, Zelenskyy said to Congress, Remember September 11th. Those events touch American hearts because to remember them is to think of what was lost and what deserves to be protected. Zelenskyy wanted Americans to remember so that they would see how Ukrainian hearts ache when Russian tanks and planes move "against our freedom. Against our right to live freely in our country, choosing our own future. Against our desire for happiness. Against our national dreams. Just like yours, ordinary people of America. Just like those of everyone in the United States."

Understanding elements of the heart, Zelenskyy invoked Martin Luther King Jr., "'I have a dream'—those words are known to each of you." He turned that phrase in a heart-wrenching way—heart-turning, he hoped—when he spoke from his heart: "Today I can say: I have a necessity. The necessity to protect our sky. The necessity for your decision. Your help. And it will mean exactly the same thing. The same thing you feel. When you hear: I have a dream."

Donald Trump denied military aid to Ukraine unless Zelenskyy accepted a bribe to get "dirt" on Joe Biden. Trump's heartless corruption undermined Ukraine and opened the door for Putin's invasion. Zelenskyy saw a better side of the American heart but made a telling point. Only if the American dream of democracy is heartfelt as a necessity will the United States rise to the occasion and defend democracy at home and abroad in ways that embody justice, healing, and peace. Philosophy's advancing or shirking of that cause will show whether philosophy is alive and whether philosophers live philosophy in the ways that matter most.

Postscript

Our exchanges in this chapter affirm the conviction that philosophy and philosophers matter. We defend a philosophical outlook that affirms free and open inquiry, respect for persons and their fundamental rights, democratic values, and just and peaceful international relations. We advance this outlook in opposition to authoritarian philosophies that threaten democracy. *Philosopher* is not a term usually used to identify Hitler, Trump, or Putin. And yet the three of them embody philosophies, even if those outlooks are neither clear nor coherent. Disrespectful of philosophy at its best, these autocrats nevertheless hold philosophical convictions that make them formidable, immensely destructive, and difficult to disable.

Hitler's philosophy of Aryan/German supremacy led him to attain dictatorial power, to ignite a world war aimed at exploitative conquest of Europe, and to do all that he could to destroy the Jewish people. Trump's America First philosophy has included the strongman outlook that only he could set right what was wrong in the United States and make America great again. His version of ethnonationalism is far less lethal than Hitler's, but it shares elements of "might makes right" as Trump came close to achieving a political coup that would have overturned the 2020 presidential election, undermined the US Constitution, and left the rule of law tattered and torn. Trump's friend Vladimir Putin, far more cunning and violence-prone than Trump, unleashed warfare, refugee disasters, and humanitarian crises unseen in Europe since the days of Hitler's Third Reich. Influenced by the political philosophy of the Russian thinker Alexander Dugin—he has a following among the extreme right wing in America—Putin embodies an ethnonationalist fascism steeped in grievances against the West and ready to use violence at home and abroad to get its way.[25] Putin's fascism rejects liberal democracy, revives ambition that a resurgent Russia will reclaim its rightful empire, including Ukraine, and foresees deserved Russian power bridging divides between Europe and Asia and reaching, in Dugin's phrase, "from Dublin to Vladivostok." If there is any doubt that philosophers and philosophies matter, one only has to consider the carnage that Putin's thinking and attacking have created in Ukrainian cities such as Kharkiv and Mariupol, Lviv and Kyiv.

Hitler's grandiose philosophy envisioned a thousand-year Reich. It lasted only twelve years, but millions upon millions suffered and died before its demise. Trump and his followers did not overturn the 2020 election, but American democracy hangs in the balance nonetheless as the 2024 elections approach. Those elections will be influenced by Putin and by what happens in Ukraine and beyond its borders in Europe. Meanwhile, "Trump fatigue" exists. Many Republicans want to get beyond Trump, some hoping that his death might rescue the party, but they lack conviction and confidence about how to do so.[26] The formidable Koch political machine, which drives Americans for Prosperity, a powerful conservative donor network, won't support Trump in 2024.[27] But even that opposition won't make Trump go away, at least not quietly. His presence still impacts the Republican presidential nomination process. Even if he does not run, either as the

25. On philosophers, including Dugin, who have influenced Putin, see Snyder, *Road to Unfreedom*, 67–109.

26. Coppins, "Magical Thinking."

27. Elliott, "Koch Political Machine."

Republican nominee or as a piqued independent disrupter, Trumpism will be on the ballot. Aspirants such as Ron DeSantis, Nikki Haley, Mike Pence, Tim Scott, and others will see to that. Antidemocratic Trumpism with or without Trump could win in November 2024.

Philosophy matters. When it makes us ask key questions—What is right and what is wrong? What is most important? What is worth living and dying for? Are we doing the best we can?—philosophy's life of inquiry embodies democracy. At least it can and must because real inquiry rejects dogmatism and supports openness. It denies infallibility and certitude and recognizes that judgments are prone to error and require reevaluation and correction.

The eloquent Holocaust writer Primo Levi never forgot an encounter that happened not long after his arrival at Auschwitz. Once he reached for an icicle to quench his painful thirst. An SS guard snatched it from him. "Warum?" Levi asked him, only to be told with a shove, "Hier ist kein warum" (there is no why here).[28] Levi's "why?" sought explanation. He got none because questions of life and death were already settled there. No asking was allowed the likes of Levi. In Auschwitz no "why?" existed—not as question and certainly not as satisfying explanation either.

Auschwitz raises every "why?" but it did not tolerate the kind that Levi posed. Paradoxically the Holocaust was beyond "why?" because the minds that produced it were convinced they "understood" why. They "recognized" that one religion, Christianity, had superseded another, Judaism. They "comprehended" that one race, one people, was superior to every other. They "saw" what nature's laws decreed, namely, that there was lebensunwertes Leben (life unworthy of life). Thus, they "realized" who deserved to live and who deserved to die.

Hitler and his antidemocratic followers were beyond "why?' because they "knew" why. Knowing they were "right," their "knowing" made them killers. One can argue, of course, that such "knowing" perverted rationality and mocked morality. It did. And yet to say that much is too little, for one must ask about the sources of such perversion. When that asking occurs, part of its trail leads to the tendency of human reason to presume that indeed it can, at least in principle, figure everything out and understand why.

People are less likely to savage and annihilate each other, they are less likely to undermine democracy, they are less likely to create or legitimate boots stamping on human faces forever, when they ask "why?" instead of "knowing" why, and when their minds are less made up than opened up through questioning and caring for those who are in need.

28. Levi, *If This Is a Man*, 29.

In 2005, the United Nations Educational, Scientific and Cultural Organization (UNESCO), a United Nations agency that promotes world peace and security through international cooperation in education, arts, sciences, and culture, established World Philosophy Day. It is celebrated every year on the third Thursday of November. The founding legislation expressed the hope that World Philosophy Day could create "greater international awareness of the need for free, critical and responsible philosophical reflection."[29] Free, critical, responsible—describing philosophy at its best, those watchwords support democracy, not autocracy. They resist lies and lying and insist on seeking and telling the truth, a fundamental condition for democracy. They speak up for liberty and equality, democracy's cornerstones. They reject "might makes right" and affirm that the question "why?" deserves respect and careful responses that will be corrected and revised when they are rightly found wanting. Free, critical, responsible—those watchwords inform and guide philosophy that can help to save American democracy.

29. UNESCO, Proclamation of a World Philosophy Day.

3
Education

MORE THAN SIXTY YEARS ago, the brilliant Black American author James Baldwin, a national treasure, wrote an essay called "As Much Truth as One Can Bear." Arguing that "we are the generation that must throw everything into the endeavor to remake America into what we say we want it to be," Baldwin ended with a warning: "Not everything that is faced can be changed; but nothing can be changed until it is faced."[1]

We Americans need to bear those truths, which are no less relevant now than when Baldwin underscored them in 1962. They call us to account, especially as we consider that the health and future of American democracy depend on sound, honest, truthful, and encouraging education. Both democracy and the education needed to sustain it are threatened in the 2020s by factions, antidemocratic and authoritarian, that are hostile to the pluralistic America that, when at our best, we want the United States to be. As Baldwin understood, the obstacles to achieving what we want to be when we are at our best are many and diverse. Owning that fact is not sufficient to ensure success, but failure to confront openly and honestly the shortfalls and shortcomings that are ours makes it impossible to muster and sustain the changes we need to make.

As autumn approached in 2022, fifty million girls and boys enrolled in American public schools. Hoping against hope, their families and communities wondered not if but when the next gun violence would be unleashed against those students. Meanwhile momentous events showed that the education of all American citizens requires grappling with other outbreaks that violate our democracy. On August 26, for example, the unsealing of a heavily redacted but still informative thirty-eight-page affidavit in support of a search warrant taught Americans that Donald Trump

1. Baldwin, "Truth," 41–42.

illegally held 184 classified documents—including twenty-five marked "top secret"—at his Mar-a-Lago estate in Florida.[2]

What's more, Americans learned why the Department of Justice concluded that Trump had more illegally held documents than the cache he reluctantly returned earlier to the National Archives and Records Administration, where they properly belonged. Backed by the court-approved search warrant, the FBI went to Mar-a-Lago on August 8 and reclaimed many more boxes containing classified documents, including nuclear secrets. Trump's illegal possession of them put national security at risk, which, among other things, imperiled American children. American education in the late 2020s includes the hard lesson that the former president committed serious crimes and betrayed the United States. His blindly supportive MAGA Republican followers are complicit in the treachery.

Far away from Mar-a-Lago and FBI headquarters in Washington DC, wartime events in Ukraine taught Americans that Vladimir Putin's assault on Ukrainians and their democracy not only will be protracted but also will keep inviting nuclear disaster. August 24, 2022, was Ukraine's thirty-first Independence Day, marking its 1991 separation from the Soviet Union. The equivalent of July 4 in the United States, that August date also marked the six-month point since Putin's invasion began. Russian forces pinpointed the day with a rocket attack on a train station in central Ukraine. It killed fifteen civilians and wounded fifty more. The Russian invasion has been especially harsh for Ukrainian children. UNICEF estimates, for example, that nearly one thousand Ukrainian children were killed or wounded in the war's first six months. In addition, Russian violence destroyed one in ten of Ukraine's schools during that time.[3] What's more, Americans learned that the Russian occupation of Ukraine's Zaporizhzhia nuclear power plant, the largest in Europe, could lead to a meltdown that would take an immense toll on human life. Sound American education entails recognition that Putin's antidemocratic aggression must be stopped no less than the gun violence that wreaks havoc on American schools and the grifting corruption of Trump and MAGA Republicans that undermines American democracy.

Education topped the list of priorities for the American founder Thomas Jefferson, who believed that "no other sure foundation can be devised for the preservation of freedom and happiness."[4] In conflict with that proposition, the United States faces tough challenges and crippling

2. See Barrett and Stein, "Affidavit to Search Trump's Mar-a-Lago." A copy of the affidavit is embedded in this article.

3. Russell, "War in Ukraine."

4. The statement is from Jefferson's letter to George Wythe, August 13, 1786.

shortfalls in providing the support for education, and especially for teachers, that robust democracy requires. Inadequate pay for educators, increased political pressure on them, concerns about health and safety—such conditions significantly diminish educational opportunities for American students. The ravages of COVID-19 alone put half of American K-12 students a full year behind grade level in at least one subject during the 2022–2023 academic year.[5] In some school districts, moreover, White Christian nationalists want control of school boards and implementation of agendas that dictate what teachers must but also cannot teach and what books American students should but also must not read in school. Such initiatives sound a death knell for liberal democracy.

Because democracy itself will be on the ballot in the 2024 elections, education policy will be too. The Republican Party will see to that as it wages culture wars to restrict if not outlaw teaching and learning about race and American history, sexual orientation and gender identity. Absent academic freedom and the debate and criticism it encourages, indoctrination and ignorance cripple us. At its best, education liberates. Learning gives democracy the foundation it requires and the hope it deserves to inspire. Education and learning can do that if they emphasize not only reading and writing but also history, science, and the arts, along with informed awareness of current events and training in the most reliable ways to inquire, calculate, and evaluate. Especially but not only for young people, education and learning also need to face the prospects and challenges arising from artificial intelligence (AI) and the ChatGPT (Generative Pre-trained Transformer) platform developed by OpenAI.[6] High priority must be given to teaching information literacy: how to assess propositions and policies, use mass media and internet sources, and manage AI in ways that depend on verifiable evidence as the standard for truth.[7] This work includes not only debunking but also "prebunking," showing how to spot lying and misinformation early on, and before they infect and threaten society. That's a lot of work to do, but we Americans fail to do it at our peril. Although insufficient to guarantee healthy and robust democracy, such education is necessary to defend and advance it.

Denying that all persons are created equal, the Nazi leader Adolf Hitler despised democracy, taking it to be a deceitful, subversive outlook spread by Jews. Hitler's minister of education, Bernhard Rust, believed that

5. Jimenez, "COVID Set Half of US Kids Behind."

6. See Kissinger et al., "ChatGPT."

7. For significant help on these concerns, see Project Censored and the Media Revolution Collective, *Media and Me*.

education's purpose was to create Nazis. Practicing that preaching, education in the Third Reich emphasized racism and antisemitism, the superiority and supremacy of so-called Aryan people. Jewish teachers and professors—dismissed. Books by Jewish authors—banned and burned. Nazi virtues—tough and hard, taught and learned. Such education, including the propaganda that spread it throughout German society, produced and emboldened Nazis who ignited World War II and the Holocaust.

Russian schooling under Putin provides another example of threats to democracy from education that indoctrinates. Although Russia currently has one of the world's highest literacy rates, memorization of data trumps the critical thinking skills that are essential to democracy. "We are taught what to think, not how to think," a recent Russian high school graduate told an American teacher.[8] *New York Times* Moscow bureau chief Anton Troianovski writes that Putin is in a "race to overhaul how children are taught at Russia's 40,000 public schools," an initiative that is "part of the Russian government's scramble to indoctrinate children with Mr. Putin's militarized and anti-Western versions of patriotism."[9] In the six months following Russia's invasion of Ukraine, expression of dissent in Russian schools has been further silenced. One CNN journalist put the matter succinctly: "Education has become a victim of the conflict."[10] Revised Russian history texts now reinforce Putin's claim that Ukraine never existed as an independent state. During the summer of 2022, moreover, Putin signed legislation stating that "all Russian children will be encouraged to join a new patriotic youth movement."[11] Echoes of Hitler Youth resonate. "We need to know how to infect them with our ideology"—that's how a senior Kremlin bureaucrat thinks Russian teachers should treat their students.[12] And in Ukrainian territory under Russian control CNN reports that local educators have seen "increasing cases of intimidation, threats and pressure to adapt school programs to align with pro-Russian rhetoric."[13] Denying students the right to critical thinking, personal expression, and dissent, Putin's antidemocratic education system is toxic.

In the 1930s, German education worked to destroy democracy. In the 2020s, Russian education does the same. American education must not do

8. Davis, "What Is Education in Russia Like?"

9. Troianovski, "Putin Aims to Shape a New Generation of Supporters."

10. Said-Moorhouse and Ochman, "This is What the 'Russification' of Ukraine's Education System Looks Like."

11. Troianovski, "Putin Aims to Shape a New Generation of Supporters."

12. Troianovski, "Putin Aims to Shape a New Generation of Supporters."

13. Said-Moorhouse and Ochman, "This is What the 'Russification' of Ukraine's Education System Looks Like."

that, but the current American relationship between democracy and education is problematic because democracy is threatened and education is both imperiled and employed in that predicament. Basing our reflections on a century's worth of combined teaching experience, much of it devoted to Holocaust education, we use this chapter's exchange to explore what education needs to be and do in order to save and sustain American democracy.

Lenny's Reflections

On January 20, 1942, fifteen members of the Nazi Party and the German government met in a villa at Wannsee near Berlin. Their agenda: to coordinate the destruction of the European Jews, the "Final Solution" of "the Jewish question." Eight of them held doctoral degrees from German universities. Their academic accomplishments did nothing to keep them from committing genocide. So, Americans need to be warned that if education is crucial for democracy, its quality and its commitments are matters of life and death.

The Nazis who gathered at Wannsee were educated either prior to or during the establishment of the Weimar Republic (1919–1933) as a representative parliamentary democracy. Weakened by economic depression, political division, the trauma of defeat in World War I, and resentment against the Versailles Treaty, which was regarded as punitive, the Weimar government had more problems than it could handle. Lack of education that supported democracy was one of them. As Max Weinrich understated the point, "from 1919 to 1933 only a small number of German scholars were intellectually opposed to what in the course of time turned out to be the philosophy of National Socialism."[14] Hostile to democracy, Nazi ideology impacted German education even before the German president Paul von Hindenburg used his constitutional authority to appoint Adolf Hitler as Germany's chancellor. Hitler took his oath of office on January 30, 1933.

The Nazi Party never won an absolute majority in any freely contested national election, but it was Germany's largest political party, and it soon used democratic procedures against democracy. On March 23, 1933, for example, the Reichstag, the German parliament, passed the Enabling Act, which gave Hitler power to legislate and govern by decree and without the Reichstag's consent. Hitler got absolute dictatorial power "legally" when democracy destroyed itself in Germany. That power enabled him to set aside provisions in the Weimar constitution that guaranteed legal equality for all citizens. The self-destruction of German democracy eventually produced a death sentence for Europe's Jews.

14. Weinreich, *Hitler's Professors*, 10.

The Weimar Republic could not withstand Nazi power hell-bent on democracy's demolition. The United States and the Weimar Republic are scarcely comparable. But in the 2020s, American democracy is fragile, even frail, and nothing about democracy guarantees its health or durability. Absent sound education, democracy is more likely to collapse than to prevail. We Americans must ask how we are to educate not only our young but all our citizens to avoid that fate.

Assuming that we want to do so, which is not a foregone conclusion for every American today, how can we preserve and strengthen democracy in our schools and classrooms? A reliable response to that question acknowledges that education-for-democracy must include a spirit of ethical concern across the curriculum. The American philosopher John Dewey—no thinker has been more insightful about the relationship between education and democracy—emphasized that "democracy is . . . a type of moral and spiritual association."[15] He also stressed that "belief in equality" is crucial for democracy.[16] Dewey was right. Defending those propositions and acting on them in our schools and classrooms are crucial steps to combat the growing threat of autocracy embodied in the idolatrous embrace of Donald Trump by most Republicans.

Failure to take those steps comes with Holocaust warnings. The philosopher Emil Fackenheim rightly argued that "once idolatry is mentioned, there appears the specter of Auschwitz."[17] Nazi leaders were idolators, believing not only in Hitler's absolute authority but also in the supreme superiority of one group, who would thus be justified in oppressing and then murdering another group deemed mere vermin. Nazi idolators in the classroom taught Aryan supremacy and encouraged violence, even war, to defend it. As Richard Grunberger noted, education in 1930s Germany is aptly characterized by the claim that "the very best thoughts are those inculcated by marching; in them reverberate the secret German spirit."[18]

Nazi education's authoritarian pedagogy did not randomly promote Hitler's fascism. Those practices were grounded in and advanced by Germany's education bureaucracy. The Third Reich's teachers fell in line, followed rules, obeyed superiors, perfected their roles as organization men and women. Like their counterparts in industries, government offices, and the Reich's railway system, teachers did their work as the system required. In so doing they embodied a silence without which the coming genocide might not have been

15. Dewey, "Ethics of Democracy," 18.

16. Dewey, *Problems of Men*, 60.

17. Patterson, *When Learned Men Murder*, 13.

18. Grunberger: *12-Year Reich*, 316.

enacted. It was not only the clamor of Nazi propaganda in classrooms that undermined the moral universe on which democracies rest. The little everyday silences in these classrooms provided the space within which democracy could be undermined and genocidal thinking advanced.

Nazi education glorified functional, means-end reasoning; it lacked concern for the ethical dimension of the end toward which such reasoning was employed. The classrooms of the Weimar period embraced *voraussetzunglose Wissenschaft*, science lacking moral concerns.[19] The result during the years of the Holocaust itself: the loud silence of the German railroad worker who never inquired, let alone protested, where the cattle cars were going; the silence of the Zyklon B factory worker who never inquired about, let alone protested, the lethal use of that product to gas Jews to death.

Education about the Holocaust can help to safeguard American democracy because it shows what can happen when the inherent moral worth of each and every human being is ignored or denied. As the philosopher Philip Hallie wisely said, "the Holocaust is the story of extreme situations . . . that can display as 'plain fact' the 'true north or the true south' of ethics."[20]

Trumpism's spurious populism—its demagogic call to the "forgotten men and women of our country"—is in fact a call to those whose skin is White, whose grievances resound, rallying them to face the alleged danger of an impending loss of hegemony in a fast-changing world. Such a message, infiltrating the way we educate our children, shakes the foundations of the pursuit of equality that lies at the heart of democracy. Attempts are widespread to censor teaching that exposes American society's endemic racism. School boards and schools are pressured to bow to the wishes of disgruntled parents about what trained teachers are allowed to explore with their students. A main criterion for discarding a book has become whether it includes discussion of racism, sexual orientation, or gender that might make students "uncomfortable" or lead them to question how well the United States is living up to its professed ideals. In the spirit of 1930s Germany, books of the "wrong" kind are enemies to be removed from libraries and in some extreme cases burned. "It can't happen here," Americans usually like to say. American education in the 2020s should make us ask: Is that assumption credible?

In an age of growing authoritarianism, democracy in the classroom is imperiled. In an atmosphere of repression fostered by Trumpism, teachers can easily fall prey to a model of education in which they exercise arbitrary authority. Educators-for-democracy must stand firm in challenging

19. Grunberger, *12-Year Reich*, 305.

20. Hallie, "Scepticism, Narrative, and Holocaust Ethics," 48–49.

such authoritarianism through the embrace of critical inquiry across curricula and pedagogies. As the political philosopher Paulo Freire argued, the democratic classroom is one in which teachers and students are "jointly responsible for a process in which all grow."[21] Democratic education calls upon teachers not merely to communicate facts, transmit information, and impart knowledge, but to teach the desire to learn, to question, to inquire. And then, when students show interest, ask questions, and explore ideas, teachers need to engage their students in dialogue that supports and guides the students' growth. In that process, learning goes two ways: students learn from their teachers, and teachers learn from their students too. The dialogical educator-for-democracy rankles, unsettles, provokes students, helping them interrogate the full range of contexts in which they live. Teachers and students share responsibility for examining what constitutes a good society and for contributing to its creation.

How do we know that the dialogical education described above will work to strengthen the moral fiber of democracy? Authentic dialogue is not a means to achieve a humanizing end outside of itself; rather, dialogue assumes the humanity of the other. In education-for-democracy, the medium of dialogue is the message. The dialogical teacher will approach students as co-subjects, rather than objects. To approach the other in dialogue safeguards the core of democracy.

Can education thus humanized make a difference in a nation currently beset with threats to its basic democratic norms? The classroom is more than a site *preparing* students for democratic action; it is a living laboratory for its immediate exercise. To educate dialogically is already a fundamentally political act, challenging those who would put democracy at risk. If we respond to the shadows of the Holocaust and educate toward honoring the humanity of one another, then we will have learned much that we need to know and do to save ourselves.

John's Questions

Your essay significantly contributes to Holocaust education as well as to reflection about the kind of education needed to defend American democracy. You remind me that it took education and educated men like those at the Wannsee conference to advance the racist antisemitism and imperialistic military policies that drove Nazi Germany to plan and implement the "Final Solution." Those persons, moreover, were not self-educated, at least not entirely. They had teachers—parents, politicians, professors,

21. Freire, *Pedagogy of the Oppressed*, 61.

preachers, as well as school instructors—who taught them antisemitism and racism, which always depend on teaching and learning. When education facilitates antidemocratic politics, danger increases.

Danger increases in 2020s America because education and teachers in particular are under attack. In 2022, well-funded right-wing groups such as the 1776 Project PAC and Moms for Liberty gained national ground in electing school board members who favor "parental rights" in education and oppose teaching and books about racial justice and gender identity. Earlier, in 2021, Republican governors in Idaho, Iowa, Oklahoma, Tennessee, and Texas signed bills that restrict the way history—especially the history of racism in America—is taught. From July 1, 2021, to March 31, 2022, according to PEN America, book bans have taken place in eighty-six school districts in twenty-six states.[22] The bans singled out 1,145 titles by 874 different authors. Many of the banned books discuss racism and LGBTQ+ identities. Until resistance led to reversals, the Holocaust classic *Maus* and some editions of Anne Frank's diary were among the targeted volumes. The crisis in American education is that the dark undersides of our history are whitewashed while the uncritical view that, in the words of Donald Trump, "the United States of America is the most just and exceptional Nation ever to exist on Earth" gets privileged.[23] The defense of democracy requires uncensored education sounder and better grounded than that.

You stress the importance of dialogical education. Exploring "the full range of contexts" in which students live, such education "rankles, unsettles, provokes students" in ways that enable them and their teachers to support democracy. It takes talented teachers, nimble and courageous ones to do that work. Where are those teachers to be found? Who will recruit, train, nurture, and support them?

Besieged by COVID-19, underpaid, overworked, harassed by contentious parents and hyperpartisan politicians who want them to bend to their wishes, burned out K-12 teachers, most of whom are women, are thinking long and hard about whether to return to the classroom. Democracy depends on good education. Good education requires teachers—dedicated, determined, dialogical. But what if they can't be found and adequately supported, at least not enough of them? Germany faced such a scarcity of good, dialogical teachers in the 1930s. The result was horrendous. How can we Americans ensure that we avoid a disastrous educational shortfall that could leave our democracy in tatters if it continues to exist at all?

22. Friedman and Johnson, "Banned in the USA."

23. Trump, "Protecting America's Founding Ideals."

Lenny's Response

You are right: "democracy depends on good education." And good education requires what I have described as dialogical teachers to serve as bulwarks against the current threats to our democracy. You are also on target when you ask, where are such teachers to be found? Ahead of talking about *good* teachers who will model democracy in their classrooms, we have to note that even before the COVID-19 pandemic, more than one hundred thousand certified teachers were needed to fill vacancies. COVID-19 made the shortage more dire, "stretching schools to the breaking point, with districts around the country having to close . . . or shift to distance learning as teachers and other staff are absent due to illness, quarantine requirements, or the need to care for sick family members."[24] Even after the worst of the pandemic, the problems of filling teacher shortages, especially in high-poverty and resource-deprived schools, and of meeting the need for teachers skilled at creating democratic classrooms in particular, refuse any simple resolution. The product of multiple factors, these problems require comprehensive solutions.

One factor contributing to a dearth of dialogical teachers in America today is most certainly the growing hostility of parents, especially those serving on school boards in conservative states, to any teaching that would prompt a critique of the America imagined by Trumpists. Topics such as racial inequities, nontraditional family structures, and sexual orientations are often deemed inappropriate. There is certainly an echo here of the challenges teachers confronted in the years leading up to the Third Reich. You stress that "Germany faced such a scarcity of good, dialogical teachers in the 1930s," one of the factors leading to the destruction of its democracy. Just prior to and certainly following Hitler's ascent to power, the teacher who departed from the Nazi Party line could not only be fired; he or she risked further punishment for not adhering to the injunction to teach courses "pointed toward a definite object," the glory of the Third Reich.[25]

You indicate that among the many factors discouraging individuals from choosing teaching-for-democracy as a career are censorship and suppression of a spirit of critique in the classroom. The need for courage to face the growing intimidation from parents and politicians is just one daunting requirement for a teacher to enter the field and remain within it. Unfortunately, circumstances in the 2020s too often require dialogical teachers to accept salaries incommensurate with the demands of the profession. Dedicated

24. Kini, "Tackling Teacher Shortages."

25. Ziemer, *Education for Death*, 174.

K-12 teachers too frequently must deal with a societywide devaluing of their career choice compared with the regard given to instructors at the university level. Such teachers must also face the challenges of overcrowded classrooms, especially in those underserved communities that are the main victims of the time-honored determination that schools be funded on the basis of tax revenues, determined by property values.

How are we to overcome these deterrents to finding teachers who, in their choice of content and pedagogy, are dedicated to preserving democracy in the age of Trumpism? The challenge is daunting. In light of this difficulty, it is easy to despair. To counter the temptation to lose hope, I contend that we can do no better than to recall our heritage as Americans. The founding fathers, imperfect as they most decidedly were, bequeathed to us an underpinning of democracy in the form of our Constitution and other early texts. Although some of the Founders held values contrary to the spirit of the documents they signed—many owned slaves—foundational principles such as freedom of inquiry and the importance of education for democracy have been handed down. They point us in good directions. After World War I, Germany briefly had democracy before Hitler's rise to power, but it lacked foundational democratic convictions akin to ours. In the 2020s those American convictions must be reclaimed and advanced.

Two current initiatives deserve attention because they emphasize freedom of inquiry, the importance of education for democracy, and ways to attract and sustain dialogical teachers who will work to preserve our democratic legacy. First, President Joe Biden's American Families Plan (AFP), constituting a third of the Build Back Better initiative, was throttled in 2022 by a conservative Senate. But it set an example, an aspiration for what the federal government—in the spirit of our founders—could yet contribute. Don't give up—that's the message. The AFP addressed teacher shortages by providing $9 billion to train, equip, and diversify our cadre of teachers. According to Adam Edelman, a political reporter for NBC News, the proposed money sought "to increase the number of people who study education and want to enter the field, keep existing teachers from leaving the field and allow existing teachers and professionals from other fields easier and less expensive opportunities to obtain certification for particularly in-demand specialties within teaching."[26] The "in-demand" specialties singled out by the AFP for securing teachers alert us to its social justice dimension: special education, bilingual education, and mentorship programs designed specifically to retain teachers in minority-serving schools. Four hundred million dollars were set aside to fund teacher-education

26. Edelman, "Biden Wants to Fix the Nation's Teacher Shortage."

programs at historically Black and tribal colleges. Teachers hired or retained per the teacher shortage segment of the AFP would likely exhibit a concern for one touchstone of teaching-for-democracy: the desire to examine what constitutes a good society and to contribute to its creation. The AFP did not succeed at first, but passage of something like it in the future would go far to advance American democracy.

Civil society has not stood still in the face of dialogical-teacher shortages. Building on previous federal projects such as the Peace Corps and AmeriCorps VISTA, Teach For America, a nonprofit organization, recruits and trains college graduates who commit to teach for two years in a public or charter K-12 school. Largely funded by donors from businesses and foundations, Teach For America has supported more than sixty-four thousand teachers in some nine thousand school districts since its founding in 1989.[27] The organization places teachers in underserved communities. It resists a status quo in which ZIP codes are markers for the quality of education students receive. Teach For America seeks and supports dialogical teachers committed to making the world more equitable. It finds and nurtures prospective teachers who commit to expanding opportunities for low-income students and for a more egalitarian society. Participants in Teach For America are trustees of the best in the American founders' legacy.

The two initiatives described above could implement constructive steps to increase the number of dialogical teachers in our schools, but multiple governmental and nongovernmental programs still must secure and train the hundreds of thousands of proficient teachers needed to staff our K-12 classrooms. Of special need are teachers enthusiastic about safeguarding democracy. Concerned Americans must urge our congressional representatives and our neighbors to heighten their awareness of the need for securing teachers who will do as much as they can to preserve democracy when its future is at stake.

John's Reflections

I was with my father, Josiah, when he died in the early morning of Tuesday, October 2, 2001, at the age of ninety-six.[28] During the fall semester of that academic year, Tuesdays were teaching days for me at Claremont McKenna College. That morning, my class on the Holocaust was scheduled to meet at 9:40. I made the decision that I knew my father would

27. See the Teach For America website; as of this writing, the number of TFA alumni is listed at sixty-four thousand. (https://www.teachforamerica.org/).

28. Parts of these reflections are adapted from Roth, *Failures of Ethics*, 106, 186.

want: go and teach. With respect and care, the students received the news about my loss, and then they agreed that the most meaningful thing to do was to keep studying together. That hour with them remains as vivid as my memory of my father's face.

The lesson for that October morning concentrated on reading from Christopher Browning's *Nazi Policy, Jewish Workers, German Killers*. We focused on Browning's findings about the dispositions and motivations that characterized the units of the German Order Police, who killed tens of thousands of Jews in eastern Europe during the Holocaust. Those units were not monolithic. They typically contained three cohorts. The largest group, says Browning, "followed orders and complied with standard procedures but did not evince any eagerness to kill Jews."[29] Smaller in number was "a significant core of eager and enthusiastic killers." Smaller still was "a minority of men who sought not to participate in the regime's racial killing." Browning concluded that they "had no measurable effect whatsoever," but the eager killers "formed a crucial nucleus for the killing process in the same way as eager and ambitious initiators at middle echelons and Hitler, Himmler, and Heydrich at the top." The influence of such ambitious and determined people, added Browning, "was far out of proportion to their numbers in German society." Nevertheless, combined with a compliant majority, that zealous minority produced untold suffering and death. That day my students and I wondered about the meaning of such results, what they imply about justice, and whether death is the last word.

Now in my eighties, I continue to believe that teaching and learning about the Holocaust are crucial, especially in the 2020s when democracy is under threat because too many ambitious and determined people, backed by compliant followers, are prepared to abandon it if not to destroy it. Today Holocaust education must sound the alarm—clearly, insistently, repeatedly: *The Holocaust is a warning*. That has been said before, but now the Holocaust's warning resounds with urgency. It does so because that genocide did not erupt out of the blue, nor was it fated to happen. Human decisions and policies in the 1930s led to disaster. Human policies and decisions in the 1930s led to disaster. Similarly destructive policies are widespread in the 2020s, and similarly destructive decisions are being made now. Hitler's rise to power in 1933 doomed the post–World War I parliamentary democracy of Germany's Weimar Republic. Christopher Browning is right: "America is not Weimar, Trump is not Hitler, Republicans are not Nazis,"

29. Browning, *Nazi Policy*, 167. Subsequent quotations in this paragraph can be found on the following pages of Browning's book: 166, 169, and 175.

but, he rightly underscores, "Weimar's fate provides us with some instructive parallels and important warning signals.[30]

The warning signals are Holocaust-related. Hitler's rise to power, the Nazis' devastation of democracy, culminated in the destruction of the European Jews. That catastrophe—the Holocaust—warns against autocracy and obedience to it. The Holocaust cries out: Beware of big, repeated lies, conspiracy theories, disrespect for evidence and truth, disdain for democracy, and disregard for language that defames and thus inflames division and violence. If such alarms are ignored, the world is worse for it. Absent lies and liars, especially big lies and liars with autocratic power, the Holocaust would not have happened. Nor could autocratic Nazi power, which undermined and destroyed German democracy in the 1930s, have advanced without the compliance and complicity it needed and received from leaders in every sector of German life—education, law, politics, science, medicine, business, sports, the arts, religion. The Nazis' lethally racist antisemitism rested on falsehoods. Nazi power arose because Hitler and his followers bogusly and repeatedly insisted that Germany's defeat in World War I resulted from a "stab in the back" conspiracy that never happened. Nazi propaganda overrode contrary evidence, calling it "fake news," and Hitler's vows to destroy the Jews, who were slandered as a disease-spreading, toxic pestilence in the body politic, show how malignant language becomes deadly. The key point for us Americans is not that failure to heed the Holocaust's warnings destines some version of that genocidal history to be ours, but that failure to heed them endangers everything that we hold dear when we are at our best.

When I started my college teaching career in 1966, I had no plans to pursue Holocaust education. But my reading of Elie Wiesel's writings a few years later put me on that path. Correspondence with him led to friendship. During one of our meetings, his mood turned somber. Wiesel wondered whether his work had changed the world very much, whether it had made a substantive difference. "Well," I replied, "you definitely changed me." I spoke those words as a Christian philosopher whose life had taken not only a professional turn but also an existential one because of Wiesel's life and work.

Learning, teaching, and writing about the Holocaust became more than my work. They became my vocation, my calling. But as I confront the world's dismal state during the third decade of the twenty-first century, which includes the COVID-19 pandemic and Vladimir Putin's 2022 invasion of Ukraine, I sometimes wonder about the degree to which my life's investment in Holocaust studies and education has been ethically worthwhile. Like Wiesel on that day long ago, I ponder in my way whether my admittedly modest

30. Browning, "How Hitler's Enablers."

work has changed the world very much, whether it has made much difference at all. Again and again, however, I find that the truths I defend and the persons who teach me—students and scholars, friends and family—give and affirm the answer: a resounding *yes*, the work remains urgent.

Lenny's Questions

You link Nazi propaganda—a preferred mode of 1930s German "education"—to lies told about "fake news" in the post-truth times of Donald Trump and his disciples. You argue that "absent lies and liars, especially big lies and liars with authoritarian power, the Holocaust would not have happened" and that "the Nazis' lethally racist antisemitism rested on falsehoods." But to believe liars of the kind we face today and to back their falsehoods with MAGA Republican passion, must not those lied to have had the ground prepared for their gullibility? The Germans of the 1930s were heirs of centuries of antisemitism that made them especially vulnerable to the new racial antisemitism espoused by the Nazi leadership. What about the current, seemingly knee-jerk response by so many to Trumpist lies in the 2020s? Why are so many swayed by the lie?

You highlight a seminal theme for educators who aspire to help make the world a better place—an issue of special importance for those who educate in the shadows of the Holocaust: "I ponder in my way whether my admittedly modest work has changed the world very much, whether it has made much difference at all." But what is the measure of success in making a difference? At the close of your essay, you say you have found a response to this question: "I find that the truths I defend and especially persons I have known . . . give me the answer: a resounding *yes*." Why do you believe you have found an answer in these truths and persons? Does empirical evidence play any part in your finding an answer? Is this "finding an answer" something intuitive in nature? What guidance can you give to other educators asking the same question?

John's Response

A few weeks before dying in 1993, the American poet William Stafford recollected a life's work in "The Way It Is," a poem that tracks "a thread you follow." People may "wonder about what you are pursuing," and so, Stafford said, explanation about the thread is important. It is also imperative, he insisted, not to abandon the thread, especially when catastrophes strike and lives are maimed and lost.[31]

You note my saying that "I ponder in my way whether my admittedly modest work has changed the world very much, whether it has made much difference at all." You rightly wonder about the measure of success in making a difference. I think about that too, because the thread I have been following is inseparable from education, from learning and teaching, and thus the thread I follow weaves its way through failure. Education is always failing even when it succeeds. That's because education reveals shortfalls and shortcomings; it exposes mistakes and errors. But education doesn't hand us solutions for those problems, at least not in any simple or final way. At its best, education keeps us searching and seeking; it requires us to keep moving to find out more but with no assurance that what is found will be sufficient to meet the needs.

For decades, I taught students about that elusive concept called the American Dream. Considerations and concerns about democracy were ever-present in that work. For decades, I taught students about the Holocaust. Considerations and concerns about democracy were ever-present in that work too. I could never tell for sure, certainly not at the time, that I was succeeding in encouraging students to love and care for democracy. To the contrary, I knew that my teaching had not done enough to alert and warn them about threats to democracy or to help them resist powers like those that led to the Holocaust. I couldn't do all that was needed to help my students defend what is right and good. But I know that students kept taking those courses. They kept discussing and writing about key issues. They went on to have families and careers that have served people and politics well. These facts have kept me going, even as I become increasingly aware that my teaching and writing have not been good enough.

"There's always Thursday," I used to tell myself. That meant another chance to teach. If things hadn't gone well yesterday or today, I could try again tomorrow. Such a rhythm characterizes education. That's true especially with regard to the challenge you raise when you ask, "Why are so many swayed by the lie?" Big lies were told by Adolf Hitler and his Nazi minions; hordes of Germans lapped them up. Big lies continue to be told by Vladimir Putin. They are also told by Donald Trump and his Republican confederates; hordes of American have lapped them up too. Many factors are at play as people accept big lies and the conspiracy theories that fuel, inflame, and sustain them.

31. Stafford, *The Way It Is*, 42. Portions of this response are adapted from Roth, "What Teaching Teaches Me."

In 1930s Germany, many Germans were easy prey for Nazism because they felt displaced, downtrodden, and disrespected, wronged, left out, and ill-treated in a rapidly changing world. The lie that Jews caused the misery, that removing them from the German body politic would set things right, was an easy sell. In the United States in the 2020s, many Americans—especially undereducated or privileged White males—also feel downtrodden and disrespected, wronged and ill-treated in a rapidly changing world. Changes in the world include US demographic shifts that will soon make the country "minority-majority," giving it a population in which more than half represent social, ethnic, or racial minorities. Blacks and Browns, immigrants and LGBTQ+ persons, Native Americans, and Jews—the belief that they threaten the White hegemony if not supremacy that made and makes America great is both cause and effect of Trumpism. MAGA Republicans have been so enthralled by Trump and Trumpism that they deemed the violent insurrection in the nation's capital on January 6, 2021, "legitimate political discourse."[32]

Nazism's "truths" denied basic human equality and human rights. In Nazism, antisemitism and racism identified "life unworthy of life" and then targeted it for annihilation. Those policies were the antithesis of life, liberty, and the pursuit of happiness. Education didn't stop Nazism and its "Final Solution." Education will not be sufficient to save American democracy either. But absent the questioning, inquiring, and learning, and lacking the nurture and resistance that only education can provide, the major threats to democracy—ignorance, overconfidence, arrogance, tribalism, and stupidity among them—will not be curbed until it is too late.

What guidance, you ask, could I give to educators like us who support and practice education about the Holocaust and American democracy? Holocaust teaching teaches me that despair is the teacher's constant companion. How could it not be?

Most teachers are idealists. However jaded we may become, most of us became educators because we want to mend the world. That hope, however, encounters discouragement aplenty. History, especially Holocaust history, provides it. So does teaching, which is a less than reassuring activity when democracy's future is at stake.

We teachers are all beginners every day. No matter how hard we try, indifference persists, prejudice remains, ignorance endures, and no place on earth guarantees safety from the destruction that such forces can unleash. Education's gains take place against stiff odds. Learning is not a matter of

32. See Weisman and Epstein, "G.O.P. Declares Jan. 6 Attack 'Legitimate Political Discourse.'"

evolutionary progress. Every year, every class, means starting over because wisdom does not accumulate.

Holocaust teaching makes me more melancholy than I used to be. It makes me realize how much despair lurks around every classroom door. Even more, however, Holocaust teaching teaches me that those recognitions are not the conclusion, but instead they must be the beginning of inspiring teaching that produces joy by defending democracy.

Postscript

Especially as the 2024 American elections approach, our exchange about education, the Holocaust, and threatened American democracy contains chilling reminders and ominous implications. It underscores that many Americans may abandon and betray democracy. It shows that nothing guarantees democracy's vitality. To the contrary, democracy is prone to demolition by democratic means as well as by violent insurrections. Furthermore, the cliché that "education is the solution" is naïve and banal in the current American context. Education-for-democracy is under siege in the United States. That does not mean that education will cease. To the contrary, antidemocratic, authoritarian regimes depend on education. They require obedient teachers and students who absorb make-America-great-again narratives about history, and the myths about American exceptionalism that define them.

Especially as the 2024 American elections approach, we think about what Abraham Lincoln said during the American Civil War when he gave his annual address to Congress on December 1, 1862.

> We can succeed only by concert. It is not "can *any* of us *imagine* better?" but, "can we *all* do better?" The dogmas of the quiet past are inadequate to the stormy present. The occasion is piled high with difficulty, and we must rise—with the occasion. As our case is new, so we must think anew, and act anew. We must disenthrall ourselves, and then we shall save our country.[33]

Echoing those convictions, our exchange about education contains encouraging reminders and aspirational implications. When we, Lenny and John, defend democracy, when we explore the Holocaust's anti-democratic darkness and its warnings, when we protest and resist Putin's atrocity-laden aggression against Ukraine, we know that we are not alone in doing that work. We remain convinced that a majority, even a decisive

33. Lincoln, Annual Message to Congress—Concluding Remarks.

majority, of Americans stands with us. But no one in that company should be silent or indifferent, unaware or unmoved about how precarious democracy's future remains as 2024 comes and goes. The thread we Americans must follow has to recognize and deal with American failures and shortcomings. But if we never let go and keep following where that thread leads when we are at our best, then we can learn and teach one another what it takes to defend and do what is right and good.

4

Religious Traditions

THE GERMAN PASTOR HERMANN Gruner spoke for many Christians in the Third Reich when he said, "It is because of Hitler that Christ, God the helper and redeemer, has become effective among us . . . Hitler is the way of the Spirit and the will of God for the German people to enter the Church of Christ."[1] Adolf Hitler despised democracy and Judaism alike. His relationship to Christianity was more complicated. He welcomed support like Gruner's but saw that his enemies included dissenting German Christians who found Gruner's words heretical and blasphemous. One of those was the resisting theologian Dietrich Bonhoeffer. Arrested on April 5, 1943, he was judged complicit in the July 20, 1944, assassination plot against Hitler, and executed by hanging on April 9, 1945. When Nazi Germany surrendered a month later, its soldiers still wore belt buckles inscribed "Gott mit uns"—God is with us—and Hitler's murderous words from *Mein Kampf* (My Struggle) remained as chilling as they were fevered when he wrote them twenty years earlier: "Hence today I believe that I am acting in accordance with the will of the Almighty Creator: *by defending myself against the Jew, I am fighting for the work of the Lord*."[2]

Antisemitic, antidemocratic, genocidal—Hitler's power depended on support from nationalistic, right-wing, "Aryan"-supremacist Christians—Protestants and Roman Catholics—who bought the lie that Hitler sold, namely, that he was God's man for Germany. Such toxic alliances neither began nor ended with Nazi Germany. Versions of them threaten democracy in the 2020s because they exist in Russia and in the United States.

Patriarch Kirill, head of the Russian Orthodox Church, has called Vladimir Putin's leadership "a miracle of God," and Putin himself the "chief exorcist" in what some Russian leaders see as the "desatanization"

1. Quoted in *Christianity Today*, "Dietrich Bonhoeffer."
2. Hitler, *Mein Kampf*, 65. Hitler's emphasis.

of Ukraine.[3] Orthodox dissent against Kirill's judgment is widespread but insufficient to prevent church authority from aiding and abetting Putin's autocracy, including the genocidal war in Ukraine and the corruption, kleptocracy, and cynicism that thrive within the lie that Putin is in any way "a miracle of God." But Putin understands that religion can confer legitimacy and power. He embraces and amplifies Kirill's religiously inspired sense of destiny. A dream to make Russia great again, it envisions the restoration of an empire "flowing from the 10th-century baptism of the Slavic tribes in Kyiv, which was then the center of lands known as Rus."[4] That Russian supremacist vision informs Putin's multiple falsehoods that Ukraine never was a separate state, properly belongs to Russia, and must be cleansed of "Nazis," the dehumanizing, lethal canard that Putin applies to pro-democracy Ukrainians who defy his treachery.

Authoritarian, antidemocratic, genocidal—Putin's power intertwines with nationalistic, fascist, Russian Orthodox imperialist Christianity to advance the lie that Putin pushes, namely, that he is God's man for Russia in its battle against Western democracies that, he claims, are besieging Russia and robbing it of rightful empire and hegemony.[5] In many ways, Moscow and Washington, DC, are as far apart as they can be. The same seems true of Putin, his Russian Orthodox patriarch, and his oligarchs, on the one hand, and 2020s life in the United States, on the other hand. But thinking twice about the ideological distance or proximity today between Russia and the United States is crucial because White Christian nationalism intertwines with the Trumpist Republican Party to degrade American democracy.[6]

A former Trump press secretary, Sarah Huckabee Sanders, elected governor of Arkansas in 2022, spoke for many conservative American Christians in 2019 and beyond when she said, "I think God calls all of us to fill different roles at different times, and I think that he wanted Donald Trump to become president and that's why he's there. And I think he has done a tremendous job in supporting a lot of the things that people of faith really care about."[7] Amplifying Sanders's adulation, Trump boasted: "You know, nobody has done more for Christianity. Nobody has done more for religion of all types than me."[8]

3. Bryanski, "Russian Patriarch"; van Brugen, "Putin Appointed 'Chief Exorcist.'"

4. Whalen, "Russian Orthodox Leader."

5. On Putin's fascism, see Snyder, "We Should Say It."

6. For an incisive, data-based analysis on this topic, see Gorski and Perry, *Flag and the Cross*. See also Wilson-Hartgrove, "Faith Is Powerful."

7. Boorstein, "Sarah Sanders."

8. Brody, "'Everything I Said Was Right.'"

Arrogant, authoritarian, antidemocratic—Trump's power has corrupted a willing Republican Party that bends its knee to him and to the White Christian nationalists who are Trump's most loyal followers and a bedrock Republican constituency. White Christian nationalism, which is antidemocratic, racist, and even friendly to violence, tells and defends what the sociologists Philip Gorski and Samuel Perry call a "deep story" about the United States, its past and its future.[9] The story claims that the United States, blessed by God, was founded as a Christian nation. Foreign and domestic threats against that Christian hegemony must be fought and defeated. A primary threat to that Christian hegemony looms in the likely change from White majority rule to multiracial, multireligious, and multicultural democratic rule, which is incompatible with White Christian nationalism. Convinced that Whites and Christians are wronged and persecuted in the very nation that is rightfully theirs, White Christian nationalists embraced Trump and Trumpism to protest the perceived assault on their prerogatives and to protect their privileges.

In the 2020s, fear and division are deeply rooted in American life. White Christian nationalism testifies to that. The history of Hitler's Germany and Putin's Russia shows that when fear and division go deep enough, murderous, even genocidal dehumanization follows. Fear and division in the United States have not descended into that abyss, but much work must be done to keep such disaster at bay. Religious traditions did not intervene to stop, let alone prevent, the Holocaust or Russia's destructive assault on Ukraine. To the contrary, religious traditions aided and abetted more than they resisted those catastrophes. In the United States, religious traditions have not intervened, at least not enough, to curb the threats against American democracy, especially the threat of White Christian nationalism. When the quiet parts of White Christian nationalism are spoken aloud, its outlook comprises racism, xenophobia, and patriarchy cloaked in a "Christian" ideology as heretical as its "American" history is misguided. Unless better religious traditions in the United States resist White Christian nationalism, democracy's American future will be increasingly fraught and fragile. As Christian and Jewish philosophers, we assess what our religious traditions can and should do in the 2020s to improve democracy's chances in the United States.

9. Gorski and Perry, *Flag and the Cross*, 3–12. See also Whitehead, "3 Threats"; Whitehead and Perry, *Taking America Back*.

John's Reflections

A distinctive moment in President Joe Biden's inaugural address on January 20, 2021, took place when he cited Saint Augustine, the classical Christian thinker. That "saint of my church," said Biden, "wrote that a people was a multitude defined by the common objects of their love." Biden went on to identify fundamental values that define us Americans when we are at our best: "Opportunity. Security. Liberty. Dignity. Respect. Honor. And, yes, the truth." Then he added these telling words: "There is truth and there are lies. Lies told for power and for profit. And each of us has a duty and responsibility, as citizens, as Americans, and especially as leaders—leaders who have pledged to honor our Constitution and protect our nation—to defend the truth and to defeat the lies."[10]

In a post-Holocaust, authoritarian-besieged world, Biden spoke the truth. In doing so, he reminded an American Christian like me to do the same. Nothing has troubled me more about Donald Trump's political grip on the United States than the slavish support he received and still gets from White, mostly evangelical and definitely conservative Christians. I agree with the late Michael Gerson's judgment that "the overwhelming support of evangelicals is the single largest reason that Trump possesses power in the first place."[11] Trump's support from White evangelicals, moreover, increased between 2016 and 2020. That support, which, as Gerson added, "sought to recover lost social influence through the cynical embrace of corrupt power," besmirches Christianity. Trump, insisted Gerson, should enrage Christians, but instead "much of what considers itself Christian America has assumed the symbols and identity of white authoritarian populism—an alliance that is a serious, unfolding threat to liberal democracy."[12]

What should I—the White, American, eightysomething son of a Presbyterian minister—try to defeat and defend about Christianity in my country's troubled 2020s? White evangelical Christianity is a problematic religious tradition in the United States because it is allied with authoritarian and antidemocratic Trumpism. Some White evangelicals resist that alliance—Russell Moore prominent among them—but they are a minority. Meanwhile, no threat to democracy in the United States is greater than White Christian nationalism. It is the American "cousin" of both the German Christian nationalism that supported Hitler and his genocide against the European Jews and the Russian Orthodox Christian

10. Biden, "Inaugural Address."

11. Gerson, "Trump's Evangelicals Were Complicit."

12. Gerson, "Trump Should Fill Christians with Rage." See also Verhagen, *How White Evangelicals Think*.

nationalism that has backed Vladimir Putin and his grisly war in Ukraine. In the United States, White Christian nationalism, whose allies include some Roman Catholics, "mainstream" Protestants, and even secular fellow travelers, is not synonymous with White evangelical Christianity. But the overlap with the American evangelical tradition is significant, striking, and sinister. The difference and the overlap pivot on the degree to which White Christian nationalism and White evangelical Christianity privilege White power to define and control American identity and the future of the United States—legitimating violence, if necessary, to do so.[13] If Christians abandon Christianity at its best and fail to resist White Christian nationalism, then God help us.

January 6, 2021, the day of right-wing American insurrection when the United States was engulfed in the darkness of Trump's attempted election-overturning carnage, was also Epiphany. That Christian observance commemorates the visit of the magi, the three gift-bearing wise men from the East who, tradition holds, followed a bright star that led them to the infant Jesus. Epiphany honors grace, truth, and light, the opposites of the corruption, falsehood, and darkness that Trump and White Christian nationalism embody and spread through the United States and thus into the world. So, it was good that President Biden's inauguration included the glowing presence and moving words of the young and brilliant Black poet Amanda Gorman. "The Hill We Climb," her inauguration recitation, ended with a theme worthy of Epiphany. "For there is always light," she said, "if only we're brave enough to see it, if only we're brave enough to be it."[14]

The light was there all along. I could see it, but not bravely enough to highlight it, not often enough to be it: One cannot be loyal to Trump and to Jesus. No one can be a White Christian nationalist and truly be a Christian. Indeed to be loyal to Jesus requires resisting Trump, Trumpism, and Trumpists at every turn. In 2020s America, saving democracy from the threat of White Christian nationalism is especially what authentic Christian commitment requires. So I am grateful to stand with Christians Against Christian Nationalism (https://www.christiansagainstchristiannationalism.org/), an initiative many thousands strong that denounces Christian nationalism's dangerous distortion of American and Christian values.[15]

But lots of Americans, especially White Christian nationalists, have tried to maintain a contradictory dual loyalty—Trump and Jesus—and still

13. Gorski and Perry, *Flag and the Cross*, 3–12.

14. Gorman, "Hill We Climb."

15. For further information about Christians Against Christian Nationalism, see Seidel et al., *Christian Nationalism*; Vlamis, "Christians Against Christian Nationalism."

claim it. In early 2016, the Christian nationalist megachurch preacher Robert Jeffress, one of Trump's chief loyalists, said of Trump, "I don't want some meek and mild leader or somebody who's going to turn the other cheek. I've said I want the meanest, toughest SOB I can find to protect this nation."[16] Drawing Trump's wrath, Jeffress declined to endorse Trump early on in the 2024 campaign, and the megachurch pastor has tried to distance himself from Trump's incitement of mob violence on January 6, 2021, but in the aftermath of the insurrection, Jeffress still insisted that "I don't regret for one minute supporting him.[17] Whether or how robustly evangelical leaders will support Trump in 2024 remains to be seen. His problematic conduct and legal difficulties have cooled their support for him, and Trump's flaws may be enough to tilt evangelical chiefs toward conservatives such as Mike Pence or Ron DeSantis. But if Trump wins the Republican nomination, leading evangelical Christians and especially White Christian nationalists are still likely to his prominent supporters.[18]

If they are truly Christians, Jeffress and his ilk should disavow and repent for their support for Trump and Trumpism. Whether they do or not, stupidity saturates their allegiance because carnage results from every attempt to make loyalty to Trump and Trumpism compatible with loyalty to Jesus. That relationship is as pernicious as it is unsustainable. Trump has been no Cyrus, no modern-day version of the Persian king who brought deliverance from Babylonian captivity to Jews in the sixth century BCE. Instead Trump's depravity and the Faustian bargain that White American evangelicals made with him in exchange for conservative judicial appointments, xenophobic nationalism, opposition to abortion and to LGBTQ+ rights, and support for White supremacy disrespect Jesus and discredit Christianity in ways that will wound for years to come.[19]

The integrity of American Christianity depends on confession of Trump-embracing sin and on contrition that seeks to restore credible fidelity to Jesus. The restoration must underscore how corrupt and wrong it is to ever invoke the name of Jesus in support of lies, racial discrimination, White supremacy, and violent insurrection against democracy. The contrition must begin by acknowledging that especially but not only White evangelical Christianity sold its soul to Trump and to a complicit and collaborationist Republican Party. As a liberal Protestant Christian, I do not exempt myself

16. Mooney, "Trump's Apostle."

17. Boorstein, "Trump Faith Advisors." See also Knowles, "Christian Leaders."

18. See Haberman and Bender, "Some Leaders Are Wavering"; and Homans, "Seeking Evangelicals' Support Again."

19. See, for example, Du Mez, "How Abortion"; Posner, "Southern Baptist Convention's Deal."

from failure, because I have not resisted the current American corruption of Christianity enough, let alone well enough.

The guiding light of Jesus is much needed in a fractured United States. I side with James Wallis, dissenting American evangelical pastor and social activist, the founding editor in chief of *Sojourners* magazine, when he argues that "there is a conflict between the politics of Jesus and the politics of Trump." Says Wallis: "Racial bigotry is a deal breaker for the Gospel. White nationalism, which Donald Trump embraces and champions, isn't just racist—it's anti-Christ. Dehumanizing immigrants isn't just racist—it's anti-Christ. Demeaning women isn't just sexist—it's anti-Christ. At some point," Wallis underscores, "Christians have to ask themselves: Are the teachings of Christ going to be followed or not?"[20] As I think about Jesus and Wallis's question, what looms largest for me when it comes to coping with the Trumpism and White Christian nationalism that besiege the United States, when it comes to doing what Jesus tells us Christians to do, when it comes to what American Christians most need to do to defend democracy?

My response to Wallis's question takes me to the environmentalist Bill McKibben. In his 2022 book *The Flag, the Cross, and the Station Wagon*, he notes that the United States is a post-Christian nation because all forms of Christianity—including evangelical as well as "mainline" Protestantism—are in decline. I share that view and, like McKibben, don't regret it. "If you're the culture," he says, "then you can't be the counterculture."[21] Post-Christian times free Christians who remain to be "not a dominant part . . . but a wonderfully useful part" in "movement for human betterment." McKibben notes an experience that undergirds those convictions. As a young writer at the *New Yorker*, he copied the Gospels by hand. What struck him was "how unrelentingly radical the Gospels were." Armed that way, minority Christians in a post-Christian United States can take stands, if we will, that challenge Americans to be better than we are. Here are some of those key New Testament teachings and insights that I find imperative to embrace and enact:

- "'You shall love the Lord your God with all your heart, and with all your soul, and with all you mind.' This is the greatest and first commandment. And a second is like it: 'You shall love your neighbor as yourself.'" (Matt 22:37–40; see also Mark 12:28–34)
- "I was hungry and you gave me food, I was thirsty and you gave me something to drink, I was a stranger and you welcomed me, I was

20. Quoted in Steinberg, "Trump v. Jesus."

21. McKibben, *Flag*, 130, 131, 134.

naked and you gave me clothing, I was sick and you took care of me, I was in prison and you visited me . . . Truly I tell you, just as you did it to one of the least of these who are members of my family, you did it to me . . . Truly I tell you, just as you did not do it to one of the least of these, you did not do it to me." (Matt 25:35–36, 40, 45)

- "In everything do to others as you would have them do to you" (Matt 7:12)
- "Go and do likewise." The mandate that Jesus gave after telling the parable of the good Samaritan. (Luke 10:25–37)
- "For what will it profit them to gain the whole world and forfeit their life? Indeed, what can they give in return for their life?'" (Mark 8:36–37)
- "And everyone who hears these words of mine and does not act on them will be like a foolish man who built his house on sand. The rain fell, and the floods came, and the winds blew and beat against that house, and it fell—and great was its fall!" (Matt 7:26–27)
- "Those who say, 'I love God,' and hate their brothers or sisters, are liars; for those who do not love a brother or sister whom they have seen, cannot love God whom they have not seen. The commandment we have from him is this: those who love God must love their brothers and sisters also." (1 John 4:20–21)
- "Do not be deceived; God is not mocked, for you reap whatever you sow." (Gal 6:7)
- "Love is kind; love is not envious or rude . . . It does not rejoice in wrongdoing, but rejoices in the truth." (1 Cor 13:4–6)
- "Whoever says, 'I have come to know [Jesus],' but does not obey his commandments, is a liar, and in such a person the truth does not exist." (1 John 2:4)
- "The truth will make you free." (John 8:32)
- "Finally, beloved, whatever is true, whatever is honorable, whatever is just, whatever is pure, whatever is pleasing, whatever is commendable, if there is any excellence and if there is anything worthy of praise, think about these things." (Phil 4:8)
- "So let us not grow weary in doing what is right, for we will reap at harvest time, if we do not give up." (Gal 6:9)
- "Do not claim to be wiser than you are." (Rom 12:16)

Practicing what these admonitions preach may not be sufficient to restore American democracy. But following these injunctions is necessary to save American Christianity from betraying Jesus and from acting in complicity if not with outright intent to destroy the chances for American democracy to be at its best and strongest—multireligious, multicultural, multiethnic, and with equal justice and liberty for all.

Lenny's Questions

The New Testament teachings with which you conclude your reflections hopefully inspire Christians and non-Christians alike to help restore American democracy. Several passages instruct us that merely to listen to God's words about justice and truth is not sufficient: we must *enact* what we hear. "Doing so," you say, "is necessary to save American Christianity from betraying Jesus"—such a betrayal is currently being conducted by White Christian nationalists. You emphasize putting these teachings into practice, citing Amanda Gorman's urging that we must be brave enough to be the light.

You echo Abraham Joshua Heschel's imploring us to pray with our feet. I believe you would agree with his claim that to realize God's mission, a "leap of action" is required. Although it is daunting to attempt to speak *of* God or *to* God, the ultimate challenge comes when we are asked to respond to the question: how do I *live* God? What you've written makes me think of the Hebrew prophet Amos, who hears God say, "I hate, I despise your festivals, and I take no delight in your solemn assemblies . . . But let justice roll down like waters, and righteousness like an ever-flowing stream" (5:21, 24).

If Christians and those who take other religious and spiritual paths fail to reclaim and practice the ethical imperatives at the core of their respective traditions, the chances of saving American democracy will have been dealt a serious blow. If Trumpism suppresses religion's prophetic voice, religion—thus hijacked—will wound rather than heal and divide rather than unite. You emphasize White Christian nationalism's threat to American democracy. You also note that such threats have abundant precedents and counterparts.

Two months after Hitler became Germany's chancellor in January 1933, he named Christianity "the foundation" for all German values. Many German Christians subordinated New Testament teachings to Nazi principles, delivering a critical blow to democracy. And currently, Moscow's Russian Orthodox patriarch, Kirill, gives significant support to Putin's invasion of Ukraine. In the words of the director of an American project documenting war crimes in Ukraine, Kirill has "staked the fortunes of his branch of Orthodox Christianity on a close and mutually beneficial alliance with Mr. Putin, offering him spiritual cover while his church . . . receives vast resources in return from the Kremlin."[22] Such "mutually beneficial" alliances can kill democracies.

In the context of current Trumpist attacks on democracy, following the call of Jesus means that it is "imperative to embrace and enact" the New Testament teachings you cite. You think that many American Christians have done less than they should to heed Jesus's teachings, and you do not exempt yourself from that charge. What would it mean for you, personally, to *enact* Jesus's call in your everyday life? What are some ways that realizing Jesus's words in practice might affect your work as teacher and writer? What changes might occur in the conduct of your church life? Or in how you live your life at home and in the local community? In what ways would the quality of your participation as a citizen of the United States be different?

Sometimes your descriptions of Trump and his supporters imply that they are unwilling or even unable to reason and engage in sincere discussion about core human values. Are we to write off the possibility of meaningful dialogue between Trumpists and authentic followers of Jesus? I don't want to be naïve in asking that question. Speculation about fruitful dialogue must not interfere with urgent work to protect American democracy. The electoral task at hand is to support the Democratic Party after the 2022 midterm elections and to do our best to protect democracy in the 2024 presidential election. But as we act to defend democracy and the teachings of Jesus and other prophets, might we still engage "the other" dialogically? Otherwise, won't we be dismissive of the breadth and depth of the humanity of "others" who espouse Trumpism?

I think it would be foolish to initiate attempts at dialogue with Trump himself or with his hardest-core supporters. But among his backers aren't there people—perhaps neighbors of ours—who are open to dialogue? Might we work from the outside in, beginning with the neighbor who has placed a Trump sign on his or her lawn, but who I know shares with me the joys of grandparenting and the outdoors? Such connections might open the door to dialogue about critical matters. Even though there is little to no chance that such dialogue would lead to agreement, is not the process itself a statement of faith in a shared humanity, a commitment to lessen divisiveness in our society? I believe that in addition to more explicitly political work, it is meaningful to sow such seeds as we endeavor to heal a nation whose democratic fabric is being torn asunder.

22. Di Giovanni, "Real Reason."

John's Response

How do I enact Jesus's call in my everyday life? What's the quality of my American citizenship? Am I closing off dialogue with others who do not agree with me? Does my analysis disrespect their humanity? How do I *live* God? To start my response to your searching and humbling inquiries, I recall the words of a centuries-old Christian hymn, a prayer that asks and challenges as much as your questions do. "God be in my head," it begins, "and in my understanding. God be in my eyes," it enjoins, "and in my looking. God be in my mouth," it implores, "and in my speaking. God be in my heart," it entreats, "and in my thinking. God be at my end," it yearns, "and at my departing." That prayer is one I need. My shortcomings and failures mean that I must repeat it often, with contrition and hope that my life may embody God's goodness better tomorrow than I did today or yesterday.

Jesus embodied God's goodness. He did so when he spoke truth to power in the tradition of the Hebrew prophets, who insisted that God's goodness requires justice to "roll down like waters, and righteousness like an ever-flowing stream" (Amos 5:24). He did so when he insisted that the two greatest imperatives of his Jewish tradition are to love God and one's neighbor as oneself.

Justice and love—that's what I must try to enact if I hear and heed the call that Jesus keeps making to me, a call that informs my American citizenship and confers responsibility for American democracy upon me. In the 2020s I am teaming with you, Lenny, to author a book intended to amplify and extend dialogue and respect for difference. But I cannot be an honest dialogue partner if I fail to speak not only as boldly and courageously as I am capable of doing but also as wisely as the times require. At their best, Judaism, Christianity, and other religious traditions honor *wisdom* and seek to cultivate it. Christian wisdom is inseparable from the New Testament passages I have cited. But today wisdom is in short supply and hard to come by. When I consider why that is the case in the United States today, I am again reminded of the resisting German theologian Dietrich Bonhoeffer. His astute writings include a brief but powerful essay called "After Ten Years." Written in December 1942, it assessed what had happened in Germany after the Nazis took control in late January 1933. Bonhoeffer's writings continue to be studied because they are timely, perceptive, and prophetic. "After Ten Years" fits that description and nowhere more so than in four paragraphs that he called "On Stupidity" (Von der Dummheit).

As Bonhoeffer used *stupidity*, he did not have in mind, at least not primarily, conventional meanings that emphasize gross ignorance, lack of intelligence, or mental deficiency. Instead Bonhoeffer's use of *stupidity* connotes arrogance, refusal to respect evidence, willful blindness, acceptance of lies and lying, and collusion in the chaos and carnage that result when political ambition clouds judgment and power corrupts action. Many German Christians and churches thought that loyalty to Jesus was compatible with loyalty to Hitler. Bonhoeffer rejected and resisted that stupidity. He would have seen and condemned as stupid how White evangelical Christians brought Donald Trump to power, inspired obedience to him, and fortified complicity with him. He would have seen and condemned as stupid how White Christian nationalism undermines American democracy and erodes the shared values that make Americans a people instead of a multitude or, worse, a mob. Bonhoeffer's "Stupidity" reflections are as relevant for our times—splintered by lies, corruption, racism, and antidemocratic authoritarianism—as they were for his. Stupidity may not be a sufficient condition or explanation for the American plight, but surely it is a necessary one.

"Stupidity," Bonhoeffer wisely wrote, "is a more dangerous enemy of the good than malice."[23] Here's why Bonhoeffer thought so. "There are human beings," he observed, "who are of remarkably agile intellect yet stupid." (Ivy League–educated Christian nationalist politicians such as US senators Ted Cruz and Josh Hawley, as well as fellow traveler Ron DeSantis, Florida's Catholic governor and a presidential aspirant, come to mind along with White evangelical Christian leaders such as Ralph Reed and Robert Jeffress.) Bonhoeffer continued: Sound reasons do not reach the deaf ears of those intellectually agile but unwise men and women, facts that contradict their prejudgment "simply need not be believed . . . and when facts are irrefutable they are just pushed aside as inconsequential, as incidental." Such stupidity leads to self-satisfaction, and thus to irritation that produces danger when attacks against opposition follow. Bonhoeffer's implication, I believe, is that Nazi ideology was rife with stupidity, exemplified by the falsehood that Jews are a pestilential race that must be eliminated root and branch. Trumpism has some similarities with Nazi stupidity—after all, Trumpism is rife with false claims about the 2020 US presidential election, with problematic American "exceptionalism," and with adherence to debunked conspiracy theories, baseless bromides against commonsense gun safety regulations, and continued loyalty to an authoritarian and antidemocratic leader, Donald Trump, who is as truthfully discredited and disgraced as he is morally debased.

Stupidity made Nazism lethal—and stupidity corrupts much of American Christianity and thus American life more generally—because,

23. 20 For the quotations from "On Stupidity," see Bonhoeffer, *"After Ten Years,"* 22–23. Some translations use "folly" for the German *Dummheit*, but Bonhoeffer's meaning is better captured by "stupidity."

as Bonhoeffer understood, stupidity is "not an intellectual defect but a human one" that has sociological as well as psychological qualities. "People," contended Bonhoeffer, can be "*made* stupid or . . . they allow this to happen to them" because "the overwhelming impact of rising power" can deprive people of "inner independence" so that "one virtually feels that one is dealing not at all with . . . a person, but with slogans, catchwords, and the like." (One thinks of Trump's mantra—Make America Great Again—or of the National Rifle Association nonsense of its CEO Wayne LaPierre Jr., that "the only thing that stops a bad guy with a gun, is a good guy with a gun.") Bonhoeffer saw that such stupidity could make people "capable of any evil and at the same time incapable of seeing that it is evil." (Consider Trump's "rallies" and the mob violence at the US Capitol that he inspired.)

An unrelenting cause and effect of Nazi power, stupidity was essential to sustain the policies and practices that constituted the "Final Solution." Stupidity is also essential to sustain the policies and practices—buttressed by debased forms of Christianity—that rot American life. In Bonhoeffer's view, such stupidity, once entrenched, won't yield to instruction or persuasion, at least not completely. Nevertheless, he was not hopeless. Stupidity, Bonhoeffer emphasized, is not "a congenital defect," nor are most people stupid "in every circumstance." Everything depends, he concluded "on whether those in power expect more from people's stupidity than from their inner independence and wisdom." (Engulfed in corruption and cunning produced, at least in part, by their own stupidity, Trump and his chief accomplices, including White Christian nationalists, expect and get much—including vast sums of cash—from the stupidity they have counted on and inflamed in their followers.) Stupidity akin to the kind identified by Bonhoeffer is a crucial cause of the fragmentation in American life in the 2020s.

In mid-June 2011, Elie Wiesel—recipient of the 1986 Nobel Peace Prize—had emergency surgery that saved his life. Less than a year later, he published a brief but significant book called *Open Heart*, which reflected not only on the operation and his recovery but also on his life and work. "I belong," he stressed, "to a generation that has learned that whatever the question, indifference and resignation are not the answer." Then he underscored, "If life—mine or that of my fellow man—is not an offering to the *other*, what are we doing on this earth?"[24] Wiesel died on July 2, 2016, before Trump became president of the United States or Putin invaded Ukraine, but his wisdom and his question live with greater urgency than ever.

Reflecting its Jewish roots, the New Testament refers to a deep-down longing called hunger and thirst for righteousness. The Gospel of Matthew,

24. Wiesel, *Open Heart*, 75.

for example, reports that Jesus said, "Blessed are those who hunger and thirst for righteousness, for they will be filled" (5:6). I doubt that Jesus was completely right about that, but the verse's yearning, passion, and hope remain on target to me, even as I recognize that the tasks of righteousness can never be completed.

At its fullest and best, *righteousness* includes wisely discerning what the goodness of God requires of us. It means thinking wholeheartedly and acting not only justly but also compassionately and with love. It compels being accountably offended—especially at oneself—when such opportunities are bypassed or squandered. Righteousness stands for justice, defends critical inquiry, seeks truth, rejects racism, and supports inclusiveness. Such qualities, I believe, are as well summarized as they are persuasively reinforced by a Methodist tradition in Christianity that interprets hunger and thirst for righteousness, the imperative for it, as follows:

> Do all the good you can,
> By all the means you can,
> In all the ways you can,
> In all the places you can,
> At all the times you can,
> To all the people you can,
> As long as ever you can.

To the extent that Americans live that way, what we are doing in the world will include trying our best to curb stupidity and save democracy.

Lenny's Reflections

I approach study of the Holocaust as an American and a Jew who takes seriously the ethical teachings of the prophetic tradition. I am not a Jew who participates, except infrequently, in the rituals that respond to biblical and rabbinic injunctions. Although well-educated in Jewish studies in my youth and although a student of the Jewish-inspired philosophies of Martin Buber and Emmanuel Levinas, I—a non-synagogue-goer—am usually regarded by others as a "cultural Jew." That designation, however, fails to speak to me. I am a Jewish scholar of the Holocaust—the grandson, nephew, and cousin of Holocaust victims. My awareness of their murder by Nazi killing squads led me to the field. Further, both my study of the Holocaust and the inspiration I get from the writings of the Hebrew prophets have contributed to my cherishing American democracy and, especially now, to my working to strengthen it.

Religions can divide and unite. They can wound or heal. The philosopher of religion John Hick rightly emphasized that "throughout history almost all human conflicts have been validated and intensified by religious sanctions."[25] Yet religions can also help to resolve conflicts, summoning us, in the words of Isaiah in the Hebrew Bible, to beat our "swords into plowshares, and . . . spears into pruning hooks" (Isa 2:4)." We find in Judaism, as we find in its fellow religions at their best, an embrace of justice and a fundamental respect for others. But, like other religious traditions, Judaism's sacred texts and lived history have also given rise to contrary beliefs and actions, including those that have resulted in the demonization of others.

Institutionalized religions do not have clean hands. Yet, through the tainted history of my tradition, I hear, loud and clear, the biblical proclamation: "Justice, and only justice, you shall pursue" (Deut 16:20). Prophetic voices lead me to ask how Judaism might contribute to healing the divisions currently besetting our nation. What assistance can Judaism provide to those of us committed to safeguarding America's democracy in the 2020s?

Post-Holocaust Judaism encounters daunting challenges with regard to the prophetic call. In the face of the Nazi murder of one out of three Jews alive just eighty years ago, Jews today are summoned to ask what lessons are to be learned from the Holocaust. Although this question is not unique to Jews—all of us must confront the ethical challenges posed by this watershed event—Jewish heirs of a European genocide and Christian heirs to acts of perpetrators face especially formidable trials. Whether or not a contemporary American Jew is an actual descendant of Holocaust victims, the trauma of genocide may well remain in regions of mind and heart. Post-Holocaust Christians face trials of their own.

How do lessons from the Holocaust inform those American Jews progressively aware of our democracy's fragility? The phenomenon of "othering"—increasingly prevalent in the current attacks on American democracy—was rife toward Jews during the Holocaust. During the 1930s and 1940s, the rejection of fleeing Jewish refugees by President Franklin Roosevelt and other leaders doomed many of the six million murdered Jews. Although the racism of Germans and their European supporters during the Holocaust knew no bounds, Jews had not been strangers to persecution in their past. During nineteen centuries of antisemitism, Jews have been among the world's most "othered" peoples.

25. Hick, "Pluralism Conference," 253. See also Brown and Smith, eds., *Routledge Handbook on Religion, Mass Atrocity, and Genocide*; Roth, "What We Know."

Ironically, Jews, so often oppressed, are enjoined to take special responsibility for honoring the personhood of others. Welcoming the other is a central Jewish imperative, first expressed in the Hebrew Bible where the commandment to love those different from me is found at least thirty-six times. The biblical prophets tell us that responsibility toward others, especially the alien other, is radical: I am called upon to regard all others as creatures born in the image of God. The Holocaust shows profoundly what can happen when individuals and religious traditions fail to regard others as inviolable.

Many Jewish organizations, both those whose members observe ritual and those whose adherents are more secular, have risen to the occasion to fight for social justice and, in particular, to defend our currently imperiled democracy. They have stood in the shadows of the Holocaust and learned. Reform Judaism is the largest of the three main American Jewish denominations. The Reform movement has traditionally been a staunch defender of democratic values. Currently advocating for progressive positions on such burning issues as voting rights and immigration justice, the denomination has been especially politically active in current times. Reconstructionist Judaism, originally an offshoot of the Conservative movement, has followed the lead of the Reform movement and now occupies a leadership position in social justice advocacy, asserting, for example, that "we must act now in defense of democracy and in support of a vibrant, principled America that protects all minorities."[26] Reconstructionists have spoken out against the current upsurge of xenophobia: "We Reconstructionist Jews see the erosion of welcome . . . and the institution of anti-Muslim, and anti-Latino, and anti-immigration policies as evidence of a severe moral decline."[27] Reform and Reconstructionist Judaism have largely heeded post-Holocaust ethical imperatives.

Grassroots Jewish organizations in the United States also promote justice. For example, more than a hundred Jewish Community Relations Councils advance such work, advocating that equal opportunity must exist "for individuals irrespective of race, religion, ethnicity, political affiliation, gender identity, sexual orientation, or physical or mental disabilities."[28] They seek "common ground among those with a broad range of religious affiliations, opinions, and ideology by facilitating constructive dialogue."[29] Both grassroots organizations and major denominations within the

26. Waxman and Rosen, "We Must Work to Ensure."

27. Schwartzman, "Reconstructionist Affiliates."

28. Jewish Community Relations Council of San Francisco, "B'Tselem Elokim."

29. Jewish Community Relations Council of San Francisco, "Core Values."

religious community bear witness to Judaism's concern for a just, egalitarian democracy.

Jewish organizations are not monolithic in their chosen missions. Some organized groups have failed to heed important ethical lessons of the Holocaust. Several, for example, demonstrate an often-unquestioned support for Israel's positions in its conflict with the Palestinians. The Conference of Presidents of Major American Jewish Organizations and the American Israeli Public Affairs Committee—US Jewish organizations often called upon or presumed to speak for the community as a whole—have fostered a well-documented bias in America's alleged role as impartial mediator in the Middle East conflict.[30] Although Israel faces ongoing dangers to its well-being—dangers, some argue, to its very existence—post-Holocaust American Jewish leadership has often failed to heed the prophetic injunction to aid the widow, the orphan, the alien, including Palestinians in occupied lands who require the assistance of American leadership to realize self-determination in a nation of their own. Jews have certainly been innocent victims of centuries of oppression and must always have the means to defend themselves in today's Israel. However, in the words of the philosopher Emmanuel Levinas, himself a Holocaust survivor, "the more innocent we are, the more we are responsible" to and for others.[31] Like other American religious traditions, Judaism has a mixed record in hearing and following prophetic voices calling for the justice and equality dimensions of democracy. Some teachings from the Holocaust have been heeded, others not.

American Jews, like members of many other ethnic and religious groups, have an added imperative to defend democracy. American Jews have experienced antisemitism, destructive and sometimes deadly, but American democracy has usually shielded them from its most virulent and vicious forms. Along with other forms of xenophobia, however, antisemitism has reared its head with vigor in Trumpist times. Like those belonging to several other ethnicities and religions—and certainly like peoples of color—American Jews have been increasingly subject to verbal and physical abuse in recent years.[32] Summarizing an Anti-Defamation League (ADL) report about the United States (released on January 12, 2023, Jonathan Greenblatt, who heads the ADL, called its findings "stunning and sobering: there is an alarming increase in antisemitic views and hatred across nearly every metric—at levels unseen for decades."[33] In safeguarding an imperiled democracy, Jews

30. See, for example, Robinson, "What Is U.S. Policy."

31. Levinas, "Ethics and Politics," 291.

32. Anti-Defamation League, "ADL Audit Finds Antisemitism Incidents."

33. Anti-Defamation League, "Number of Americans Harboring Extensive

act for a common good that includes their own endangered well-being. Success in defending American democracy depends significantly on how well Jews answer prophetic calls for justice and equality.

John's Questions

As a Jew and an American who studies the Holocaust, you defend democracy in the United States against forces that betray it. I study the Holocaust as an American Christian, and thus I also try to defend democracy. So I start my questions by recalling that on the evening of May 5, 2022, Mike Pence, the former vice president of the United States during the Trump administration, spoke at a pro-life, antiabortion fundraiser in Spartanburg, South Carolina. "We're about to enter an era of the renewal of the sanctity of life, so help us God," said Pence. Referencing Samuel Alito's leaked Supreme Court draft opinion about the fate of abortion rights and the overturning of *Roe v. Wade*, Pence affirmed his hope that Alito's highly problematic denial of abortion rights "soon becomes the majority opinion of the Supreme Court of the United States." He urged prayer that "those five [judges] might have the courage of their convictions and send *Roe v. Wade* to the ash heap of history where it belongs."[34] After the overturning of *Roe v. Wade* on June 24, 2022, Pence celebrated by violating the court's provision that decisions about abortion belonged to the nation's states. Pence affirmed that the next step should be a national ban on abortion.[35]

Religions, you rightly state, can divide and unite. That fact loomed large during the Holocaust. Absent Christian support for Hitler's antidemocratic, antisemitic Nazism, the European Jews would not have been murdered in the Holocaust. Absent his alliance with Patriarch Kirill and the Russian Orthodox Church—Pope Francis warned Kirill that he should not become "Putin's altar boy"—Vladimir Putin would have been less emboldened to launch genocidal war in Ukraine.[36] Absent ongoing support from White evangelical Christians, Trump and Pence would not have been elected in 2016. Nor would democracy and women's rights be threatened as they have become in the United States. When you say that religions can unite, I understand that you have in mind a process that resists destructive division and "othering" in particular. But religions produce division because they can unify people around a vast variety of allegiances that are unfriendly

Antisemitic Prejudice Doubled."

34. Mackenzie, "Hundreds Gather."

35. Alfaro et al., "Pence Calls for National Abortion Ban."

36. Bella and Westfall, "'Don't Be 'Putin's Altar Boy.'"

and even hostile toward democracy and human rights. When Pence urged prayer to send abortion rights to the ash heap of history, he could count on fervent support from White, nationalist, and Trumpist Christians who intend to wield their minority power to control the behavior of the majority of Americans who oppose them. How do you differentiate between religious uniting that divides and religious uniting that seeks to overcome the authoritarianism that threatens democracy?

That question is complex because the biblical injunction to pursue justice needs clarification to make the differentiation stand. Mike Pence and his followers appeal to justice to defend "the sanctity of life." Some of them, in fact, invoke the Holocaust—massive murder of the innocent—to justify their antidemocratic opposition to abortion. Their opponents resist by decrying misappropriation of the Holocaust and by invoking justice too. Paraphrasing Abraham Lincoln's 1864 Civil War-insight that Americans "all declare for liberty, but in using the same *word* we do not all mean the same *thing*," it can be said that all sorts of people appeal to justice, even Hitler, Putin, and Trump, but they do not mean what the Hebrew Bible or the Christian New Testament means by that word.[37] What's the difference that makes all the difference in the world?

A similar issue lurks in your desire to overcome the destructiveness of "othering." You stress that Jews are called—but not only Jews—to honor "the personhood of others," to see "all others as creatures born in the image of God," and "to regard others as inviolable." Those words appeal to me—until they don't or at least not until they contain more lucidity than the phrases alone contain. Should I regard Hitler's personhood as inviolable, or should I continue to wish that various plots to assassinate him had succeeded before he could do his worst? What does it mean to say that Vladimir Putin was born in the image of God? How do I honor the personhood of Donald Trump and his Trumpist followers, whose lying and deceit will destroy American democracy if they have their way?

The Constitution of the United States encourages Americans to seek "a more perfect Union." As the First Amendment affirms, that goal requires that "Congress shall make no law respecting an establishment of religion, or prohibiting the free exercise thereof." Freedom of religion and the separation of church and state—as fraught as they are fundamental, as contested as they are shared, these principles require caring attention in the 2020s. When religious nationalism, authoritarian politics, and antidemocratic senses of justice support one another, a poisonous, lethal

37. Lincoln, Address at Sanitary Fair.

outcome awaits. What can religion do to forestall that fate? Where are the best allies for that religious resistance to be found?

Lenny's Response

You do well to ask for elaboration and clarification of my contentions—explicit or implied—that we humans are born in God's image, that the personhood of all others is inviolable, that "justice" as articulated in aspects of the Jewish tradition is the way justice should be understood, and that religions' call to "unite" may be problematic.

I speak about seeing all of us as born in the image of God. I think that's important if we are to overcome the destructiveness of "othering." But you ask me to clarify what that assertion means. I respond by recalling my opening remarks during a university course I taught for many years, a course called The Holocaust: Philosophical Issues. I would tell my students that for the next fifteen weeks we were going to study Holocaust perpetrators, bystanders, and victims. I added that we should be less fearful that we might become *victims* of future genocidal actions and more fearful that we might be among the *perpetrators*. Concluding my introductory remarks, I would say that we all exist on a moral continuum. At its negative endpoint is Hitler—joined nearby today, it could be said, by Putin and Trump.

Among the wonders of human birth is the enormous plasticity, the potential to be realized, in the unfolding of new life. Morally speaking, the claim that we are born in God's image is less *descriptive* of a fixed "human nature" and more an *imperative* to embody and expand the goodness that Jewish tradition says God saw in the creation of humankind. The contention that we are born in God's image is thus more directive than depictive. Being (born) in God's image is more verb than noun. Existentialist philosophers rightly insist that human living is an ongoing process. We continually make ourselves who we are and will be. Morally speaking again, the claim that we are born in God's image is a call for us to transcend ourselves—to become more just, more caring, more giving and less greedy, less cruel, less selfish. In more traditional religious terms, we are summoned to reach toward divinity, to sanctify our existence.

That Hitler, Putin, and Trump failed to heed that call does not mean that they were not born in God's image. These individuals chose—two continue to choose—to debase their own potential to move beyond a self-interested existence in which others must become subject to their authoritarian desires and dictates. They choose to live in ways that disrespect the inviolability of others. That disrespect makes them hostile to democracy because, at its best, respect for the inviolability of others is a core attribute of democracy.

In societal terms, heeding the call to respect the inviolability of others entails valuing the kind of parenting, then schooling, that nurtures commitment to the justice and equality that undergird democracy. No system of parenting or educating guarantees democracy's existence. Individuals must choose to hear and abide by what is modeled and taught about democracy's significance and value. In a post-Holocaust world—and in a world where Ukrainian and American democracies are under attack—we need to remind ourselves continually about the inviolability of our fellow human persons. We must never forget that the injunction "You Shall Not Murder" is a baseline for democracy.

To say, as I imply, that "Hitler's personhood is inviolable" does not mean that I would refrain from defending my life and the lives of others against his genocidal acts. I wish that the July 1944 attempt to assassinate Hitler had succeeded. A genocidal murderer has violated personhood—not only that of others but his or her own as well. Such action deserves no impunity. Such self-destruction of personhood, when it harms and destroys others, deserves no privileges. It must be stopped. In the 2020s, Putin and Trump violate their own personhood by refusing to hear and heed the injunction to act justly and to respect others rather than to divide, corrupt, and destroy them. Putin kills Ukrainian civilians to advance his genocidal version of "Russia's greatness." Trump's corruption is manifest in his infamous statement that "I could stand in the middle of Fifth Avenue and shoot somebody and I wouldn't lose any voters."[38] Violating their own personhood by destroying the inviolability of others, their destruction of humanity-in-the-image-of-God is beyond unacceptable.

Further, you remind me that Judaism's call to live justly assumes an understanding of justice that is not necessarily shared—indeed, is sometimes contradicted—by persons and parties who coopt and employ the same term. A distinctively biblical and Talmudic sense of justice is found in the frequent use of that word in the context of welcoming the stranger, the widow, the orphan, the poor one. Deuteronomy (27:19), for example, succinctly states, "Cursed be anyone who deprives the alien, the orphan, and the widow of justice." Representing the voices of Judaism's prophetic tradition, Jeremiah (22:3) proclaims, "Act with justice and righteousness . . . And do no wrong or violence to the alien, the orphan, and the widow." According to Emmanuel Levinas, moreover, to act justly toward the stranger is no mere "corollary

38. Bump, "If Trump Shot Someone Dead."

of Judaism . . . but . . . is the very content of faith."[39] Certainly, more narrowly tribal tenets regarding "justice" are also found in the Hebrew Bible. Yet the later rabbinic tradition often attempted to provide necessary correctives. Rabbis cited in two Talmudic tractates, Megillah (10b) and Sanhedrin (29b), have God incensed when the Hebrews celebrate their freedom as their former Egyptian enslavers drown in the Red Sea: "How dare you sing for joy when My creatures are dying." Justice in the context of welcome is to be extended to the foreigner, the "other"—an ethic utterly absent from any alleged "justice" embraced by the likes of a Hitler, Putin, or Trump.

Finally, you ask for explication about the "uniting" potential of religions. I agree that religions can "unite" people around ideas-become-ideologies. It is clear that Germans invoked Christianity in support of Nazism; that the blessing of the Russian Orthodox Church eased the way for Putin's unjustifiable invasion of Ukraine; that Trump's election depended on the zealous support of White evangelical Christians. Religious traditions have often embraced exclusivism that declares their particular and often highly problematic "truth" to be *the* truth. Politicization of a tradition takes place time and again. The use of political power to champion religious ideology and the use of religious ideology to legitimate political power all too often divide the human community, bolstering one side or another in existing conflicts or spawning new ones. When that happens, democratic society, which requires and boosts dialogue among equals, gets defaced.

Yet religions contain antidotes to human division, including resources for justice and peacemaking. At their best, each in its own idiom speaks of transcending ego-driven concerns in the name of just and peaceful resolution of conflict. These traditions can be mined for teachings that welcome the other—teachings that unite. Religion can wreck and destroy democracy, but at its prophetic best, religion defends and sustains it. My Jewish tradition acknowledges the incomplete nature of creation; it affirms and insists that the world needs repair. The imperative to mend the world, *tikkun olam*, tasks humankind, formed in God's image, to be God's partner in creating a just world at peace. Revitalizing American democracy is a crucial step in that process.

Postscript

A constellation of events in May 2022 focused how religious traditions and vulnerable American democracy are intertwined. On May 14, Payton S. Gendron, an eighteen-year-old White supremacist, drove from two

39. Levinas, *Difficult Freedom*, 173.

hundred miles away to the Tops Friendly Market, a grocery store in a Black neighborhood in Buffalo, New York. Clad in body armor, Gendron opened fire with his AR-15-style rifle. He shot thirteen people, killing ten of the eleven Black persons among them. Gendron's murders resulted from his belief in the Great Replacement conspiracy. Steeped in White supremacy, antisemitism, and hostility to immigrants, this lethal lie claims that immigrants, Jews, and nonwhites intend to oust Whites, especially White Christians, from power and even from the American population.

Two days later, on May 16, the authoritarian and antidemocratic Hungarian leader Viktor Orbán won a fourth consecutive term as his country's prime minister. A favorite of Donald Trump, the Fox News quisling Tucker Carlson, and Republican stalwarts such as Elise Stefanik and Ron DeSantis, Orbán, who was likely well aware of the Buffalo shooting, reiterated his endorsement of the view that Western civilization—in Hungary, throughout Europe, and in the United States—is jeopardized by cabals intent on making White populations, Hungarian or American, "an endangered species."[40] As the journalist Zack Beauchamp insightfully discerned, Orbán "has elevated fear of demographic replacement into a central governing ideology, serving as justification for a policy agenda that demonizes minorities and helps cement his hold on power."[41] On a variety of issues—including the rights of women and LGBTQ+ persons—the Republican Party moves closer to Orbán's increasingly far-right Fidesz Party, a fact underscored when the Conservative Political Action Conference (CPAC) opened a meeting in Budapest on May 18 and invited Orbán to speak there. Trump's video address to the meeting hailed Orbán as "a great leader, a great gentleman."[42]

On May 17, far away from Budapest but nearby politically, Pennsylvania Republicans voted overwhelmingly to make state senator Doug Mastriano their candidate for governor in the November 2022 election. American democracy became less endangered when Democrat Josh Shapiro soundly defeated Mastriano, who intended to advance antidemocratic authoritarianism. Channeling Christian nationalism, election denialism, and rejection of COVID-19 mitigation policies, he spent weeks trying to subvert Pennsylvania's victory for Joe Biden and then participated in the January 6, 2021, insurrection at the Capitol. Claiming that he would "restore freedom," Mastriano delivered a nomination victory speech that denounced coronavirus vaccine and mask mandates, attacked critical race theory (CRT), advocated "school transparency" (parents must have more control over what is taught in

40. Beauchamp, "European Country."

41. Beauchamp, "European Country."

42. Milbank, "Hero of the Trump Right."

schools), ensured that "only biological females can play on biological female teams," and insisted that "you can only use the bathroom that your biology anatomy says."[43] His twenty-three-point primary election win showed that he checked all the right-wing Republican boxes and then some.

The editorial board of the *Washington Post* issued a response to Mastriano's nomination. Fortunately, many Americans heeded its warning.

> Mr. Mastriano's alarming rise, and that of other election deniers who have won GOP primaries this year, call for two urgent responses. General election voters must reject candidates who, either through delusion or partisan calculation, deny valid election results. Inflation, the Ukraine war, gasoline prices, the covid-19 pandemic—none of these issues are as important as preserving the democratic order. Americans should vote like it.[44]

The journalist Michelle Boorstein highlighted dangers that her colleagues on the *Washington Post*'s editorial board did not. Mastriano embodies White Christian nationalism. His nomination showed that ideology to be a mainstream element in Trumpist or MAGA Republicanism.[45] "We have the power of God with us," Mastriano told his followers, "We have Jesus Christ that we're serving here. He's guiding and directing our steps." The sociologist Philip S. Gorski, coauthor of *The Flag and the Cross: White Christian Nationalism and the Threat to American Democracy*, regards Mastriano as perhaps the "most purely distilled version of a Christian nationalist politician I've run across."[46] Both democracy and Christianity in the United States got a reprieve—but no more than that—when Mastriano lost and conceded in Pennsylvania.

In the early 2020s, about 45 percent of the American population are White Christians, with 15 percent of that cohort identifying as White evangelical Protestant. Overall, the number of White Christians in the United States, including the population of White evangelical Protestants, the "base" of White Christian nationalism, has been in decline in the twenty-first century.[47] Christian nationalists are a minority in the United States, but their

43. Bump, "Doug Mastriano."

44. Editorial Board, "After the Pennsylvania Primary."

45. Boorstein, "Christian Nationalism."

46. Reyes and Seidman, "Doug Mastriano Embodies."

47. On these points see the PPRI (Public Religion Research Institute) 2021 analysis, "Religious Affiliation Updates and Trends." For data and analysis of Jewish demography in the United States, see Cohen Center for Modern Jewish Studies and the Steinhardt Social Research Institute, *American Jewish Population Estimates 2020*. The report estimates that 7.6 million persons in the United States are Jewish, about 2.4 percent of the American population. Including approximately 1.5 million children, the American

antidemocratic intentions and their embrace of authoritarianism should not be underestimated. Emboldened by the US Supreme Court's 2022 decision in *Dobbs v. Jackson Women's Health Organization* to rescind abortion rights guaranteed in *Roe v. Wade* (1973), Christian nationalists often emphasize "Dominionism," the conviction that right-thinking Christians should control virtually every aspect of American society, including the government. As Katherine Stewart, religion journalist for the *New York Times*, soundly observes, "The shape of the Christian nationalist movement in the post-Roe future . . . should terrify anyone concerned for the future of constitutional democracy . . . Breaking American democracy isn't an unintended side effect of Christian nationalism. It is the point of the project."[48]

Religious resistance did too little to curb the support that Hitler received from German Christians and their churches. Nor is Putin's backing from Russian Orthodox Christianity checked by religious opposition. In the United States, adherents of Christian, Jewish, Muslim, and other religious traditions who are wary of White Christian nationalism have not done enough in the 2020s to defend religious pluralism and the separation of church and state. Absent religious as well as political commitment to those bedrock principles, democracy falters everywhere, but especially in the United States.

Christian tradition holds that wise persons followed a star that led them to Jesus. Long before that story was told, Jewish tradition affirmed that God created heaven and earth and human life in God's image. On the fourth day of creation, the Jewish narrative says, "God made the two great lights—the greater light to rule the day and the lesser light to rule the night—and the stars. God set them in the dome of the sky to give light upon the earth, to rule over the day and over the night, and to separate the light from the darkness. And God saw that it was good" (Gen 1:16–19).

Much later, on May 12, 2022, astronomers on the Event Horizon Telescope team announced the existence of a supermassive "black hole" at the center of the Milky Way. Named Sagittarius A*, it is twenty-seven thousand light-years away from Moscow, Kyiv, or Budapest, from Washington DC or Pennsylvania. Scientists gave assurances that Sagittarius A* does not threaten Earth, but descriptions of its awesome nature and immense power are thought-provoking and even mind-boggling. This black hole, for example, "reaches temperatures measured in the trillions of degrees." It bends space and time. What is called the black hole's event

---

Jewish population comprises 4.9 million adults who identify their religion as Jewish and 1.2 million Jewish adults who identify with no religion.

48. Stewart, "Christian Nationalists Are Excited." See also Stewart, *Power Worshippers*.

horizon is "the boundary of no return—the point at which an infalling piece of matter vanishes into an inescapable gravity well." What's at the black hole's core, scientists say, is "unknowable."[49]

Sagittarius A* should humble and humanize us all. Although its reality is awesome, the black hole has metaphorical power too. Can religious traditions help us to avoid black holes of our own making, boundaries of no return in which democracy as we have known it vanishes, and hopes for its restoration and strengthening are forlorn? All religious traditions—individually and even collectively—are incomplete, fallible, corruptible, in need of contrition and correction, reform and revitalization as they encounter one another, probe themselves, expand their horizons, and resist injustice. If the right religious and especially interreligious responsibilities become more pronounced and practiced, there may still be hope for fragile but much-needed democracy.

49. Achenbach, "Supermassive Black Hole."

5

Death and the Dead

Biblical tradition holds that God turned "dust of the ground" into human life (Gen 2:7). That transformation did not preclude death. No matter our status, wealth, or power, we human beings are finite and frail. Our days are numbered. Death awaits us. But how we die, and therefore how we live, makes the difference between civilization and carnage, justice and injustice, what is true, right, and good, and what is not. Struggles to create, defend, and sustain democracy illustrate and clarify that point.

On April 30, 1945, Adolf Hitler, at fifty-six years of age, committed suicide in his bunker in Soviet-besieged Berlin. The end of World War II in Europe, but not its far-reaching aftermath, soon arrived when Nazi Germany unconditionally surrendered to the Allies on May 7–8. Precise death statistics for World War II are impossible to verify. The carnage was too prolonged and vast. But that war, the largest and most lethal in human history to date, took the lives of between seventy million and eighty-five million persons. That number includes fourteen million victims of mass killings in what the Yale historian Timothy Snyder calls, "the bloodlands," eastern European territories, today's Ukraine among them, that were subject to wartime control by Nazi Germany or the Soviet Union at one time or another.[1] Adolf Hitler bears huge responsibility for the death toll, including for the murder of approximately six million Jews during the Holocaust. Had German democracy been successfully defended and sustained in the 1930s, the children, women, and men wasted in Nazi war crimes, crimes against humanity, and genocide would not have eluded eventual death, but it would have taken them far more humanely. Grief and sorrow would have remained, but the tears would have been less bitter and more healing.

Vladimir Putin is in his seventies. He may not commit suicide, but he too will die. How much blood will be on his hands remains to be seen. Unless he unleashes catastrophe through a meltdown at the Zaporizhzhia

1. Snyder, *Bloodlands*, 409–14.

nuclear plant in Ukraine if not by using nuclear weapons in his ruthless war against Ukrainian democracy, he may not murder as many as Hitler or Joseph Stalin, the dictator-predecessor he admires, who killed more people than Hitler. But Putin's death toll puts him high on the list of those who have committed ghastly atrocities. His escalating terror has made refugees of more than 4.5 million Ukrainians, more than half of them finding safety in Poland. If Russia were a twenty-first-century democracy, Putin would not be in power, and his corrupt and murderous ways would not be at play. Democracy matters. A lot.

Donald Trump has committed many crimes, but murder, let alone mass murder, is not among them. Trump is reminiscent of the Italian fascist Benito Mussolini, and his antidemocratic demeanor and deportment show his attraction to strongmen, including to Putin if not to Hitler.[2] Now in his late seventies, Trump too will die. How much blood will be on his hands is less the question than how weakened American democracy will be when death takes him. Trumpism won't die with Trump. It is deeply embedded and embodied in the MAGA Republican Party of the 2020s, so much so that the April 20, 2022, tweet by the American filmmaker-activist Rob Reiner went viral because so many Americans found him on target when he said, "It couldn't be more simple. A vote for Republicans is a vote to destroy democracy."[3] The continuing damage Trumpist Republicanism can inflict on democracy in the United States has the potential to immensely weaken the prospects for democracy worldwide.

We—Lenny and John—were alive when Hitler committed suicide. Although too young to be aware of Hitler's demise at the time, we have spent much of our lives trying to fathom what he did and to guard against the recurrence of such disasters. The wrack and ruin unleashed by Putin and Trump testify that we have scarcely been successful. But as death approaches for us, we keep trying because we remember the murdered dead, the ones destroyed in the Holocaust, in other genocides, and in Ukraine. We listen to their silenced voices, seeking to discern and amplify what they might say to us if they could speak. We think they would support our view that democracy is a necessary if not sufficient condition to curb mass-atrocity crimes and to enhance human flourishing.

2. For further insight on this point, see Applebaum, *Twilight of Democracy*; and Ben-Ghiat, *Strongmen*.

3. See Reiner, "It couldn't be more simple"; see also O'Donnell, "Lawrence Asks."

John's Reflections

Until the first week of April 2022 few Americans had heard of Bucha or Kramatorsk. But during that time those Ukrainian cities appeared repeatedly on television news in the United States. Often the reports about them came with warnings: the video clips will be "disturbing;" the scenes will be "hard to take." Those cautions were understatements because the videos and reports about Bucha and Kramatorsk depicted crimes—torture, rape, murder—inflicted on Ukrainian civilians by Vladimir Putin's Russian military.

Occupied by Russian soldiers for a month, Bucha, a city of thirty-seven thousand near Kyiv, Ukraine's capital, was the site of atrocities that killed hundreds. When Ukrainian forces took Bucha back, they found the dead. With hands tied behind their backs, some victims had been executed by gunshots to their heads. The bodies of the murdered, decaying and desecrated, showed the carnage brought to once-vibrant neighborhoods by barbarous Russian aggression. Where mass graves were found, they contained the bodies of children. In Kramatorsk, a city of 157 thousand east of Bucha, a missile attack targeted a train station where civilians waited to evacuate before Russian troops arrived. It killed at least fifty persons and injured many more. Near the train station, a Ukrainian salvage team found a missile fragment. Written in Russian, the inscription on it—For the Children—was as cynical and chilling as the missile had been lethal. Predictably, Russian reports denied the truth and disrespected the dead by claiming that Ukrainians "staged" these atrocities or, worse, committed them against their own people.

Amid the carnage, what Timothy Snyder saw was even more sinister and deadly. In one of the "Thinking About . . ." reports that he has circulated to email subscribers, Snyder documented on Sunday, April 3, 2022, that RIA Novasti, the official Russian press agency, had published what he called "an explicit program for the complete elimination of the Ukrainian nation as such."[4] Even if Putin—who deserves his "Butcher of Bucha" epithet—does not perpetrate genocide in Ukraine, the Russians' murder of civilians exceeds anything that has happened in Europe since World War II and the Holocaust. By late January 2023, less than a year after the Russian invasion began, more than sixty-six thousand war crimes had been reported in Ukraine.[5] On March 17, 2023, the International Criminal Court issued an arrest warrant for Putin, indicting him for war crimes.[6] Undeterred,

4. Snyder, "Russia's Genocide Handbook."

5. Sly, "66,000 War Crimes."

6. International Criminal Court (ICC), "ICC Judges Issue Arrest Warrants."

steeped in fear, fraud, and fascism, Putin and his regime do not want a democratic Ukraine on Russia's border. If they have their way, Ukraine will be a puppet state—if it exists at all—and its democracy will be destroyed. No democracy anywhere in the world, including the United States, can afford to let that happen. Nothing drives home that proposition more than careful attention and listening to the murdered dead.

One cannot know about Ukraine, one cannot encounter the Holocaust and other genocides without confronting death as atrocity—brutal, unjust, and relentless. In the streets of Bucha and Kramatorsk, in the ghettos, killing fields, and gas chambers of the Holocaust, a "good death," one that comes with a person "at peace," surrounded by loving family and friends, was scarcely possible. Before and after the Holocaust—in Armenia, the former Yugoslavia, Rwanda, Darfur, Myanmar, Xinjiang, and now in Ukraine—war crimes, crimes against humanity, and genocide escalate death as atrocity to overwhelming enormity, which includes the desecration that robs the dead of respect, consigning their bodies to unmarked mass graves, to decay and rot, to incineration in mobile Russian crematoria, to disrespect and disappearance.

Facing death as atrocity involves at least two unsettling apprehensions. First, the murdered dead have faces, defaced, devoured, and now completely obliterated though they may be. What meanings or lack of meanings do those faces possess and communicate? Second, as one contemplates the murdered, trying to see their lifeless and mutilated faces, how does doing so affect deep-down understanding of the implications for democracy that such catastrophes reveal and underscore?

When the Auschwitz survivor Charlotte Delbo wrote her memoir-trilogy, *Auschwitz and After*, her account, which often drew attention to the dying and the dead, challenged her readers to *look*, to *try* and *see*. One spring evening in Auschwitz, Delbo and her worn-out prisoner companions returned to the camp after another long day of punishing slave labor. This time, her work detail carried the bodies of Berthe and Anne-Marie, two comrades beaten to death—helplessly, hopelessly—when they collapsed from exhaustion that afternoon. Every evening, the Germans required that the prisoners—the dead and the living—had to be counted, and so it was with Berthe and Anne-Marie, who were lined up for "roll call" with those who had carried their lifeless bodies back for the tally. When the count ended, darkness had fallen, but while the roll call lasted, Delbo writes, "we never looked at them." And then her depiction continues, but less with continuity than with disruption: "A corpse. The left eye devoured by a rat. The other open with its fringe of lashes. Try to look. Just try and see."[7]

Whose corpse did Delbo's description identify? During the roll call, Delbo says, "we never looked at them," and yet she urges her readers—and even herself?—to look. But whose body does she want her readers—and even herself?—to see? Berthe's? Anne-Marie's? Delbo leaves the corpse unnamed. It's just the one with the rat-devoured left eye, the one whose right eye is fringed with lashes and still as open as it is sightless. Delbo leaves her readers—and even herself?—to bridge the disruption if that can be done.

This much can be done: It must be said that what happened to that person was wrong. Like the murdered dead in Ukrainian cities and towns, the corpse Delbo had in mind was once a living person, a woman or a man, a girl or a boy, with a name—one who had parents and friends, one who was loved, and one who deserved neither to be robbed of life by the perpetrators of mass atrocity crimes nor to be left in degradation after being senselessly beaten to death and reduced to a mark in the death column of a Nazi roll call in Auschwitz.

The American psychologist David Boder was among the first to interview survivors of the Holocaust and other Nazi crimes after World War II. He published eight of these interviews in 1949. Boder ended his book's introduction with these words: "The verbatim records presented in this book make uneasy reading. And yet," he added, "they are not the grimmest stories that could be told—I did not interview the dead."[8] That last, thought-provoking phrase—I did not interview the dead—became his book's title.

We cannot interview the murdered dead, but by seeing them, by not turning away but by letting them dwell in our lives, we may give them a voice that speaks to and through us in ways that fit Robert Pogue Harrison's wise observation that "the dead are our guardians. We give them a future," he says, "so that they may give us a past. We help them live on so that they may help us go forward."[9] Such action cannot bring back those done to death by lies and lawlessness, autocracy and the corruption on which it depends and thrives, but it would help to create a present and a future—and even a past—more worth having.

In silence, we can hear and listen to the murdered dead. No one deserves to die this way—that's what the corpse that Charlotte Delbo wants us to see would say if it could. No one deserves to die this way—that's what

7. Delbo, *Auschwitz and After*, 84.

8. Boder, *I Did Not Interview the Dead*, xix. For a significant study of Boder and his work, see Rosen, *Wonder of Their Voices*.

9. Harrison, *Dominion of the Dead*, 158.

the butchered dead in Bucha and the missile-shredded bodies in Kramatorsk are saying if we listen. Take nothing good for granted—that's what the corpse that Charlotte Delbo wants us to see would say if it could. Take nothing good for granted—that's what the butchered dead in Bucha and the missile-shredded bodies in Kramatorsk are saying if we listen. Defend democracy; do not let it be destroyed by deception and deceit, but protect it against lies big and small that weaken and corrode it—that's what all the dead defaced by war crimes, crimes against humanity, and genocide would say if they could.

If democracy had not been destroyed in Germany in the 1930s, no Auschwitz would have existed, and no Holocaust would have happened. History and philosophy convince me of that. The idea is so counterfactual as to be almost unimaginable, but if Russia were a democracy, Bucha and Kramatorsk would not be the sites of mourning that they have become. Ukraine's sovereignty and democracy would not be subjected to Russia's war-crime-ridden aggression. History and philosophy also convince me of that. But democracy was destroyed in Germany in the 1930s. It did not exist in the Soviet Union and does not exist in Putin's Russia. Those realities put the world in dark places. Auschwitz and Treblinka but also Bucha and Kramatorsk are warnings. Failure to defend, protect, and expand democracy imperils what is right, just, and good.

The warnings require Americans to defend, protect, and expand democracy at home as well as abroad. If we Americans do not do that demanding work, our democracy will decay, and we are unlikely to be resolute in helping others who seek to secure democracy for themselves. The US senator Raphael Warnock sounds a note that we Americans especially need to hear and heed. "Democracies don't die overnight," he has wisely said. "They slowly erode before completely dismantling. We can't let that happen."[10] Charlotte Delbo's insistence anticipates Warnock's: "I beg you," she said, "do something . . . something to justify your existence . . . because it would be too senseless after all for so many to have died while you live doing nothing with your life."[11] My conclusion follows hers: The murdered Jews of the Holocaust and the Ukrainians murdered by Vladimir Putin warn us Americans to resist tyranny and to save our democracy from the Trumpists and Trumpism that will erode, dismantle, and even destroy it if they are empowered and have their way.

10. Warnock, "Democracies don't die overnight."

11. Delbo, *Auschwitz and After*, 230.

Lenny's Questions

You say that the dead challenge us to let them dwell in our lives, that they impel us not to let democracy die. On April 10, 2022, in response to Putin's atrocities in Ukraine, Thomas Friedman underscored the summons to defend democracy: "When Ukrainians are making the ultimate sacrifice . . . is it too much to ask that Americans make the smallest sacrifices and compromises to hold on to our precious democratic inheritance?"[12] You recall the warnings on television that video clips about the Ukrainian cities of Bucha and Kramatorsk are "disturbing." Yes, we are distraught at the sight of Ukrainian civilians cruelly murdered, sometimes after suffering torture. Hopefully, we are "disturbed" in ways that move us to act in support of American assistance in preserving democracy abroad, while we sustain efforts to keep our democracy alive at home. If we are attentive, we can hear the dead questioning us, insistent that we remember them.

You say that democracies do not die suddenly; I certainly agree. The unraveling of democracy in 1930s Germany was gradual until Hitler took control in January 1933. Portents about what was coming went unheeded. If Hitler's lies seemed inconsequential at first, they produced dire consequences. Words matter. First published in 1925, Hitler's *Mein Kampf*—partly autobiography, partly political playbook—fared modestly for several years. By late 1932, however, about two hundred thirty thousand copies had been sold. Then, in 1933 alone, the sales soared to eight hundred fifty thousand.[13] By 1939, sales of *Mein Kampf* rose to 5.2 million, making Hitler as wealthy as he was powerful. Realization of the full significance of Hitler's' book came far too late.

When I think about early warnings that our own democracy is fading, I ask myself—a Holocaust scholar and thus someone who might be expected to heed such warnings—what I missed and may continue to overlook. Two failures to respond to warning signs loom large. First, I was not "disturbed" early or intensely enough by the deep divisions developing between red and blue America—divisions in evidence prior to the 2016 election. A vibrant democracy rests, in part, on the willingness of citizens to talk openly and respectfully to one another, even when strongly disagreeing about key issues. I shied away from attempts to engage in meaningful dialogue with Trump followers I had gotten to know. Living in an urban bubble with people mostly like me, I avoided contact with those I presumed to be caught up in a Trumpist sect—people unable or unwilling to "listen to reason." I

12. Friedman, "How Do We Deal with a Superpower?"

13. United States Holocaust Memorial Museum, *Holocaust Encyclopedia* (website), "*Mein Kampf*."

had withdrawn from the dialogical arena, from the attempt to see Trumpists as capable of change that would lead them to preserve and not plunder our democracy. And so I ask: What role, however small, can we who are committed to preserving democracy play in bridging the chasm between us and Trump followers who may not be as unreachable as they seem? How do we begin to overcome biases rooted in class stereotypes? How do we avoid failing to realize in practice that, as the novelist Marilynne Robinson declares, "any human face has a claim on you"?[14]

Secondly, I often neglected to listen to what you, citing Delbo, refer to as the call of the dead demanding that we "take nothing good for granted." In today's America we cannot afford to take good things for granted. To remain indifferent in the face of current threats to our democracy is to engage in bystander behavior, calling to mind the passivity of so many "ordinary Germans" during the Holocaust. I ask: How might we continually remind ourselves that what we have is a blessing to be protected? How do we "live" the acknowledgement that we've been gifted with democracy, imperfect though it is, which must be protected and expanded lest we lose it. How, concretely, do we sustain what are often only fleeting moments of gratitude for what we have? How do we act best to express that gratitude? How do we respond to the dead, who remind us not to take what is good for granted?

John's Response

Your comments move me—emotionally, philosophically, politically. They make me realize that I need to do more and to be better at trying to bridge chasms between red and blue America. Your comments also make me think again and anew about the ways in which democracy is a blessing, something gifted to me, to us Americans, and how and why it is something good that must not be taken for granted. My response highlights that a renewed emphasis on what we Americans share and value in common may help to bridge the chasms and increase gratitude that includes determination to take nothing good for granted.[15]

I begin by recalling that in April 2022, Ukrainians battled to preserve their sovereignty and democracy from invading, war-crime-committing Russian forces hell-bent on destroying the Ukrainian state and its democracy. At least for a time in the spring of 2022, nothing did more to start bridging the American red-blue chasm than the deeply felt conviction that the United States must help Ukraine. Differences existed about the best way

14. Robinson, *Gilead*, 66.

15. Parts of my response are adapted from Roth, *Private Needs, Public Selves*.

to do that, and too many Americans seemed more concerned about gas prices and economic inflation than about authoritarian threats that endangered democracy in Ukraine and at home as well. Nevertheless, Ukraine's plight had a unifying effect on the United States.

It remains to be seen how much influence the unifying will have as the country moves beyond the November 2022 midterm elections, debates and disagrees about sustained support for Ukraine, and approaches the presidential election in 2024, which has so much to say about democracy and its future in the United States. Events in April 2022 foreshadowed the importance of November 2024. At that time, the US Congressional Select Committee to Investigate the January 6th Attack on the United States Capitol reaffirmed its March finding that the former president, Donald J. Trump, likely broke the law by trying to obstruct Congress's counting of electoral votes in the 2020 presidential election, which Trump lost, and by engaging in a criminal conspiracy to defraud the United States.[16] Adding to that coup attempt—its success would have destroyed American democracy—the *New York Times* reported on April 8, that Trump's son Donald Trump Jr. had texted his father's chief of staff, Mark Meadows, two days after Election Day 2020—votes were still being tallied—to say that all the bases were covered to ensure Trump's second term. "It's very simple," the younger Trump told Meadows. "We have multiple paths. We control them all." As the message explained, the paths for overturning a fair and free election included making legal challenges, appointing alternative electors, and using the statutory date of January 6 to delay and deny—the former president's favorite strategy—certification of the Electoral College results.[17]

Americans can be misled. They can willingly and willfully embrace falsehoods and lies. They can be driven to seek wealth and power while disregarding the common good. They can deny historical facts that show how deeply racism, hate, inequality, and injustice mar and scar our country. But most Americans, most of the time, recognize that our country is flawed, that it should and can be better. Most Americans, most of the time, know that might does not make right, that lying (especially "big" lying) is wrong, that facts are facts, that facts make a difference, and that critical inquiry—not belief without verifiable evidence—is the path toward truth. So, in what could be seen as protest against the seditious and insurrectionist corruption of Trump and his acolytes as well as resistance against the uncompromising hyperpartisanship that saps American democracy in the

16. Wire, "Jan. 6 Committee." See also Schmidt and Broadwater, "Jan. 6 Panel Has Evidence."

17. Haberman, "Text from Donald Trump Jr."

2020s, Ken Burns chose early April 2022 to launch his PBS documentary on Benjamin Franklin, a pivotal founding father.

As Burns showed, no one did more than Franklin to give birth to the United States of America and its democracy.[18] Diplomat, scientist, inventor, philosopher, humanitarian, slaveholder-turned-abolitionist, prolific and brilliant writer (his papers fill more than forty volumes), and ever the astute politician, Franklin traveled far and wide, knew the American colonies better than anyone, and envisioned what they could become if they united. He helped Thomas Jefferson to write the Declaration of Independence, secured French funding and military support essential for liberation from the British, and presided over the 1787 Constitutional Convention in Philadelphia. His life contained shortcomings and contradictions, but he kept trying to honor his conviction that a person's highest calling is to do what is good and right.

In his eighties when he signed the US Constitution, Franklin had experienced personal vicissitudes and social upheavals before the nation was born. Stories about him abound. None is more significant for his legacy and our current situation than the report about an exchange he had with Elizabeth Willing Powel, an influential Philadelphian, shortly after the delegates to the 1787 convention had voted in favor of Franklin's motion to accept the Constitution. "What have we got," Powel asked Franklin, "a republic or a monarchy?" In words as circumspect as they were pithy and hopeful, Franklin not-so-simply said: "A republic, if you can keep it."[19]

A resolution adopted by the American Continental Congress on June 14, 1777, specified that the United States should have a flag. Its thirteen stars and stripes represented the uniting colonies. The flag still symbolizes national unity. But on January 6, 2021, it was desecrated when poles flying the Stars and Stripes were used to bludgeon police who stood against the violent, flag-waving American mob urged on by Donald Trump to storm the US Capitol and to obstruct the certification of Joe Biden's fair and free election as president. Most Americans, including members of that mob and perhaps even Donald Trump himself, know by heart the words of the Pledge of Allegiance that Americans often recite together: "I pledge allegiance to the flag of the United States of America and to the Republic for which it stands, one nation under God, indivisible, with liberty and justice for all." The January 6 insurrection, including Trump and his seditious

18. For criticism of Burns's interpretation of Franklin, see Messer-Kruse, "Unbearable Whiteness of Ken Burns."

19. For further information about Powel and the importance of women in the American founding, see Anishanslin, "What We Get Wrong."

followers who planned and unleashed it, disrespected those words and betrayed the promise they entail.

According to the pledge, the country we Americans inhabit together has a flag that stands for a *republic.* Most Americans know something about the Republican Party, but it would be difficult even for most Republicans to specify what the word *republic* means. In fact, if the Pledge of Allegiance disappeared, most of us Americans would not have *republic* in our vocabularies. Even when the word is pronounced in that context, *republic* remains one of those words that gets recited thoughtlessly. American democracy flails because having a *republic* doesn't mean enough to us nowadays. But there are certain words that we need to hear, care about, and look after. Here's why *republic* is one of them.

In American political history, as Benjamin Franklin understood and shows, the term *republic* refers primarily to a form of government. Such usage is embedded in the Constitution itself, whose Fourth Article guarantees "to every State in the Union a Republican Form of Government." That form places a premium on ingredients such as (1) a government of laws, not rulers, to secure liberty and justice; (2) the sovereignty of a people who are free; (3) representative democracy; (4) defense of fair and free elections; (5) peaceful transfer of power; and (6) a mixed political structure that checks and balances legislative, executive, and judicial authority.

Those elements stress process. They map *how* a republic should work. Granted, such forms are more than the means to an end, for these elements are to some extent ends in themselves. But only to some extent if they are taken by themselves, for American history also draws deeply on traditions that add other key elements to the formal republican vision. Two of these elements are especially important.

To discern them, recall that the word *republic* derives from the Latin *res publica*, meaning "the public thing." Neither the Latin phrase nor its English translation clarifies much, but both do point in key directions: first, "the public" and, second, "the thing" that is public.

In Latin, *public* means "of the people." It does not refer to generic, unidentified people but to *the* people. Particularity, identity, unity—terms such as those help to specify the meaning. One belongs to "the people." In republican tradition, moreover, the people *inhabit* a place. Inhabitation means that they do more than live there. The people establish a way of life in the territory of their dwelling. Their practices invest it with history and tradition. But the relationship goes the other way as well. The place inhabits the people. Its horizons define what is possible and what is not, what is permitted and what is not. Membership in "the people"—participation in its traditions and recognition of its shared memories, values, and hopes—entails responsibilities as well as privileges, obligations as well as rights.

At least on American soil—and it can be said of Ukrainian ground as well—a republican people is one whose inhabitation commits them to value and practice government by law, popular sovereignty, representative democracy, and the separation of powers. But political philosophers, including Benjamin Franklin and other founders of the United States, have always added a fundamental warning: A republican way of life depends mightily on the *virtue* of the people. Self-discipline, compassion, responsibility, friendship, work, courage, perseverance, honesty, loyalty, and faith—these virtues are ones that American need to recover and revive. Paul's New Testament Letter to the Philippians (4:8) points in that direction when he says, "Whatever is true, whatever is honorable, whatever is just, whatever is pure, whatever is pleasing, whatever is commendable, if there is any excellence and if there is anything worthy of praise, think about these things." If Americans do so, divisiveness can be reduced, and chasms between red and blue America can be bridged. Democracy will be stronger and better. It will be treasured as a blessing, a gift that must not and will not be taken for granted. If Americans come together and make that happen, those who have died to defend and expand it will be heard and honored as they deserve.

Lenny's Reflections

Archibald MacLeish's 1941 poem "The Young Dead Soldiers Do Not Speak" honored the war dead by reminding us that they must be heard because the meaning of their death depends on us, the living.[20] Indeed, MacLeish's poetry underscored, the dead insist that we must give them meaning. Whether the dead have spent their lives for hope and peace or for nothing is up to us. The dead, MacLeish contended, do not only speak *to* us but also *through* us. Our words and deeds give theirs significance,

In what ways do the Holocaust's dead summon us to remember them? Eighty years on, scholars of that genocide continue to debate how best to remember the deaths of six million Jews. Museums? Memorials? Commemorations on days of remembrance? Yes, but the depth and reach of each of these and other proposed ways to memorialize the dead should be subjects of ongoing deliberation, especially as we near the time when no survivors of the Holocaust remain alive. In a post-Holocaust world, what are the best ways to remember the Holocaust's dead? Static memorials don't fit that description. The best remembrance leads to action that gives meaning

20. MacLeish, "Young Dead Soldiers Do Not Speak."

to the genocidal dead. Such action resists the conditions and powers that took their lives. Democracy's destruction is among what must be resisted. That democracy requires us to respect the personhood of living others is an inescapable truth. But if death is part of the life cycle, we who wish to preserve democracy are also called to respect the dead.

The Nazi Holocaust did the opposite. The perpetrators of genocide murdered Jews and then assaulted their death. The killers not only killed; they intended for the murdered ones to die nameless. It has taken vast post-Holocaust research to recover the victims' names, which shows how thoroughly the killers wanted Jewish persons to be erased as well as dead. Jews who perished in ghettoes from hunger and sickness, those murdered by bullets in the early years of the Holocaust, the millions murdered in gassing operations—all went to their deaths with the Nazis intending that Jewish lives and names would be forgotten.

The numbers tattooed on the arms of Jews in Auschwitz would have been the only identifiers of the dead, if their corpses had not been incinerated, turned to ashes, and scattered so that no graves were to be found. Jews were deemed ciphers during their capture, imprisonment, and finally, death. No eulogies were delivered for the anonymous dead. Only at random times was Kaddish, the Hebrew prayer for the dead, uttered by those aware of the imminence of their own deaths and the deaths of fellow Jews. At shooting sites, Jews' bodies were piled in unmarked pits. No burial observances took place. At Auschwitz and Treblinka, the fire of Nazi ovens consumed respect for the dead. "Burying the dead," says Holocaust scholar David Patterson, "is central to an understanding of death as a rite of passage and as part of an affirmation of the dearness and meaning of life . . . The Nazis are literally grave robbers: they rob the Jews of their graves."[21] The murdered dead can be killed more than once.

If respecting the dead includes the possibility of hearing their call, what might the dead be saying? In particular, what are they saying to or through *me*? As the grandson of grandparents murdered in Eastern Poland (today Western Ukraine) and as a scholar of the Holocaust, I have heard a summons. I feel commanded by the murdered ones to remember—literally to help "re-member"—a world dismembered eighty years ago. The Holocaust was an attempt to destroy the realm of human solidarity. I hear the silent screams of Holocaust victims telling me to insist that it is unacceptable to engage in acts that murder the victims a second time. The Holocaust's dead implore me not to see them merely as victims, but as living persons who had names, took part in family events, and energized the communities they inhabited. I

21. Patterson, "Reflections on the Nazi Assault on Death," 131.

am asked to see their deaths not as objective facts but as subjective blows that strike me.[22] I am summoned to do my best to gather together pieces of the dismembered world of the Holocaust. For me, that means working toward healing our democracy's torn egalitarian fabric.

The summons of the dead alerting me to live a life of *tikkun olam*, the healing of the world, is no abstraction. I have personally encountered some of the Holocaust dead; they stir me to action. My decision to pursue a career in teaching—and teaching about the Holocaust in particular—was no arbitrary choice. I was provoked to study and teach the Holocaust both by the knowledge that my father was the sole member of his immediate Polish Jewish family to escape the Holocaust and by my 1989 journey to find the house where my father grew up and the street where my forebears were murdered. As I taught courses on the Holocaust, I sometimes sensed, viscerally, that I was being watched by my grandparents shedding tears of joy, happy that their grandson whom they had never met was re-membering the world during these moments. Standing in the classroom, I felt challenged to work harder, to educate better so that I might help play a part, small as it might be, to create a future free of genocide.

It is not just *hearing* the dead that has moved me toward the work of healing—at present, attending to a wounded democracy at home. I have also "seen" the dead. In the 1990s, on the occasion of a visit to my wife's parents at their Florida retirement community, I ventured out on the first morning to walk the three-mile path around the perimeter of a complex populated mainly by Jews. One after another, Jewish men and women, walking in the opposite direction, passed by. And then I saw—really saw—not only those elderly Jewish men and women but also those who were *not there*, the absent ones, those among the six million who might well have lived long lives. They might have spent their winters lying in the sun in Florida or continuing to live in their ancestral homes in eastern Europe. I wept—wept for the fullness of life denied them. I wept that they were not able to enjoy the sun, the water, their children and grandchildren. But they were present on the three-mile path, beckoning me to defend justice and restore life in a troubled world.

On that Florida path, I was strengthened in my commitment to work for *tikkun olam*. Today the work of *tikkun* for me is to contribute to the preservation of democracy at home—in the shadows of the current devastation of democracy in Ukraine. The murdered ones of the Holocaust implore me to revisit "Never Again," to ensure that it is no empty slogan, robbed of meaning by overuse as genocide persists. I am implored to

22. Hatley, *Suffering Witness*, 3.

remember both the particular and the universal elements of that imperative by enacting it in my chosen field of education.

John's Questions

Your reflections profoundly emphasize that the dead, especially Jews murdered in the Holocaust and now people killed in Ukraine, summon you to remember them and to live a life of *tikkun olam*. American memory and memorialization of the dead often eulogizes those who, in Abraham Lincoln's words, "gave the last full measure of devotion" to defend the United States and democracy. You echo Lincoln when you rightly say that "we who wish to preserve democracy are called to respect the dead."

As we exchange our reflections, I am reminded that we share other reflections too. For instance, we shared the *Washington Post* editorial that Timothy Snyder published on March 23, 2022. Snyder argued that Vladimir Putin's invasion of Ukraine fulfills the definition of genocide specified in Article II of the United Nations Convention on the Prevention and Punishment of the Crime of Genocide.[23] Members of your family were victims of the genocide unleashed by Adolf Hitler's invasion of eastern Europe eighty years earlier. You and I both want, as you say, "a future free of genocide." But signs are scarce that the world is heading that way. Genocidal threats continue to imperil democracy. Is "Never Again" a forlorn cause? Where is confidence to be found that it isn't?

Clearly such hope will not come from Donald Trump and his stalwarts. As Joshua Shanes documented in his *Haaretz* article on March 28, 2022, especially since Russia's invasion of Ukraine, the American right wing has attacked "'globalists,' 'cosmopolitans,' and 'international bankers,' all classic euphemisms for Jews, . . . claiming they threaten the nation's strength and identity."[24] In concert with those canards, Shanes adds, Putin is viewed as "a white Christian savior fighting for racial and sexual purity." Can you indicate what the dead, so many of them murdered because of antisemitism, require Americans to do about such lies when freedom of speech is not only crucial for the democracy we want to protect but also potentially dangerous for its future, especially as misinformation and disinformation spread so fast and far through social media and the internet?

The postwar Nuremberg trials of Nazi leaders convicted them of crimes against peace, war crimes, crimes against humanity, and conspiracy to commit any of those crimes. Hitler committed suicide before those

23. Snyder, "Putin Has Long Fantasized."
24. Shanes, "Volodymyr Zelenskyy."

indictments could be brought against him. The International Criminal Court's indictment of Putin for war crimes may not make much difference, but there is little doubt that his Russian forces have inflicted atrocious suffering on civilians and created a refugee and humanitarian crisis unseen in Europe since World War II.

No one is above the law. The rise or fall of democracy hinges on the truth and enforcement of that proposition. That fact helps to show why democracy teeters on the brink in 2020s America. As another of our exchanged articles documents, US district judge David O. Carter found that "then-President Donald Trump 'more likely than not' committed federal crimes in trying to obstruct the congressional count of Electoral College votes on Jan. 6, 2021."[25] Time will tell whether the US Department of Justice will indict, prosecute, and convict Trump, but there is little doubt that he and his zealous followers disrespect the law. Ironically, even US Supreme Court justice Clarence Thomas is subject to scrutiny on that point because of his arguably illegal refusal to recuse himself in cases involving the actions of his spouse, Virginia "Ginni" Thomas, to overturn the 2020 presidential election.[26] Where law ends, when respect for law ceases, tyranny begins.

Many Americans have given their lives to defend the United States and its democracy against foreign enemies. What do those dead summon us Americans to do about domestic enemies, about people who regard themselves as above the law, or about those who do not use the power that is theirs to enforce the foundational principle that no one is above the law? What if American judges and courts fail in that regard? Recognizing that simple answers to these tough questions are unavailable and definitely untrustworthy if they are offered, I ask them nevertheless because your insight will help to save and sustain democracy at home and abroad.

Lenny's Response

We agree that the dead of the Holocaust and other genocides speak to us. We also agree that what we hear from the dead is a summons to repair our troubled world—in present-day America to heal a deeply wounded democracy. We also agree, I believe, that the dead cry out "Never Again." But you ask whether "Never Again" is a "forlorn cause" in a post-Holocaust world that failed to prevent genocides in Cambodia, Rwanda, Bosnia, Darfur, Myanmar, and Xinjiang. And, as you cite Timothy Snyder, Ukraine can be added to the list. You ask, how we are to respond to the

25. Zapotosky and Wagner, "Judge: Trump 'More Likely Than Not.'"
26. Blake, "How Clarence Thomas's Recusal Controversy Compares."

call of "Never Again" in 2020s America when domestic enemies "regard themselves as above the law," threatening our democratic heritage and portending the rule of might makes right? Some eighty years after the Holocaust, is "Never Again" a hollow cry?

How are we to begin the work of repair with any optimism when we recall that the polarization in today's world is hardly new. During the Cold War seventy years ago, for example, Martin Buber claimed that "the human world is today, as never before, split into two camps, each of which understands the other as the embodiment of falsehood and itself as the embodiment of truth."[27] Buber might have said the same about the United States today. A current study undertaken by the Pew Research Center finds that among residents of seventeen developed nations surveyed, "Americans were the most likely to say their society was split along partisan, racial, and ethnic lines."[28] We currently witness the rise of those on the extreme right who support the Russian war on Ukraine and employ terms borrowed from the Nazi playbook to characterize Putin as a savior of Russian "racial and sexual purity." How are we to correct and curb such stupidity?

I take a deep breath as I respond to your challenges because there are no "answers" to the questions you pose. What there can and must be, as Charlotte Delbo underscores, are actions, "something that gives you the right to be dressed in your skin and in your body hair," something that seeks to justify our living by resisting the corruption, injustice, and killing that deface life's goodness.[29] Delbo insisted that we should take steps toward repairing our world, knowing all the while that a world shattered by repeated genocides is ultimately irreparable. She heard the murdered ones of the Holocaust urging us to work toward creating an interhuman world, imploring us, each in our own idiom, to say the biblical "*Hineni*, here I am."

I believe we can approach your (and my own) lack of confidence in "Never Again" by listening to what the dead have said to Delbo and to us. Not "answers" but action-responses must begin from the place where each of us stands. We can start small; *small* is no less *political* in nature than larger ventures on an overtly political stage. No one-size-fits-all formula exists for healing actions by individuals like you and me. Each of us serves in our chosen way. I begin with how I conduct myself with those closest to me: my wife, my children, other family members, friends, acquaintances, and indeed all the people I encounter in my daily life. How, for example, do I interact with the postal clerk? The philosopher Emmanuel Levinas argues

27. Buber, *Pointing the Way*, 220–21.

28. Lauter, "Researchers Asked People."

29. Delbo, *Auschwitz and After*, 230.

we must be "insomniacs," ever watchful that we regard others, in religious terms, as "sacred" beings. How I speak with my wife, my tone as well as the content of my words; how I both educate and learn from my children; how I conduct my classroom, how I look at and speak with each individual; how I construct a curriculum with the face of each student before me; how I deal with conflict dialogically, affirming the other person even as I explain my reasons for holding opposing views—all these, and infinitely more, are components of an attempt to hear and heed the dead who have suffered the ultimate dishonoring of their personhood.

In the same essay in which Buber decries the division among us humans, he concludes that "hope for this hour depends upon the renewal of dialogical immediacy."[30] Here Buber is speaking of the hope that I will see others as co-subjects, rather than as objects or merely the means to some end that will serve me at their expense. My regard for others is a point of departure for repair on a larger scale. It is the building block for creating, or at the present moment in America, *protecting* our democracy from relentless attacks. None who have chosen to honor the humanity of others can think of themselves, as do Trump and many of his followers, as above the law—something forged by the consensus of fellow humans.

Right now, we face dramatic challenges to democracy at home and in the larger world. We see antisemitism increasing markedly in the United States and abroad. We cannot avert our eyes from the daily devastation of Ukraine and its people. The actions of individuals I described earlier constitute but a seedbed of resistance to such evils. They can bear *full* fruit only in some future time—although the quality of human interaction improves, however slightly, each moment we treat others with the respect due them. Further, the individual work of repair exists just at one end of a continuum of measures designed to face these challenges to core elements of our humanity. Individuals have left their mark on the larger world in many ways. But if "Never Again" is to regain meaning, collective action for justice must increase in greater measure than collective deeds of evil. Individuals can and do join one another in the struggle. Some stand together on the street protesting injustice, others work in NGOs dedicated to social justice, still others enter the political realm as candidates for office. Some Americans have gone to Ukraine to fight alongside other internationals.

In the struggle to preserve our democracy, resistance in our daily lives is essential. Fortunately, current models of resistance are to be found—and none is brighter than the example of the courageous acts of ordinary Ukrainians and their government. No one is exempt on principle from hearing the

30. Buber, *Pointing the Way*, 228.

call to resist. All may participate, each contributing in their own way. We witness the truth-telling of scientists who fight falsehoods regarding the threats to life on the planet incurred by climate change, the resistance of so many in the medical community to Trumpist lies about the COVID vaccines, the ongoing investigative reporting by journalists in the face of false accusations by Trump during his administration and to this day, the work of attorneys to assist those dishonestly accused of wrongdoing. Social media, as you note, do spread disinformation, but the internet can be and is utilized to disseminate truth, to promote social justice movements, to sustain political protest at home and across borders. United Nations peacekeeping initiatives—those realized or, unfortunately only promised—would occupy a further point on the continuum of responses to the dead summoning us to engage in the work of repair. Although we Americans have more than enough reason to despair at the injustices we behold, hope—a balm in Gilead—manifests itself in modes of resistance like those I have noted.

Reflecting on what the dead said to him, Levinas emphasized the irreparable nature of genocide. "The meaning of Auschwitz is a suffering, a faith completely without promise," he declared.[31] But, he continued, "after Auschwitz, even though it doesn't 'pay' to be good" within a universe of self-interest, "one cannot deduce from that that one should not be good . . . Stop preaching, but accept the obligation to . . . do the good."[32] Levinas's words respond to the charge of the murdered ones that we must help repair our badly broken world.

Postscript

The poet Archibald MacLeish wrote about young dead soldiers who defended democracy. They cannot speak but must be heard. Another poet, T. S. Eliot, began his 1922 poem "The Wasteland" by calling April the cruelest month. Genocide—"acts committed with intent to destroy, in whole or in part, a national, ethnical, racial or religious group, as such"—puts the title and opening of Eliot's poem on target.[33] Although no Nazi was explicitly indicted and convicted for perpetrating genocide, the Holocaust put that word, coined by Raphael Lemkin in 1943, into humanity's vocabulary. On December 9, 1948, the United Nations attempted corrective action by approving the Convention on the Prevention and Punishment of the Crime of Genocide. For more than a decade, April, that cruelest month, has been widely designated Genocide

31. Levinas, "Judaism and Christianity after Rosenzweig," 60.
32. Levinas, "Being Toward Death," 134.
33. United Nations, "Convention."

Awareness Month because it contains so many pivotal dates in genocide's recent history: the Armenian genocide, for example, began on April 24, 1915; the Warsaw ghetto uprising during the Holocaust began on April 19, 1943; the Cambodian genocide began on April 17 in 1975; the genocide against the Tutsi in Rwanda started on April 7, 1994.

The UN's genocide convention came too late and did too little to deter genocide or to hold its perpetrators accountable. April's cruelty continued in 2022 as Vladimir Putin's barbarous invasion of Ukraine became genocidal. Americans were deeply concerned about Ukraine in April 2022. Putin had appointed a brutal general, Alekzandr Dvornikov, infamous for his butchery in Syria, to oversee an onslaught in Ukraine's eastern Donbas region that could atone for earlier military losses and give the Russian dictator a victory in his intended annihilation of the Ukrainian state, its democracy and its people.

Writing perceptively in the *Atlantic*, George Packer said of the United States, "Ukraine has done what nothing else—no election or insurrection, no pandemic, no environmental catastrophe—could do: shown the difference between right and wrong, heroism and barbarism, truth and lies, with such clarity that Americans are in agreement."[34] Underscoring, however, that the American attention span is short and Ukraine is far away, he worried that Americans would too quickly and too easily forget Ukraine and allow what he called "our own incipient Russification" to deplete democracy at home as well as abroad. The United States, Packer rightly underscored, has its own "class of immensely rich business oligarchs." Authoritarianism threatens democracy whenever the wealthiest few get the power that allows them to take lopsided shares of national wealth. Accountability and responsibility do not check their vast political and economic clout, which includes media control that pits Americans against one another and blurs the clarity needed to distinguish truth from lies.

As bold as he is insightful, Packer courageously held nothing back. The most immediate threat to sustained support for Ukraine, which depends on clear and staunch support for democracy at home, is the Republican Party's "strong attraction to autocracy." At home and thus in Ukraine and elsewhere abroad, democracy will be betrayed "unless the Republican Party purges itself of the poisonous influence of its Tucker Carlsons and Marjorie Taylor Greenes, and above all of Trump." In words that ring true not only in April 2022 but also as the 2024 elections approach, Packer identified much of the remedy that's needed: "Reversing America's Russification will mean defeating our own authoritarians, reducing the power

34. Packer, "I Worry We'll Soon Forget."

of our oligarchs, ridding our politics of endemic corruption, and giving Americans on the losing end of 40 years of globalization a sense of security and identity that binds them to our democracy."

The remedy that's needed is much needed. The shelf life of political polls is limited, but the *New Republic*'s April 2022 polling data supported that proposition: "44 percent of Republicans agree with 48 percent of Democrats that our political system is in such trouble that it needs no less than major changes or even 'a complete overhaul.'"[35] The problem worsens because the agreement also revealed disagreement about the problems, let alone the solutions. When asked about the meaning of democracy, 47 percent of Republicans prioritized the protection of individual rights and liberties. Trailing well behind were the core ideas that democracy prioritizes majority rule and equal application of the law to everyone. Democrats saw things the other way. Protection of individuals rights and liberties was important to them, but their understanding of democracy's meaning placed the greater emphasis on majority rule and equal application of the law to everyone. Absent those priorities, individual rights and liberties are likely to be lost or used irresponsibly.

How about people who forced their way into the US Capitol on January 6, 2021? Was that action an insurrection? Yes, said 87 percent of Democrats, but only 43 percent of Republicans agreed. Was the event an act of patriotism? Yes, said 57 percent of Republicans, a position with which only 12 percent of Democrats concurred. Is the growing strength of White nationalist groups a serious threat? Yes, said 82 percent of Democrats, but only 38 percent of Republicans agreed. Not a threat, said 62 percent of Republicans, a position with which only 18 percent of Democrats concurred.

While the data showed strong agreement that the United States should not divide into two countries, what would Americans want if such a divorce took place? Republicans, 89 percent of them, said they would want to live in the more conservative or "red" country; only 15 percent of Democrats agreed. Most Democrats, 85 percent of them, said they would prefer the more progressive or "blue" country, a position with which only 11 percent of Republicans agreed. Democrats and Republicans shared concerns about the influence of big money in elections, but when it came to the increasing economic power of the very wealthy, 81 percent of Democrats thought that's a serious threat to democracy, compared to 58 percent of Republicans. A growing wealth gap is not a problem, said 42 percent of Republicans, compared to 19 percent of Democrats. These items are only a fraction of the

35. *New Republic*, "TNR Poll: Americans Agree Democracy Is Doomed."

New Republic's findings, but they are sufficient to document the depth of the differences that divide Americans in the 2020s.

We have a republic, said Benjamin Franklin in 1787, "if you can keep it." Franklin lived a long life. He was eighty-four when he died in Philadelphia on April 17, 1790. His funeral was the largest the city had ever seen. Franklin lived and died centuries before Hitler, Putin, and Trump made it immensely difficult to keep democratic republics alive and well. But he knew how hard it had been to give birth to a country governed by a Constitution that promised to "secure the Blessings of Liberty to ourselves and our Posterity." From early battles at Lexington and Concord in 1775 to the British surrender at Yorktown in 1781, about 6,800 Americans were killed in combat. A heavier toll on the military, some seventeen thousand deaths, resulted from disease. If those dead could speak now, would they say that the cost was worth it? Their answer would depend on whether Americans in the 2020s rally to protect and defend American democracy.

In 1728, while still a young man, Franklin wrote his epitaph. It is not found at his grave in Philadelphia's Christ Church cemetery, but it is remembered.

> The Body of B. Franklin, Printer; like the Cover of an old Book, Its Contents torn out, And stript of its Lettering and Gilding, Lies here, Food for Worms. But the Work shall not be wholly lost; For it will, as he believ'd, appear once more, In a new & more perfect Edition, Corrected and amended By the Author.

Written with death and the dead in mind, Benjamin Franklin's words—playful and realistic, self-effacing and determined—still speak and appeal to us Americans. They express hope about the future that can help to convince us that, far from being lost, the work we need to do can make not a perfect but a more perfect American democracy in the 2020s and beyond. We honor, hear, and heed the dead by keeping the American republic strong and well.

6
Pandemics

Hitler's Holocaust and Putin's invasion of Ukraine underscore warnings from Europe about embattled American democracy. Warnings of a related kind surfaced in late December 2019, when SARS-CoV-2, a new coronavirus, emerged in Wuhan, China. Maybe the contagion originated in a "wet market" (a market where fish, poultry and other animals are slaughtered, butchered, and sold on site). Perhaps a laboratory leak was the source. Probably the answer to the origins question will remain uncertain. No doubt, however, the new coronavirus caused a pneumonia-like and often lethal respiratory disease. On January 21, 2020, the United States confirmed its first case, which was found in a man from Washington State who had traveled to the Wuhan area. The World Health Organization (WHO) officially named the disease COVID-19, an abbreviated version of *coronavirus disease 2019*, on February 11.

COVID-19 became a household word as quickly as the disease spread. By early March 2020, the infection—more than 118,000 cases in 114 countries and 4,291 people dead—led Dr. Tedros Adhanom Ghebreyesus, the WHO's director-general, to open a media briefing on March 11 by declaring that "COVID-19 can be characterized as a pandemic."[1]

Its ancient Greek and Latin roots indicate that early uses of the term *pandemic* referred to what is public, common, pertaining to all people. In the late seventeenth century, *pandemic*—often regarded as synonymous with *epidemic*—began to denote the spread of disease. By the time global influenza raged in 1889 and 1918, *pandemic* meant a rampant contagion affecting vast populations and wide geographical areas. COVID-19 definitely fits that description. Despite successful vaccines developed in record time, COVID-19 continues to plague life and community. As spring 2023 approached, more than 758 million people around the world, including 101 million Americans, had been diagnosed with COVID-19. The

1. World Health Organization, "WHO Director-General's Opening Remarks."

pandemic's global death toll exceeded 6.8 million, with 1.1 million Americans among the dead. COVID-19 trailed only heart disease and cancer as the leading causes of death in the United States. Elderly Americans have been hardest hit by the COVID-19 death toll. People over sixty-five account for three-quarters of those fatalities, with the greatest losses among those over seventy-five.[2]

On May 12, 2022, President Joe Biden ordered that federal American flags be flown at half-staff until sunset on May 16 "in memory of the one million American lives lost to COVID-19 and their loved ones left behind." That "tragic milestone," he said, brought to mind "one million empty chairs around the dinner table. Each an irreplaceable loss. Each leaving behind a family, a community, and a Nation forever changed because of this pandemic."[3]

COVID-19 fatalities did not empty chairs around dinner tables in the Grob or Roth households. But we have witnessed and reflected upon the myriad ways in which COVID-19 and other pandemics threaten the nation and demoralize its democracy.

Lenny's Encounters

March 2020 dawned. We Americans were realizing how COVID-19 would upend daily routines. Life in my household and neighborhood began to shed ordinary patterns of behavior. Other regimens took their place: staying at home became the norm, as did wearing masks and practicing social distancing when doctors' appointments or other matters of urgency summoned us to leave home; we washed our hands—and then just-purchased produce—with new frequency and resolve. Much became topsy-turvy. Our adult children assumed traditional parental roles, as they phoned often to check on our health and to beg us not to leave home. My teaching transitioned from treasured face-to-face pedagogy to online meetings in the virtual world. My wife's career as a music therapist at our local hospice came to a halt. She was not an "essential worker." The dangers of singing to and with dying people and their aides and relatives were all too apparent. Thoughts about retirement resurfaced. In a world invaded by a new and deadly virus, when would it be safe to return to work of this kind?

Some changes to customary behaviors could be—and have been—reversed. Vaccines appeared, and the virus came under a measure of control,

2. Span, "For Older Americans"; World Health Organization, *WHO Coronavirus (COVID-19) Dashboard.*

3. Biden, "Proclamation on Remembering the 1,000,000 Americans Lost."

however limited and impermanent that control may be. Other changes persist. The most enduring and disturbing effect of the pandemic on my life is one that mirrors the impact of COVID-19 in revealing current threats to our democracy. Virus skeptics and vaccine resisters appeared among some close friends and family members. The possibility of engaging in reasonable dialogue across differences—an essential feature of any democratic society—has been tested and frequently found wanting. Meaningful communication, until now the norm in discussions with these individuals, has often broken down because of their insistence—hardened over time—that the virus is only "a bad flu," that vaccines are ineffective, even harmful, merely part of a conspiracy by large pharmaceutical companies to enlarge profits.

Divisiveness is a Trumpist legacy worsened by COVID-19. That such divisiveness mars friendships and family life is further evidence that common ground has become harder to find. In times of conspiratorial thinking, mistrust of government and large corporations has made strange bedfellows of MAGA Republicans and radical societal critics on the Left. While I share some mistrust of "big pharma" and its influence on government, meaningful dialogue with anti-vaxxers remains difficult.

Yet just as the pandemic period saw a hardening of positions regarding the virus in families like my own and across civil society, hope for revitalizing our imperiled democracy can be detected as well. Living amid an ever-broadening web of suffering caused by the virus, I have come to value the contributions of people I had previously overlooked. How often had I neglected to acknowledge the contributions of grocery clerks, custodial employees, highway workers, and other so-called blue-collar laborers responsible for building and maintaining the infrastructure that sustains the world I live in? How many times had I passed by the postal carrier in the lobby of my apartment house and failed even to nod? During the pandemic, I learned that what I might previously have considered to be "ordinary" was, in fact, vital. The weight of this historical moment, and the increased personal danger associated with everyday acts, alerted me to the heroic qualities of countless individuals just "doing their jobs." Wasn't the health aide at a hospital bedside during the height of the pandemic a hero as she or he held tightly to a patient's hand—the only person present to give comfort as COVID-19 claimed another life?

A telling instance of this new learning occurred when I tested positive for COVID-19 in early January 2021. Vulnerable as an elderly asthmatic, I was told by my physician to go immediately to the emergency room to be infused with antibodies. I waited more than eight hours for my turn. Instead of complaining, my usual response in such situations, I was brought up short by the sight of nurses and other hospital workers literally running to meet duties that all but overwhelmed them. I had viewed scenes of this kind on television newscasts, but witnessing firsthand these healthcare workers doing more than appeared possible, I came to better understand how their deeds were profoundly courageous.

At least in its most lethal phases, COVID-19 may eventually run its course. I will be challenged then to recall how the pandemic, for a moment in time, taught me the deepest respect and gratitude for so many. This insight is not just the moral of a personal story about life during COVID-19. *Democracies flourish when the humanity of others, irrespective of their stations in life, is honored. They flounder and fail—often fatally—when that is not the case.* This lesson needs to be learned and relearned. But COVID-19 and its negative reverberations have profoundly infected the United States. They reveal how the nation's spirit is sapped, its character weakened to such a toxic extent that Americans should not be self-confident let alone certain that we will do what it takes to preserve and strengthen our democracy in pandemic times. COVID and its aftereffects show the fragility of our democracy and warn that we must redouble our efforts to preserve it.

John's Realizations

On March 11, 2020, the director-general of the WHO, Tedros Ghebreyesus, warned that COVID-19 was "not just a public health crisis, it is a crisis that will touch every sector—so every sector and every individual must be involved in the fight."[4] The nation's schools are a primary example of the ways COVID-19 has affected every aspect of American life. Responses to COVID-19 were quickly politicized, and these responses drove deeper the divisions—for instance, conflicts between red and blue parts of the country—that jeopardize American democracy.

Use the leverage you have. If you are going to change the world, I often told my students, that's what you have to do. My leverage has included being a professor at a liberal arts college. I could educate students. I could affect my college. I could write. Such leverage is significant.

Aging and vulnerable when COVID-19 arrived in 2020, I felt my leverage ebbing away. In my case, however, the pandemic did not win, at least not yet. My wallet contains a CDC (Centers for Disease Control and Prevention) COVID-19 vaccination record card. At the earliest opportunity, on January 15, 2021, my wife, Lyn, and I got our first doses of the Moderna vaccine. We got second doses a few weeks later. Booster shots followed. We gladly accepted the direction of scientists and physicians. We

4. World Health Organization, "WHO Director-General's Opening Remarks."

were dismayed and even angered when so many Americans did not. We welcomed mandates for masking and vaccination and deplored the selfish blindness, the misguided appeals to "liberty" that led too many others to reject lifesaving and community-sustaining practices. We wore masks—often still do—when traveling or in crowded indoor spaces. Living in relative isolation, we felt safe enough—until we weren't.

In early February 2023, Lyn and I both tested positive for COVID-19. Medical friends prescribed antiviral drugs. Unavailable at the pharmacy nearest to our rural home in Washington State, Paxlovid had to be delivered by our children, who traveled some distance to obtain it. Friends and family teamed with physicians and pharmacists, scientists, pharmaceutical companies, and government cost-covering programs to restore our health. Our gratitude includes renewed appreciation for the ways in which the goodness of individual life is dependent on the communal care and the social support that nourish and sustain it.

I look out my window and see the beautiful vista I enjoy in the rural mountains of the American Northwest. I can almost imagine that all is right with the world, but I know it isn't. We lost friends to COVID-19. Virulent variants will not disappear; they continue to evolve and will wreak havoc again. Good health is essential for strong democracy, and vigilance is required to protect them both. During the pandemic, "We're all in this together" resounded to rally solidarity and cooperation, but that mantra was unconvincing because too many Americans failed to act that way. COVID-19's devastation exposed and worsened deep divisions in American life. Its ongoing impact threatens our democracy.

Something similar took place about a century ago in Germany.[5] The influenza pandemic of 1918–1920 killed at least fifty million people worldwide, including 675,000 in the United States. The German death toll was smaller, about 273,000, but recent research shows that the influenza pandemic had lethal political consequences. A significant correlation existed between German districts with high influenza mortality and their support for Nazism. Its biomedical ideology advanced pandemic-related racist and antisemitic themes, which were allied with and even inspired by an American attraction to racialized eugenics and genocidal policies against Native Americans.[6] Adolf Hitler and his followers took the German nation to be a living body politic. But his widespread conspiracy theory held that Germany was existentially threatened by disease caused by and embodied in Jews, who were

5. Forgey, "Fed Study." See especially Blickle, "Pandemics Change Cities."

6. See, for example, Whitman, *Hitler's American Model*; Bachrach, project dir., and Kuntz, ed., *Deadly Medicine*; Kakel, *American West*.

variously depicted as parasites, bacteria, viruses. The prescribed cure had to be the "Final Solution," the annihilation of Jewish existence.

Watching television reports about the COVID-19 pandemic, I have respected the no-nonsense evaluations of Dr. Michael Osterholm, director of the Center for Infectious Disease Research and Policy at the University of Minnesota. In Alice Park's 2022 *Time* article about Ukraine's struggle with COVID-19 during war with invading Russia, Osterholm rightly said, "War is an infectious disease's best friend. It challenges every public health program you can possibly have. It limits the medical care available for those who might be seriously ill, and often fosters transmission when so many people are crowded into bomb shelter locations and on trains. This is going to be the perfect storm of one serious challenge after another."[7] Osterholm's comments made me think about the term *super-spreader*, which applies to events, persons, policies, or settings that escalate the spread and worsen the control of COVID-19. *Super-spreader* fits and indicts Vladimir Putin and his war-crime-infested onslaught against Ukraine.

Putin's corrupt rule produced tardy and ineffectual responses to the pandemic in the Russian Federation, which by mid-February 2023, had more than 22 million confirmed cases and a likely undercounted 395 thousand deaths since the pandemic began.[8] Undaunted and arrogant, Putin decided that no virus would stop his ambition to destroy Ukrainian democracy and seize control of as much of Ukraine as his armies could take. COVID-19 does not care about ambition or anything else. It just goes where conditions and mutations permit. As Vladimir Putin's war raged, COVID-19 added misery and death to the danger and destruction confronted by the Ukrainian president Volodymyr Zelenskyy and his country. Putin's super-spreading damages health and democracy. He and his anti-democratic, authoritarian confederates must be stopped.

Pandemics have long-lasting consequences. Not always obvious, they can be as harmful as they are complicated to foresee. Data from the onset of the pandemic through March 2022 showed that the COVID-19 death toll in the United States was significantly higher, 38 percent higher, in red states that supported Donald Trump in the 2020 presidential election than in the blue states won by Joe Biden.[9] More than 60 percent of Americans unvaccinated against COVID-19 were Republicans. The COVID-19 vaccination map still resembles a 2020 election map. In addition, William Brangham,

7. See Park, "Why Ukraine's COVID-19 Problem Is Everyone's Problem."

8. On these topics, see Yaffa, "Why Russia Hasn't Cracked Down." See also World Health Organization, *WHO Coronavirus (COVID-19) Dashboard*.

9. Mitropoulos, "For Red and Blue America."

correspondent and producer for the *PBS NewsHour*, found that being Republican was "the single most reliable predictor of vaccination status" in the United States."[10] As the 2022 elections came and went, as the 2024 elections approach, the Republican Party, its constituency full of COVID-disgruntled anti-vaxxers increasingly supports an antidemocratic authoritarianism, a Trumpist version of fascism. Will it prevail? What if it does?

For me, these realizations and questions entail responsibility to do what I can to keep my leverage—my thinking and writing—from ebbing away. That responsibility means following the good counsel that the activist lawyer and legal scholar Sherrilyn Ifill tweeted on June 24, 2022, the day that the Supreme Court of the United States overturned *Roe v. Wade* and stole from American women and girls a fundamental right to choose: "Decide today that you will never give up fighting for the country you want for yourself, your children, your community. Decide it. Then no matter what happens, you won't be swayed or paralyzed."[11] And yet, how can I not despair when the problematic state of the world and the dismal condition of my country coincide with the diminishing days and energy that are mine?

With his Holocaust experience as a warning and as imperative for resistance, Elie Wiesel taught me that despair is the beginning, not the end, because as long as breath lasts and awareness lives, decisions about what to make of despair remain. In my resisting, protesting ways, I retain what the Black American W. E. B. Du Bois called "a hope not hopeless but unhopeful."[12] That's persisting in between—refusing optimism that experience can't sustain, refusing to give despair victories it doesn't deserve.

Our Diagnosis

Our encounters with COVID-19 and realizations about its impact contain insights that converge. So we continue in one voice, not two, as we further diagnose and assess the toll that COVID-19 and its cultural mutations and political variants have taken on American life. A key conviction is that COVID-19 is by no means the only deadly disease that has sickened the United States. Accompanying its virulence, lethal plagues of moral, political, and spiritual infection are at pandemic levels in our body politic. Demoralizing our democracy, they include American versions of interrelated ills that put Hitler's Germany and Putin's Russia on their antidemocratic, deadly paths: disrespect and distrust, lies and lying, judicial tyranny and cruelty, hypocrisy

10. Brangham, "How Misinformation and the Partisan Divide."
11. Ifill, "10. Decide today."
12. Du Bois, *Souls of Black Folk*, 227–28.

and corruption, confiscating rights, minority rule, gun violence, misery and insecurity. Unless we find ways to heal these contaminations—our prescriptions follow in the next chapter—their poison will be lethal.

Disrespect and Distrust

Compounding disrespect for truth, distrust and disinformation about science ramped up Trumpists' dysfunctional responses to COVID-19. Inflamed by his denial of the extent and seriousness of the disease and by his infamous recommendations to ingest disinfectants to fight the virus, too many in our country trusted Trump's botched policies and ignored science, distrusted sound medical guidance, and resorted to quack remedies such as hydroxychloroquine and ivermectin. Amid overwhelmed intensive care units and spiking death tolls, lifesaving mandates for masking and vaccination were defied by mostly red-state Republicans, whose support of the defeated Trump and his lies about a fraudulent, stolen election intensified political division and worsened the nation's deteriorating health.

Although not comparable in scope and depth to Nazi racist policies, America's endemic racism reared its head in distinctive ways during the COVID pandemic. A majority of Americans experienced economic distress from closed businesses, unemployment, housing instability, and food shortages, but people of color have suffered disproportionately. A history of economic exploitation leading to a lack of opportunity has put Blacks, Hispanics, and Native Americans at a disadvantage under COVID-19's financial pressures. Workers of color are overrepresented in lower-wage occupations. For those living in crowded homes and employed at crowded workplaces, what did it mean for public policy to recommend social distancing? For those deemed essential workers, what did it mean for public health policies to advise staying home to avoid exposure to the virus? Childcare, largely unaffordable in prepandemic times, became a distant dream, one made yet more distant by school closings that led to students studying from home. Studying from home depended on internet access and computers, which were much less available to the nation's minorities and poor. America's institutionalized racism has stood out in bold relief during COVID-19 times, which reveal how toxic our ongoing pandemics of racism and poverty continue to be.

Threats to democracy today have been further exacerbated by the furor engendered by vaccination resisters. Although their motivations vary for refusing vaccination, resisters are often driven by a spurious notion of freedom that rejects health-oriented governmental constraints on their ability to act as they please. For vaccine resisters and others who see freedom as license to act without external restraint, *self* is understood, implicitly, as a solitary ego whose needs take precedence over the needs of others. For those committed to preserving democracy's regard for the welfare of all, *self* is understood differently. The British writer J. B. Priestley cogently stated that difference in a passage especially telling when democracy is under fire: "We are members of one body. We are responsible for each other," he urged, "and if [people] will not learn that lesson, then they will be taught it in fire and blood and anguish."[13] If we disrespect human interdependence, if we distrust lifesaving policies and community-sustaining institutions, the loss of guidelines and guardrails for a just democracy invites violence and tyranny.

Vaccine resisters, and others who deny scientific evidence in the name of freedom-as-license, disregard and disrespect how their freedom steals the freedom and well-being of others. Selfish freedom meant that others had increased chances of infection because the unvaccinated are not protected against the virus and were more likely to be agents of viral transmission. The United States has one of the lowest vaccination rates among developed nations, thus escalating the current threat to democratic values rooted in respect for the rights of others. In healthy democracies, concern for oneself is balanced—and sometimes overridden—by concern for one's neighbors. One pandemic leads to another to the extent that COVID-19 produces disrespect and distrust that leads people to think that personal freedom is separable from communal responsibility.

COVID-19 morphs into new variants, resists containment, and keeps the misery going. That process has produced a pandemic of hostility—verbal and physical—that raises a crucial question: Do Americans want to preserve and strengthen democracy, in which respect for others prevails? Or is our disrespect and distrust so deep that we are destined for fire, blood, and anguish?

Lies and Lying

Nothing harms American democracy more than the pandemic of lies and lying that worsens every threat confronting the nation. Amplified by social media, lying and the virulent toxins that accompany it—denial of facts, disregard for evidence, disrespect for truth—drain the country's spirit and poison its soul by rotting the trust on which democracy depends.

Lying breeds dishonesty and emboldens corruption. It aids and abets overthrow of fair and free elections. Its allies—distraction, denial, deflection,

13. Priestley, "Inspector Calls," 207.

and deceit—downplay and distort facts that are plain to see unless we let gaslighting falsehoods blind us. Lying labels and libels truth as "fake news." It appeals to "alternative facts," which are lies by another name. Disregard for evidence and disrespect for truth undermine—especially among those who are aggrieved because they embrace conspiracy theories—America's quest for a more perfect union. Like mutating viruses, lies produce more lies. Their defense, which is about gaining power and keeping control, requires cover ups and rejection of self-corrective inquiry. Lying, disregard for evidence, disrespect for truth—they are the common denominator of each and every threat to American democracy.

During World War II, more than 160 thousand Allied forces crossed the Atlantic from England on June 6, 1944, and fought the Germans for a foothold on the beaches of Normandy, France. With Soviet troops on the eastern front advancing toward Berlin, the opening of a western front on the European continent created the military vise that crushed the authoritarianism and ended Hitler's genocide eleven months later. As the anniversary of D-Day came and went in 2022 and 2023, American troops were not fighting directly against Vladimir Putin's ruthless invasion of Ukraine, but the United States provided extensive military support for the Ukrainians as they resisted Russia's onslaught. Russian footholds in eastern Ukraine mean that the war will continue to be long and hard. The cost in blood and treasure to defeat Putin will be high, including an estimated $411 billion to rebuild the country.[14] But a Putin victory in Ukraine is more than democracy can bear.

The democracy-hating lies of Hitler and Putin led to war and genocide. Americans have defended democracy against those tyrants. But as the summer of 2022 unfolded, and the Select Committee to Investigate the January 6th Attack on the United States Capitol gave its damning reports—buttressed significantly by the courageous patriotism of Cassidy Hutchinson, a young White House aide—it remained unclear how staunchly we Americans would defend democracy at home. Will we shield it against the domestic authoritarianism that depends on the lying and disrespect for evidence and truth that have become hallmarks of MAGA Republicanism? If the elections of 2022 and 2024 make that ideology victorious, the American democracy that we have too easily taken for granted could be dead and gone.

The Select Committee skillfully used its witnesses to show the American people that Donald Trump and his collaborators—including infamous minions such as his chief of staff Mark Meadows, the seditious lawyer John Eastman, and the ever-duplicitous Rudy Giuliani—organized and incited violent insurrection. They conspired to overthrow the results of the 2020

14. Knickmeyer, "World Bank."

election and to prevent the peaceful transition of power. They came dangerously close to executing a political coup that would have defrauded the American people and wrecked democracy in the United States. Whether attorney general Merrick Garland and his special counsel Jack Smith, appointed by Garland on November 18, 2022, to oversee crucial criminal investigations, will indict and successfully prosecute Trump and his co-conspirators for the crimes they have committed is a question that leaves American democracy hanging imperiled in the balance. But this much is sure: the 2024 elections will be more fateful than those of 2022.

The 2024 elections will show whether fair and free elections are possible in the United States, particularly when repeated lies and false allegations about voter fraud have led to the suppression of voting rights and to chicanery that jeopardizes accurate vote counting and election certification. The 2022 and 2024 elections will also reveal further how deeply entrenched and malicious antidemocratic minority rule has become in the United States, including in the Supreme Court of the United States (SCOTUS).

Judicial Tyranny and Cruelty

In *Federalist* 78, the founding father Alexander Hamilton argued that the Supreme Court, a necessary final arbitrator of the law, has "neither force nor will, but merely judgment."[15] He tried to persuade his readers that SCOTUS is the "least dangerous" branch of American government, which separates legislative, executive, and judicial power, using checks and balances to keep them in proper alignment.

Life in the 2020s makes Americans reconsider Hamilton's judgment. It's risky to think that any branch of American government is least dangerous. In the wrong hands, the three of them—each and all, and with no exception for SCOTUS—can be extremely dangerous to American democracy. Polluted by hyperpoliticized appointments to the bench, dubious and sometimes leaked opinions, and conflicts of interest unchecked by a credible code of ethics, SCOTUS flexes more muscle than Hamilton imagined or most Americans approve in the 2020s. For good reasons, trust in SCOTUS is at a record low as the 2024 elections approach. That state of affairs is further evidence that the health of American democracy is precarious and fragile.

Republican presidents appointed fourteen of the last nineteen SCOTUS judges. The rightward-tilting court's decisions track Republican too. As authoritarian and antidemocratic impulses of pandemic proportions convulse the American republic, it should not be surprising that forces

15. Hamilton, *Federalist Papers*, No. 78.

have long been at work to bend the law and the judiciary to support them. History shows that antidemocratic, autocratic regimes prioritize control of courts, law, and police. Adolf Hitler and his Nazi Party took steps to make "justice" serve their ends.[16] From Joseph Stalin to Vladimir Putin, courts and their jurisprudence in the Soviet Union and now the Russian Federation have been controlled and used by autocratic, antidemocratic power.[17] In Putin's regime, courts convict hapless defendants 99 percent of the time. Authoritarian control of courts subverts the rule of law and green-lights the politically powerful to do as they will.

With his sidekick Mitch McConnell, the former and aspiring Senate majority leader, Donald Trump used his presidential term to entrench a conservative but extremely activist federal judiciary.[18] The United States has a total of 816 federal judges, including those who serve on SCOTUS, the nation's thirteen appellate courts, and its ninety-one district courts. During one presidential term, Trump appointed 28 percent of those jurists, including three of the nine on SCOTUS and 30 percent of the appellate judges. The three SCOTUS judges—Neil Gorsuch, Brett Kavanaugh, and Amy Coney Barrett—were between the ages of forty-eight and fifty-three at the time of their appointments. Like all federal judges, they serve until they retire or die. Given that the average age of Trump's appellate judges was forty-seven when they took the bench, these jurists will wield power for a long time. Most of Trump's appointees are White men or women, many of them schooled by the right-wing Federalist Society.[19] Eventually Trump will be gone, but his judges will live to demoralize democracy unless reforms take place: for instance, term limits for federal judges, expansion of SCOTUS, and curbing its use of quick "shadow docket" decision-making. Such steps face stiff odds. Efforts to limit SCOTUS terms, for example, might be struck down as unconstitutional by the very court they seek to curb.

In early December 2021, Justice Sonia Sotomayor saw what was coming. Its conservative majority ensured by Amy Coney Barrett's hasty appointment, SCOTUS heard arguments about abortion in a Mississippi case called *Dobbs v. Jackson Women's Health*. Sotomayor knew that Trump's appointments to the court—just the changes in the judges, nothing more or less—doomed American women's right to abortion. Prophetically, she

16. See, for example, Müller, *Hitler's Justice*; and Steinweis and Rachlin, eds., *Law in Nazi Germany*.

17. See, for example, Trochev and Schwartz, *Rule of Law in Russia*.

18. On this point and the discussion that follows, see Scheindlin, "Trump's Judges Will Call."

19. For insightful analysis of the Federalist Society, see Hollis-Brusky, *Ideas with Consequences*.

cried foul: "Will this institution survive the stench that this creates in the public perception that the Constitution and its reading are just political acts?" she asked. "I don't see how it is possible."[20] Sotomayor was right. In the summer of 2022, American approval of SCOTUS cratered to a fifty-year low of 25 percent. What happened on June 24 that year was a major factor in the ongoing dismay and disillusionment.

On that day, SCOTUS took action that threatened its trustworthiness and legitimacy when it overturned *Roe v. Wade*, the 1973 landmark decision affirming that the Constitution protects a woman's right to an abortion before the viability of the fetus.[21] By early summer 2022, SCOTUS had taken the American divide on abortion from bad to worse. In twenty states, abortion remained legal, in twenty-one it was prohibited or restricted, and issues were unresolved in nine.[22] Meanwhile, a conservative, zealous minority of the American people celebrated the *Dobbs* decision. Insisting that human life begins at conception and often vowing to establish fetal personhood and citizenship, they excluded abortion exceptions for rape or incest and claimed that state governments should have the power to determine what a woman can and cannot do about childbearing.[23] The threat of pandemic cruelty in the United States became real.

The conservative SCOTUS bloc's antidemocratic reversal of *Roe* overrode the American majority. In early June 2022, for instance, a *Wall Street Journal* poll found that more than two-thirds of Americans wanted *Roe v. Wade* upheld. In addition, the poll reported, "some 57% of respondents said a woman should be able to obtain a legal abortion if she wants it for any reason."[24] Those majority outlooks, which are often held by religious Americans, indicate that Republican antiabortion plans—using the Dobbs decision to increase support for them—may backfire. The majority dissent against the reversal of *Roe* assumes a needed humility that recognizes human fallibility. No human being, let alone any government or court, knows definitively when the unborn in a woman's womb becomes a human person. "When does a human life begin?"—that's a religious or philosophical question. Religions and philosophies are not in agreement about the answer. People who say they know the answer claim knowledge they do not possess. SCOTUS holds Americans, especially women and girls but men and boys too, hostage to

20. See Pilkington, "'Stench' of Politicization."

21. See the documentation and discussion of *Roe v. Wade* provided by the Legal Information Institute, Cornell Law School.

22. For updates, see *New York Times*, "Tracking the States."

23. On fetal personhood, see Carlisle, "Fetal Personhood Laws."

24. Lucey, "Upholding Roe v. Wade."

the views of religious minorities—evangelical or Catholic Christians—that human life begins at conception. Judicial tyranny and cruelty deny the truth of human limitation that speaks in favor of a woman's right to choose with regard to abortion. Courts and legislatures that take away that right are arrogant and tyrannical, cruel and unethical.

A pandemic of minority rule took the country elsewhere and in multiple ways. As Jill Filipovic underscores, five of the nine SCOTUS judges—Chief Justice John Roberts; Samuel Alito Jr., who wrote the majority opinion in *Dobbs*; Neil Gorsuch; Brett Cavanaugh; and Amy Coney Barrett—"were appointed by presidents who initially lost the popular vote; the three appointed by Donald Trump were confirmed by senators who represent a minority of Americans. A majority of this court, in other words, were not appointed by a process that is representative of the will of the American people."[25] Filipovic aptly added that Gorsuch got his lifetime SCOTUS seat because Mitch McConnell sabotaged Barack Obama's nomination of Merrick Garland, claiming that no appointment should be made in an election year. But then the shamelessly hypocritical McConnell rushed Barrett's confirmation. She was sworn in days before the 2020 election.

Filipovic states what many Americans now believe: SCOTUS is an illegitimate institution. "Stacked with far-right judges appointed by ignoble means," she wrote, SCOTUS has denied American women the right to control their own bodies, privileging "fertilized eggs, embryos, and fetuses" instead. She doubts that a country can truthfully be called democratic if it takes away fundamental rights, freedoms, and liberties from half of its population. That's the stuff of antidemocratic governance, which was on display on January 6, 2021, when Trump and his followers, says Filipovic, "decided that they, an authoritarian, patriarchal, white supremacist minority should rule."

Hypocrisy and Corruption

Republican opinion about the SCOTUS reversal of *Roe* included conviction that God had answered antiabortion prayer. Donald Trump claimed that "God made the decision," adding incoherently that the court's ruling "will work out for everybody." Cheering that "*Roe v. Wade* has been consigned to the ash heap of history," Mike Pence called for a national ban on abortion. Mitch McConnell, who did so much to deliver the devious Federalist Society triumvirate—Gorsuch, Kavanaugh, and Barrett—who clinched the Republican deal to take away a fundamental right from American women,

25. Filipovic, "It's Time to Say It."

accused Democrats of being "jaw-droppingly extreme on abortion" and praised SCOTUS for its "impartiality."[26] Hypocrisy of pandemic proportions deepened the corruption that produced it.

Writing for the majority in *Dobbs v. Jackson Women's Health Organization*, the case that reduced American women to second-class citizens, Samuel Alito, his prose as combative as it was problematic, held that *Roe* was "egregiously wrong . . . and on a collision course with the Constitution from the day it was decided . . . Roe found that the Constitution implicitly conferred a right to obtain an abortion, but it failed to ground its decision in text, history, or precedent." Finding that "the Constitution makes no reference to abortion, and no such right is implicitly protected by any constitutional provision," Alito and his minoritarian SCOTUS majority concluded that *Roe* "must be overruled."[27] The decision returns "the issue of abortion to the people's elected representatives"—that is, to the states. Republican supporters of the judgment touted the decision as a constitutional restoration, a victory for democracy and deliberative persuasion about what should be done. But the lived reality is that debate and democracy were already overridden in gerrymandered red states triggered to enact and enforce draconian antiabortion laws that in some cases made no exceptions for pregnancies caused by rape or incest, even if ten-year-old girls are the victims. Nor was returning the issue of abortion to the states sufficient to satisfy Republican extremists. On September 13, 2022, the South Carolina senator Lindsey Graham introduced a bill for a nationwide ban on abortion after the fifteenth week of pregnancy.[28] Graham's bill allowed exceptions for rape, incest, or the mother's health, but a bill like Graham's aims to trump SCOTUS's trampling on women's rights.

Furthermore, far from restoring the Constitution, Alito and his allies held it hostage to a reactionary "textualist" reading and "originalist" interpretation. Those two approaches are related but not the same. Textualists look closely at what the words of the Constitution are and are not. Alito is textualist when he finds no mention of abortion in the Constitution and uses that finding as one reason to reject a constitutional right to abortion. But textualism goes only so far; the Constitution's words and meanings require interpretation. Originalism seeks and takes as normative the original public meaning of the Constitution's propositions. While focusing on the text, constitutional originalists hold that its meaning is properly

26. On these points, see Alfaro et al., "Pence Calls for National Abortion Ban."

27. Consult the bibliography for the URL linking to the full text of *Dobbs v. Jackson Women's Health Organization*.

28. See Wang and Kitchener, "Graham Introduces Bill."

determined by discerning how the Constitution's statements "would have been understood by the general public, or a reasonable person, who lived at the time the Constitution was ratified."[29]

Originalism is problematic because its textual reading is never as clear, certain, or objective as its advocates want people to believe.[30] Originalists interpret texts in terms of history—what happened in the past, who said what, and what was intended and meant. But history is contested. It tells more than one story. It has more than one meaning. Its truth is complex. More than that, SCOTUS originalists are far from the most respected and dependable historians; they are fallible and finite human beings with political agendas. Jurists who appeal to originalism find needed evidence and arguments to justify and ensure desired outcomes. Originalists are scarcely as impartial as Mitch McConnell and the conservative SCOTUS justices contend.

What makes originalism the gold standard of constitutional interpretation, permeated as it is with selective appeals to history and overconfident claims to know definitively the intended meaning of words used and statements made generations ago? The Constitution's words and statements matter. They matter because although those words and statements are anchored in the past, their meanings are not frozen in time. The Constitution was ordained and established to form "a more perfect Union" and to "secure the Blessings of Liberty" for American generations beyond those of centuries past. Originalism, at least as presently practiced by SCOTUS, does not rise to that occasion or meet that standard. As the historian Jill Lepore cogently argues, "originalists are always narrowing the pool of available historical corroboration . . . There is no method to it, nothing but inconsistency and caprice."[31]

The *Dobbs* decision, for example, disregards the historical context and implications of the Thirteenth Amendment, which abolished slavery in the United States. No understanding of that amendment can be adequate if it ignores and disrespects, as *Dobbs* does, the lived experience of Black women and girls who were freed from bondage. Slavery subjected them to forced pregnancy and motherhood and to births that risked their lives and traumatized them as their children were stolen and sold. If the constitutional

29. On these matters, the US Library of Congress and the Congressional Research Service provide important guidance. See "Textualism" and "Original Meaning" in *Constitution Annotated.*

30. For a telling critique of originalism, see Chemerinsky, *Worse Than Nothing.*

31. Lepore, "The Supreme Court's Selective Memory." See also Dennie, "Originalism," which cogently argues that "originalist ideology glorifies an era of blatant oppression along racial, gender, and class lines, transforming that era's lowest shortcomings into our highest standards." See also Marcus, "Originalism Is Bunk."

abolition of slavery does not free women from the constraints on liberty that *Dobbs* produces, then present-day SCOTUS originalism not only lacks credibility but also embraces cruelty.

Egregious, to use one of Alito's favorite words, the originalist SCOTUS ruling against *Roe* also disregards and disrespects the fact that most of the Constitution, including the Fourteenth Amendment, was enacted and ratified when, as Lepore says, "the majority of people living in the United States could neither run for office nor cast a ballot. They could not elect, and they could not enact; the historical analysis employed by the Court to make decisions about the constitutionality of laws concerning everything from guns to abortion relies on a fundamentally anti-democratic historical record." Such jurisprudence grows from what Jill Filipovic calls a "rotted root."[32] Antidemocratic and authoritarian, those origins subjugate the majority of Americans to a patriarchal, White minority, with the result that the United States is one of the few countries actively strengthening abortion restrictions.

Confiscating Rights

The Constitution does not contain the word *abortion*, but its Fourteenth Amendment, ratified on July 9, 1868, affirms that no State can deprive a citizen—anyone "born or naturalized in the United States and subject to the jurisdiction thereof"—of "life, liberty, or property, without due process of law" or deny "the equal protection of the laws" to such persons. Many rights that Americans treasure are not mentioned explicitly in the Constitution—the right to marry whom one chooses, for example, or to use contraception without governmental interference—but they are reasonably inferred and justly derived from those Fourteenth Amendment clauses. The right to abortion has been grounded that way, and rightly so, the SCOTUS decision to the contrary notwithstanding. That decision rests on the fraught originalist contention that the meaning of the Fourteenth Amendment in 1868 had no place for abortion. The right to abortion, which entails women's power to control their bodies and decide their own destiny, is not, SCOTUS mistakenly judged, "deeply rooted in this Nation's history and tradition." Hence, no right to abortion exists. But as the Yale legal scholar Reva Siegel argues, Alito's SCOTUS unconvincingly chains American women to nineteenth-century White men's "cramped view of women's rights," and in a highly selective way at that. Repeatedly "reading the Fourteenth Amendment's guarantees in light of evolving understandings of liberty has been . . . foundational in modern constitutional

32. Filipovic, "It's Time to Say It."

jurisprudence." Alito's reasoning, she contends, "evades a fundamental question: Why should 19th-century antiabortion laws limit the ways we understand the Constitution's liberty guarantee any more than the history and traditions of segregation limit the way we understand the Constitution's equality guarantee? There is no good reason." Alito's antidemocratic reasoning, she persuasively argues, "shaped and whitewashed . . . the nation's history and traditions . . . to justify his desired results."[33]

"With sorrow—for this Court, but more, for the many millions of American women who have today lost a fundamental constitutional protection," said Justices Stephen Breyer, Sonia Sotomayor, and Elena Kagan, "we dissent." The dissenters lamented that "after today, young women will come of age with fewer rights than their mothers and grandmothers had. The majority accomplishes that result without so much as considering how women have relied on the right to choose or what it means to take that right away." Their resistance spoke for the majority of Americans. But Justice Clarence Thomas did not. Already delegitimized by his conflict-of-interest failure to recuse himself from deliberation that affected his spouse, Ginni, a right-wing Trumpist attorney who aided and abetted attempts to overthrow the results of the 2020 presidential election, Thomas wrote a concurrent opinion in *Dobbs* that paves the way for further assaults on American rights and democracy. Although his colleagues claimed that no other rights were at stake in SCOTUS's antiabortion decision, Thomas said the quiet part aloud and showed how worthless that promissory note could be. If the Fourteenth Amendment cannot be used to establish a right to abortion, how can one justify its use to establish rights to contraception, sex by same-sex couples, gay marriage, and even the right to interracial marriage, which the Thomases themselves enjoy? None of those rights appear explicitly in the Constitution. Thomas wants the basis for such rights, if not the rights themselves, to be "reconsidered." That's an invitation for a pandemic of litigation aimed at the cruel destruction of said rights.

More Minority Rule

Trump's presidency and his almost-successful attempt to steal a second term have undercut democracy. So has a feckless and corrupt Republican Party that twice refused to convict Trump on the impeachment charges that were rightly brought against him and supported by evidence that went far beyond any reasonable doubt. Now, SCOTUS joins the ranks of less-than-sacred institutions that will not be sufficient to save us. Its complicity in the

33. Siegel, "Trump Court."

pandemic dismantling of American democracy is not restricted to decisions taken in 2022. Under Chief Justice John G. Roberts, who was nominated to be chief justice by President George W. Bush and confirmed by the Senate on September 29, 2005, this SCOTUS pattern precedes and extends beyond the pivotal year of 2022. In 2010, for instance, a 5–4 decision in *Citizens United v. Federal Election Commission* held that corporations and other groups can spend unlimited funds on elections.[34] Otherwise, the majority held, their right to freedom of speech would be violated. The antidemocratic result has been elections controlled if not corrupted by wealthy American oligarchs and by "dark money"(money from undisclosed sources). Three years later, in 2013, the Roberts court took another 5–4 decision in *Shelby County v. Holder*.[35] Gutting the Voting Rights Act of 1965, it held that states, mainly southern ones where voter suppression was common, no longer have to clear changes in election laws with the United States attorney general or with the United States district court for the District of Columbia prior to their enactment. In his opinion for the majority, Roberts lauded racial progress in the United States and concluded that American racism was no longer sufficient to warrant the clearance requirements of the Voting Rights Act. But not long after the decision came down, voter suppression measures came roaring back, especially in the very states that had previously been required to obtain clearance before changing their election laws.

SCOTUS is more than complicit in endangering American democracy. A very dangerous branch of government, it actively worsens the damage in the 2020s, a judgment that is likely to be corroborated further in 2023 because SCOTUS has agreed to hear arguments about *Moore v. Harper*, a Republican-backed case from North Carolina. Advancing a fringe doctrine called the independent state legislature (ISL) theory, the case advocates that state legislatures alone have the authority to determine how congressional elections are conducted. According to this theory, neither state constitutions nor state courts have power to check and balance the legislature's prerogative. If this view prevails, American elections, subject to control by gerrymandered Republican state legislatures, are in a world of hurt.[36] Election results could be determined, and likely would be determined, not by votes and the will of the people but by partisan state legislatures. Justices Alito, Gorsuch, and Thomas are known to be friendly to this antidemocratic cabal.

34. See the bibliography for the URL linking to the full text of *Citizens United v. FEC*.

35. See the bibliography for the URL linking to the full text of *Shelby County v. Holder*.

36. See Amar, "Legal Trick."

An ongoing pandemic of SCOTUS activist-conservatism could produce a judicial coup, dooming the democracy Americans have taken too much for granted. Short of that, the elections in 2022 and 2024 will show how much power Americans give or withhold to racism, White supremacy, and religious nationalism. Lies, disregard for evidence, and disrespect for truth are at the core of those malignant ideologies. In addition, hanging in the electoral balance are issues about the minority rule syndrome that revolves around the antidemocratic filibuster in the US Senate and an Electoral College system that allows a presidential candidate to gain office despite an overwhelming loss in the national popular vote. It is false to say that democracy is consistent with minority rule. Democracy can die with a bang when coups overthrow it, but it can die with a whimper too, which can happen if a government fails to respect the majority's will and allows minorities not just to have their say but to have their way through minority rule.

Gun Violence

Already at pandemic levels, gun violence increased by 30 percent during COVID-19 times in the United States.[37] According to the Gun Violence Archive, which collects data from seventy-five thousand law enforcement, media, government, and commercial resources, over 640 mass shootings—defined as four or more persons shot or killed, not including the shooter—took place in the United States during 2022, and sixty more happened in just the first six weeks of 2023.[38] That number will rise after the conservative SCOTUS bloc struck down (6–3 in *New York State Rifle & Pistol Assoc. v. Bruen*) a 108-year-old New York law that restricted carrying concealed firearms in public.[39] SCOTUS prioritized gun rights over public safety, an antidemocratic decision ignoring that by significant majorities Americans want stricter safety measures to quell the nation's pandemic of gun violence, which senselessly slaughters school children.[40] Almost 90 percent of Americans support universal background checks for firearms sales. By a three-to-one margin, Americans believe that a person should be twenty-one before being allowed to buy a gun. On the question of banning

37. Penn State College of Medicine, "U.S. Gun Violence."

38. The website for the Gun Violence Archive, "a not-for-profit corporation formed in 2013 to provide free online public access to accurate information about gun-related violence in the United States," is found at https://www.gunviolencearchive.org/.

39. See the bibliography for the URL linking to the full text of *New York State Rifle & Pistol Association, Inc. v. Bruen.*

40. Daniels et al., "POLITICO Playbook: New Poll." See also Quinnipiac University, "Nearly 3 Out of 4," the Quinnipiac University poll released on June 8, 2022.

assault weapons in the United States poll findings vary, but between 50 and 70 percent strongly or somewhat support a ban. Americans who yearn for such commonsense measures are more likely to receive hostility and cruelty from SCOTUS, not support for human life that SCOTUS conservatives hypocritically claim to defend.

Controlled by those who condone and brandish military assault weapons on our streets and in our neighborhoods, the United States has become a gun country. No other democratic country is like that.[41] Worsening gun tyranny, perpetrated by what columnist Eugene Robinson rightly calls the "devolution" of the Republican Party into "what amounts to a Second Amendment death cult," robs Americans of safety and security.[42] Too many Americans value guns more than life itself. It is utterly false to say that the nation's current gun culture is compatible with the safety of school children. No sound evidence supports that noxious notion. But how will Americans vote? Will there be election consequences for pro-gun politicians who advocate for school safety and mental health measures but refuse to deal with the obvious problem: a massive proliferation of high-powered weapons that does nothing to keep American schools and streets safer? Or will power remain in the bloodstained hands of intransigent elected officials, overwhelmingly Republican, who seem more committed to protecting unborn than born and living children. They do little but offer distracting "thoughts and prayers" or disingenuous bromides about mental illness (as they hypocritically cut health resources) and diversions about "hardened" schools (as they talk nonsensically about arming teachers). Republican politicians gaslight the American population about "the right to bear arms" while the glut of easily available weapons of war in our towns and cities results in grade-schoolers being laid waste, including the nineteen girls and boys murdered in Uvalde, Texas, on May 24, 2022, and the scores of people maimed and murdered by a mass shooter while participating in a Fourth of July celebration in Highland Park, Illinois. How ironic and tragic it is that lethal interpretation and unethical allegiance to the Second Amendment maim and murder American democracy.

Tragically, if significant limits on the nation's gun culture are ever enacted, that will happen because of the gun-murdered American dead and the truth of their blood-drenched stories. In 2023, those realities have scarcely softened the hard hearts or opened the closed minds of Americans who love the Second Amendment more than the "more perfect Union" that the Constitution was ordained to create and established to protect. The

41. See the Institute for Health Metrics and Evaluation, "On Gun Violence."

42. Robinson, "Michigan State Shootings."

wanton murder of Ukrainians has moved Americans to resist Vladimir Putin's antidemocratic authoritarianism. The United States is heavily and rightly invested in helping Ukraine to defend democracy against Putin's greed, violence, and imperialism, against his threats to use weapons of mass destruction. But the war for democracy is not being fought only on Ukrainian soil. It is waged on American ground as well.

Is our commitment to defend democracy at home as strong as it is abroad? Or will even our commitment to Ukraine weaken as we Americans put "gun rights" and cheap gasoline ahead of the ideals that we defend and practice when we are at our best: rights to life, liberty, and the pursuit of happiness; justice for all; equality of opportunity; the rule of law; binding up the nation's wounds; and doing, as Abraham Lincoln said, "all which may achieve and cherish a just, and a lasting peace, among ourselves, and with all nations"?[43] Responses to such questions must not be too optimistic because American democracy faces daunting odds. Two more crises of pandemic proportion testify to that.

Misery and Insecurity

Made worse by the Russian invasion of Ukraine, and its escalation as the one-year anniversary of the war's beginning came and went on February 24, 2023, the world's displaced and refugee population rose to a record 100 million, according to a report issued in late May 2022 by Filippo Grandi, the United Nations High Commissioner for Refugees. "Humanitarian aid," said Grandi, "is a palliative, not a cure. To reverse this trend, the only answer is peace and stability so that innocent people are not forced to gamble between acute danger at home or precarious flight and exile."[44]

Grandi's comments also fit the fact that Putin's war has caused food and fuel crises. It has driven more than seventy million people into poverty, "measured by the number of people surviving on less than $3.20 per day."[45] How the United States responds to this demographic pandemic of misery and insecurity, which has implications for immigration policy in the United States, is another of the many stress tests confronting American democracy.

In addition to worsening the world's demographic upheavals, Putin's war in Ukraine has increased the pandemic-sized dangers of climate change, another unrelenting stress—too long denied or ignored—on American democracy. The April 2022 report of the Intergovernmental

43. Lincoln, Second Inaugural Address, March 4, 1865.

44. See UN High Commissioner for Refugees, "Ukraine, Other Conflicts."

45. Lynch, "Casualties from War in Ukraine."

Panel on Climate Change, experts convened by the United Nations, underscored that the chances are vanishing to curb global warming before floods, wildfires, and droughts do increasing damage.[46] Once again, SCOTUS turned a blind eye and a deaf ear to reality when its conservative bloc predictably voted 6–3 to undermine the regulatory authority of the US Environmental Protection Agency (EPA), which Republican president Richard Nixon and the US Congress established in late 1970 to safeguard American health and the environment. The EPA has a crucial role in limiting greenhouse gases, including CO2, whose pollution drives dangerous climate change. But in *West Virginia v. Environmental Protection Agency*, the callously unrealistic SCOTUS majority held that the EPA does not have the power to establish regulations that limit emissions from existing power plants in efforts to curtail coal burning and to advance use of renewable energy. Only Congress, said the court, has that authority. That's a recipe for supplanting needed administrative authority with congressional inaction that will worsen democracy-threatening climate change.[47]

Recklessly activist in its disastrously antidemocratic 2021–2022 term, which included problematic 6–3 decisions to undermine the separation of church and state (*Carson v. Mackin* and *Kennedy v. Bremerton School District*), SCOTUS is emblematic of the fact that American democracy is demoralized and threatened, often from within the United States, by pandemics that include but extend beyond COVID 19.[48] Each one is aggravated, action to resist them delayed, by lies, disregard for evidence, and disrespect for truth.

Evidence that Americans are at least dimly aware of our plight exists in the fact that the country was in a sour mood as the November 2022 midterm elections came and went. Polls have limited shelf lives, but according to one that the Gallup organization conducted in May 2022, only 16 percent of Americans are satisfied with the way things are going in the United States. The vast majority, 83 percent, are not.[49] If Americans placed a premium on practicing critical, self-corrective inquiry, valuing evidence, and respecting truth, our prospects would be better. Doing that work requires renewing American character, recovering good habits, and revitalizing long-neglected

46. Plummer and Zhong, "Stopping Climate Change."

47. See the bibliography for the URL linking to the full text of *West Virginia v. Environmental Protection Agency*.

48. For a helpful overview of the 2021–2022 SCOTUS term, one of the most disastrous in American history, see Marimow et al., "How the Supreme Court Ruled." See the bibliography for the URLs linking to *Carson v. Makin* and *Kennedy v. Bremerton School District*.

49. Brennan, "Satisfaction with U.S. Dips."

virtues of honest inquiry, trustworthiness, and truth-telling. If those qualities remain in short supply, American democracy will succumb to the pressures that convulse it. Given our current circumstances and dispositions, that regrettable outcome would not be surprising, at least not completely.

American Exceptionalism?

The rhetoric of political myth tries to assure us Americans that our nation will thrive indefinitely, if not forever. Those promises resonate because so much that we hold dear does depend on the national life we share. But closer and more critical examination shows that our fondest hopes take too much for granted. Nations come and go. Nothing guarantees long life for them, let alone eternal existence. Why would we Americans assume that the United States is an exception to the tides of history?

American exceptionalism is a major theme in the story that we have loved to tell ourselves and the world. Democracy anchors that narrative. But the story of American exceptionalism is problematic. As Taylor Harris's *Time* essay for the 2022 Fourth of July issue argued, "My experience tells me America, above all, is exceptional in its commitment to gaslighting. A country willing to violate or exploit those at the margins, cast some to the shadows, take away a long-established right and call others into question, all under the banner of equality and democracy. Any country with a record like ours should dream first of becoming decent, rather than insisting on its own greatness."[50]

The narrative of democracy is not over. That means the United States and its democracy could end and be no more. But the fact that the American story is not over also means that our experiment with democracy continues. Nothing ensures what will happen next. The process of democracy is not synonymous with progress, but the process persists. How will it unfold? Where will it go? The responses to those questions are yet-to-be-written chapters in American history. They are not completely ours to determine, but we do have a say, even a major part, in them. What follows, at least for Lenny and John, are next-chapter reflections on what Americans must do, the qualities of character we must nurture and grow, in order to resist, and give our democracy a chance to survive, the pandemics that besiege it.

50. Harris, "America Insists It Is Great."

7
Resistance

WELL INTO 2023, AMERICANS wondered whether the US attorney general Merrick Garland and the Department of Justice would resist existential threats to American democracy and indict former president Donald Trump and his cronies for felonies they committed in illegally holding classified documents at Trump's Florida estate, as well as for attempting to overturn and steal the 2020 presidential election. Back in 2022, those concerns were interrupted—momentarily but magnificently—on Tuesday, July 12, 2022, when the US National Aeronautics and Space Administration (NASA) released the first breathtaking images from its $10 billion James Webb Space Telescope. NASA administrator Bill Nelson's summary grasped their significance: "We're looking back more than 13 billion years," he said. "Light travels at 186,000 miles per second, and that light that you are seeing from one of those little specks has been traveling for over 13 billion years . . . And by the way, we're going back further. Because this is just the first image . . . We're going back almost to the beginning."[1]

While the country struggled to rebalance its teetering democracy, a project complicated by forty-year-high economic inflation, President Joe Biden saw the telescope's images optimistically. "These images," he insisted, "are going to remind the world that America can do big things. And they'll remind the American people, especially our children, that there's nothing beyond our capacity—nothing beyond our capacity . . . America is defined by one single word: possibilities. Possibilities."[2]

Although reality is always complicated and often frustrating, disappointing, and crushing, the appeal of possibility has long kept Americans hopeful and enabled us to resist discouragement, defeat, and despair. Inescapable history, however, shows possibilities are fickle and even fatal. They include racism, antisemitism, fascism, genocide, Russian brutality

1. See Achenbach, "NASA Unveils First Images."

2. Biden, "First Images."

in Ukraine, and antidemocratic judicial decisions that steal rights to autonomy and privacy from American women and girls.

When Bill Nelson said that images of our universe might take us "back almost to the beginning," his words are reminders about the vast possibilities contained in the history of the universe. Those possibilities have included the origins of the United States and ongoing perspectives about them. Going back to the beginning reminds us that democracy of any kind, including American democracy, is but a speck in the cosmic scheme of things. That's also true of everyone who inhabits the earth. And yet, individual life and national identity brim with passionate meaning. A country's flag, as the French sociologist Émile Durkheim observed, "is only a piece of cloth," but "a soldier will die to save it."[3]

Legend and tradition obscure the exact origins of the Stars and Stripes. Historians have never documented that Betsy Ross first made the American flag at the request of George Washington. Yet the story persists. Every year thousands of visitors to Philadelphia trek to the Ross house to pay their respects. Better proved than the Betsy Ross legend, a resolution adopted by the Continental Congress on June 14, 1777, specified that the flag of the United States should be "thirteen stripes, alternate red and white; that the union be thirteen stars, white in a blue field, representing a new constellation."[4] The Webb Telescope will transmit no images of such a constellation, but the constitutional founding of the United States created promising possibilities and hopes for new beginnings. Agitating for revolution against British rule, Thomas Paine's *Common Sense* (1776) argued that "the cause of America is in great measure the cause of all mankind . . . We have it in our power to begin the world over again," Paine's optimism soared. "The birthday of a new world is at hand."[5]

The American founders had a sense of possibilities less effusive than Paine's because it was so difficult to move from the Declaration of Independence (1776) to the ratification of the Constitution (1778). Writing collectively as "Publius," (the name of one of the first two consuls of the Roman republic), Alexander Hamilton, James Madison, and John Jay—White, male, slaveholding "founding fathers"—made substantial contributions toward its ratification by coauthoring *The Federalist*, commonly called *The Federalist Papers*, a series of eighty-five essays urging support for the Constitution.[6]

3. Durkheim, *Sociology and Philosophy*, 87.
4. US Congress, Joint Committee on Printing, *Our Flag*.
5. See Paine, *Common Sense*.
6. See Hamilton et al., *Federalist Papers*.

"Publius" had few illusions about human beings. In *Federalist* No. 85, for example, Hamilton said that he never expected "to see a perfect work from imperfect man." The imperfections he saw were considerable. "Men," he wrote in *Federalist* No. 6, "are ambitious, vindictive, and rapacious." Although gentler than Hamilton, whose optimistic statements about people were rare, James Madison took the history of politics to be one of "factions, contentions, and disappointments" that often deserve to be "classed among the most dark and degrading pictures which display the infirmities and depravities of the human character" (*Federalist* No. 37).[7]

"Publius" defended the new Constitution not because of confidence, let alone certainty, that it would be successful, but because there was a chance, a fraught possibility, that it might be. That modest hope rested on the belief that the Constitution created institutions sensibly, separated powers sufficiently, and provided checks and balances to equip Americans, in Hamilton's words, to "decide the important question, whether societies of men are really capable or not of establishing good government from reflection and choice, or whether they are forever destined to depend for their political constitutions on accident and force" (*Federalist* No. 1).

Ratification of the Constitution in 1788 left that question at play and unsettled. It still looms large because the Constitution is vulnerable to subversion and subject to overthrow. In the 2020s Americans have learned to our sorrow that oaths to preserve, protect, and defend the Constitution are not as trustworthy as they ought to be. When they are broken, moreover, accountability is too hard to obtain. Twice impeached, Donald Trump should have been twice convicted for breaking his oath of office. He was not. If he goes unindicted or is not convicted for the crimes he has committed, good government will be immensely harmed if not lost because American reflection and choice will have failed.

What would it take for us to resist the persons and powers that rob us of the good government we need and the democracy we Americans cherish when we are at our best? We cannot go back to the beginning of time or even to our nation's founding. No possibilities of that kind exist. But Hamilton's important question still stands: Can we establish good government from reflection and choice?

Reflection and choice—those possibilities remain. Especially in times as unsettled and unsettling as ours, they can create paths of resistance to safeguard American democracy. This chapter maps some of them.

7. On the founders' bleak views about human nature and their insistence that democracy's survival depends on moral virtue, see McKenzie, *We the Fallen People*.

Lenny's Reflections

In 1791, during the early years of the United States, Thomas Paine argued in *The Rights of Man* that "the strength and powers of despotism consist wholly in the fear of resisting it."[8] The Ukrainian president Volodymyr Zelenskyy despised such fear when he said, "I need ammunition, not a ride" in response to an offer to flee Vladimir Putin's blatant aggression and its atrocities.[9] In the United States, nonviolent resistance against Donald Trump and Trumpism has been underway since the 2016 presidential campaign. Its effectiveness, however, is still to be determined, as democracy hangs in the balance. So it is important to underscore that Paine added the following words to the statement quoted above: "in order to be free, it is enough that . . . [one] wills it."[10] Paine was too optimistic. Willing something to happen does not make it so. But absent decisions to resist, taken by groups as well as by individuals, the despotism of Putin and the tyranny of Trumpists will have their way.

While German democracy in the early 1930s was undermined, resistance by ordinary Germans was minimal. Bystanding—in this instance, the failure of most Germans to acknowledge and then contest the growing danger to liberty—contributed to democracy's downfall. Stripping Jews of their civil rights was among the early assaults on democracy that followed Hitler's ascent to power in 1933. Jews were excluded from German citizenship; they were barred from schools. Opportunities closed to practice professions and own businesses. Had German doctors, confronting laws barring Jewish practitioners, refused to practice medicine; had German jurists and attorneys, facing anti-Jewish laws, refused to practice law; had employees of the Deutsche Bank, seeing expropriation of Jewish property, refused to go to work—had all these and other acts of resistance occurred, Hitler's regime would not have survived. Two-thirds of European Jewry would not have been murdered.

Resistance is not one-size-fits-all action. Some individuals and peoples resist oppression with force of arms; others resist nonviolently, sometimes in ways called "spiritual." Jewish defiance of Nazi rule during the years of the Holocaust provides numerous case studies of resistance under the most restrictive conditions. Many Jews showed that the canard "Jews went to their deaths like sheep to the slaughter" remains a lie. In partisan groups, in ghettos and camps, Jews mounted armed resistance

8. Paine, *Rights of Man*, 320.

9. Braithwaite, "Zelensky Refuses."

10. Paine, *Rights of Man*, 320.

beyond what could be expected.[11] But spiritual resistance was the primary way that Jews could and did resist their Nazi captors. Despite dehumanizing measures designed to degrade both body and spirit in the camps, many Jews resisted, for example, by doing what they could to practice personal hygiene, which helped to preserve their dignity. Sustaining the life of the spirit in the ghettos was often achieved by clandestine study of Torah and secular texts. Jews established synagogues and schools in basements. Religious observance continued. Diarists and historians documented the Nazi siege so that future generations would know the fate of those targeted for death just because they were Jews. Others preserved their humanity by engaging in the arts. Concerts and theatrical performances were held in the ghettos and sometimes even in concentration camps as well.

These truths do not deny that most Jews were unable in such dire circumstances to initiate or even participate in acts of resistance. Yet the fact that so many Jews defied Nazi power compels attention. Even in ghettos faced with imminent liquidation, Jewish resistance arose. The Holocaust scholar Yehuda Bauer recounts, for instance, the resistance of Jews in the Ukrainian town of Kosow. Prior to learning that the town's ghetto was about to be liquidated, Kosow's Jews hid or fled to the forest. With the Nazis approaching, three members of the Jewish leadership stayed behind "as sacrificial victims—to deflect the wrath of the enemy." Bauer concludes by asking, "Was their act less than firing a gun?"[12]

What can Jewish resistance to the Nazis teach Americans about resistance to attacks on our democracy? If Jews in ghettos and camps could resist massive human degradation and almost certain death, surely democracy-affirming Americans—most of us free to challenge authority without fear of serious reprisal—can do much more to preserve our democracy. But how can we best do that and, in particular, defeat the common denominator undergirding all attacks on democracy: the rule of the lie? The political philosopher Hannah Arendt emphasized that "the result of a consistent and total substitution of lies for truth" means that "the sense by which we take our bearings in the real world . . . is being destroyed." Truth, according to Arendt, "is the ground on which we stand and the sky that stretches above us."[13] At a time when Trumpism's lies attack the very existence of truth—our lodestar—what kinds and styles of resistance are most needed?

11. Bauer, "Forms of Jewish Resistance," 33. Bauer's chapter provides an excellent overview of armed and spiritual resistance during the Holocaust.

12. Bauer, "Forms of Jewish Resistance, 40.

13. Arendt, "Truth and Politics," 252–53, 259.

The lie—big, medium-sized, or even small—can reign in a variety of viral forms that collectively produce pandemic conditions. Combatting such disease requires resistance appropriate for the varied modes of attack. How, for example, do we resist the proliferation of conspiracy theories regarding COVID-19 and the vaccines that defend against it? Such attacks on truth often render traditional forms of resistance-by-reason—clinching arguments, for instance, or barrages of facts—ineffective, sometimes even counterproductive. In such cases, resistance to the dominion of the lie might better begin with finding elements of common ground in discussions with virus skeptics and vaccine opponents. Exploring points of agreement might advance dialogue.

To support such skeptics and opponents to think about their use of the word *freedom* (often understood as license to contest alleged government interference) by asking them questions about the origins of their views can be effective. An opening query might be, "How did you come to the position you hold on the COVID-19 pandemic?" The respectful tone in which such a question is asked, along with the questioner's willingness to be similarly questioned, may plant seeds that create genuine communication. Such communication could be advanced by sharing personal stories about times when each party had to rethink what once was a fixed and certain belief. The sharing of common experiences may help to foster mutual trust, a principal element in the resistance needed to defend democracy. Letting my discussion partner know my willingness to learn something new from the exchange of views underway may ward off the potential for defensive responses and, at the same time, model a basic element of democratic discourse.

Viruses attacking democracy have proliferated. How, for example, are we to resist the lie that global warming, a climate crisis, does not exist, or that reports of it are exaggerated? As with attempts to reach anti-vaxxers, presenting scientific facts will unlikely change the minds of environmental skeptics. But mention of concern for future generations may lead to finding common ground in constructive dialogue. Climate-crisis deniers, like environmental guardians, will care about the lives of their grandchildren and great-grandchildren, making it more difficult for them to reject all attempts to heal the planet. Although piercing the ideological bubble of the skeptics is an enormous challenge, many young Americans today have provided leadership in resisting lies about global warming. Their often bodily protests make concern for future generations visceral. I have been moved by grade school and high school students lying on the pavement in opposition to continued exploitation of the environment. Bringing along a young person while engaging a climate-crisis skeptic in conversation may prove a useful strategy.

Trumpist lies threaten America's tradition of welcoming diverse peoples to the United States. The virus of xenophobia has kept immigration issues at a crisis point, especially at our southern border. The Trump administration's policies toward immigrants stoked fears of the "other." Large gaps have opened between those with xenophobic leanings and those who seek to preserve a democratic heritage that responsibly supports immigration and honors the humanity of people who seek the refuge and new beginning that have led so many men, women, and children—including members of our own families—to become Americans. How can xenophobia and the policies that embody it best be resisted? Lies and liars must be called out. Immigrants are not the criminals and rapists that Trump and his followers demonize them to be. Ways must be found to speak with Trumpism-supporting neighbors, personally and in public forums, about the groundless nature of the "great replacement theory" and other anti-immigrant narratives of White extinction. We must help whoever will listen to understand that an "invasion" of immigrants does not exist, but the need is real to do what we responsibly can to assist fellow human beings who seek refuge from oppression and aspire to a better life.

Maintaining resistance in order to protect democracy also includes revealing and understanding the origins of threats to democracy in the 2020s. Why, for instance do so many Americans—millions of them—continue to believe the Big Lie that the 2020 presidential election was stolen from Donald Trump through rigged elections and voter fraud? Time and again, those allegations are disproven, but the Big Lie's power persists. That persistence has much to do with cultural discontent and feelings of grievance and victimization rooted in demographic and economic change. Trump appeals to Americans who feel left out. Accepting his election loss was too much. A privileged American like me saw things differently. Nevertheless, many rural or working-class individuals, for example, are fearful about the loss of economic opportunity. Many blue-collar workers and the working poor in the rural heartland feel alienated from those they deem "urban elites" on the Atlantic and Pacific coasts. Many voters feel condescension from the Democratic Party, which they perceive to be allied with college graduates and people of color. Debates about these matters ensue, but inflammatory language doesn't help to advance needed communication. For instance, Hillary Clinton's hostile phrase "basket of deplorables" did nothing to advance discussion with the Trump supporters it targeted.

The list of viruses afflicting America in the 2020s is long. My comments have referred only to a few of them. In the age of Trumpism, what about authoritarianism? Minority rule? Religious nationalism? Gun violence? Curtailment of reproductive and sexual-orientation rights? The list goes on, but so does the list of modes of resistance available to defend democracy. I have spoken about just one of its forms: resistance-through-dialogue. Dialogue is necessary to combat Trumpism and the divisiveness it produces, but dialogue is not sufficient. We must not think that dialogue as an expression of democracy-at-work guarantees success against Trumpism. Such credulity is dangerous. In the words of journalist and author Chris Hedges, "It is easier, as many academics did in Weimar Germany, to believe . . . that opening channels of dialogue and communication could see the fascists domesticated."[14] We must resist through other actions in the public square, as each of us envisions it. We must resist with our votes, with our presence at rallies for preserving democratic norms, by creating or attending antiracist workshops, by funding organizations advocating equal treatment for marginalized groups.

Lawyers and paralegals can volunteer to advise undocumented immigrants and help establish sanctuary cities. Visual artists, musicians, filmmakers, poets, playwrights, journalists, and authors can produce works that address societal inequities and inspire public protest against authoritarianism. Religious leaders can speak out in defense of their traditions' core teachings of justice and compassion, and in opposition to those who co-opt those traditions for antidemocratic ends. Health workers can publicly protest disparities in access to care for racial and ethnic minorities and other medically underserved populations. Teachers can promote democratic ideals in the style and substance of their teaching. Corporate leaders can model democratic ideals in their interactions with employees and support them when Trumpism impedes their freedom.

In the 2020s, Americans face threats to democracy similar to those that Germans confronted in the Weimar Republic of the 1920s and early 1930s. We Americans are forewarned. All of us can resist by speaking truth in a multitude of ways, each proceeding from the place where he or she stands, each stepping out from business as usual to repair the fraying fabric of our democracy. Thomas Paine was right in the 1790s, and he is on target in the 2020s: the future of democracy depends on our will to resist what undermines it.

John's Questions

I agree with so much that you say about resistance against the persons, postures, and policies that erode American democracy in the 2020s. I especially applaud your emphasis on truth and truth-telling. Every threat

14. Hedges, "Fascists in Our Midst." See also Hedges, *American Fascists*.

eroding the United States is rooted in a pandemic of lying and lies. No disease that we have to combat is more lethal.

Speaking to military families gathered at the White House on July 4, 2022, President Joe Biden underscored that "many Americans look around today and see a divided country and are deeply worried about that fact." Attempting reassurance, Biden added, "I understand. But I believe we're more united than we are divided . . . from the deepest depths of our worst crises, we've always risen to our higher heights. We've always come out better than we went in."[15] Americans should not assume that Biden's belief is credible. That's why it is right for you to emphasize dialogue and its potential to resist division and build bridges. But, you rightly add, resistance-through-dialogue is not sufficient to overcome the demoralizing division.

Why is resistance-through-dialogue inadequate? History provides insight. Dialogue was insufficient to stop Adolf Hitler and the Holocaust because violent power overwhelmed any chance that it had. Inspiring though it was, Jewish resistance never assumed that it could end a murderous, racist antisemitism. It took massive military force to defeat the genocidal Third Reich. Nor did dialogue keep Vladimir Putin from invading Ukraine and pursuing brutal warfare to occupy as much of that country as he can. His imperialistic ambition swamped discussion and diplomacy. So far in the 2020s, violence has not completely engulfed the United States, but you wisely avoid putting more weight on dialogue than it can bear. How would human thought and action have to be different to change that situation?

You think that resistance to defend American democracy must take place in "the public square." You urge that this work can be done through voting, rallies, workshops, philanthropy in support of political causes, volunteerism, artistic activism, and commitments within professions. If these steps supplement dialogue, can they be sufficient to restore our democracy's health? I ask because I wonder how virulent and deadly you take the threats to American democracy to be. What has to change in American thought and action before resistance in the public square can be sufficient to restore and revitalize democracy in the United States?

In an essay called "News from the Sky," the Auschwitz survivor Primo Levi noted that the German philosopher Immanuel Kant emphasized two wonders in creation: the starry sky above and the moral law within. "Let's leave aside moral law," said Levi, "is it to be found within everyone? . . . Every year that passes only amplifies our doubts."[16] The starry sky contributes to such unease because it is the territory of Russian missiles that

15. Biden, "Military Families."

16. Levi, *Other People's Trades*, 2180.

intentionally target Ukrainian schools and hospitals. Weapons of mass destruction capable of annihilating human existence could be unleashed in its darkness. Levi's doubts about the moral law within make me wonder: Do Americans have a shared morality? Does dialogue fail because we don't? Do we honor the same values? If we don't, can action in the public square be sufficient to rescue democracy?

Those questions lead to Sarah Kofman. An important French philosopher, she survived the Holocaust as a hidden child in Paris. Her book *Smothered Words* contains a challenging insight: "No community," said Kofman, "is possible with the SS."[17] That vast military and political juggernaut in Nazi Germany planned, coordinated, and directed the Holocaust. It embodied and advanced a restricted, exclusive, antipluralistic, and genocidal sense of "community" hell-bent on destroying the expansive and inclusive sense of community—the community of communities—that democracy fosters and on which it depends.

Kofman makes me wonder: Can there be democratic community with Trumpists? Is a democratic community of communities possible with what Mark Leibovich accurately calls "Republican nihilism."[18] Epitomized not only by Donald Trump but also by Lindsey Graham and Kevin McCarthy, a perverse MAGA Republican "community" prioritizes personal ambition and power, obtained and held by whatever it takes, to the exclusion of caring about our country's health and the future of its democracy. Is community possible with everyone, with every group, in the United States? Or have too many lines been crossed to make that aim realistic and credible?

"Resistance," you correctly say, "is not one-size-fits-all action." To restore American democracy, to save it from Republican nihilism and related ills, what does resistance entail? Part of the answer, I believe, is that power must be denied to antidemocratic leadership and authoritarian rule. Lucidity about what's at the core of the threats to our democracy will determine what's necessary and sufficient to achieve that goal. What's at the root of our rot? Are we headed for more January 6–style insurrection or even civil war? Is our democracy too far gone to permit full recovery?

Lenny's Response

You ask big questions that go to the roots of key concerns. I'll begin by responding to your wondering how "virulent" I take the threats to American

17. Kofman, *Smothered Words*, 70.

18. Leibovich, "Most Pathetic Men." See also Leibovich, *Thank You for Your Servitude*.

democracy to be. Like you, I am unconvinced by the Biden quote you cite regarding a "happy ending" to the crisis. In a *New York Times* editorial, Michelle Goldberg wrote about other Democratic leaders who believe that our traditional institutions are strong enough to withstand current attacks. These leaders, according to Goldberg, "give every impression of seeing this moment, when . . . one party openly schemes against democracy, as an *interregnum rather than a tipping point*."[19] We are at a decisive moment for American democracy.

I don't have easy yes-or-no answers for your questions about whether "too many lines have been crossed," or whether democratic community with Trumpists is even possible. Those issues require nuanced responses. Threats to democracy exist on a continuum over the course of American history. We have always had to protect our nation's democratic foundations. They were damaged severely during the Civil War era. Taking up arms against one another brought us as close as possible to the destruction of the nation and its democracy. How closely do the 2020s encompass threats akin to those of the 1860s? In the 2020s, I believe, the United States is at an inflection point. Our schisms significantly challenge American democracy. How to bridge the gaps and heal the divisions is the question, and that question has to take seriously that we Americans may not be able to do so. Warnings about our dire straits must include credible proposals about resistance—what you and I are trying to provide.

You ask about the root of the moral rot that has spread in Trump's followers, undaunted by mounting evidence of his grifting deceit, hostility to the rule of law, and far-reaching criminality. I, too, wonder why so many Americans are unable or unwilling to see that the emperor has no clothes. You ask if "Americans have a shared morality"; you question whether "we honor the same values." Although the degree to which Trumpists fail to honor core democratic values enrages me, I have difficulty answering either question without complicating—and tempering—my response. I don't want to "totalize" or "other" my fellow humans in ways that would demonize them and undercut the very democracy that should be preserved. Human persons are not static beings with fixed and unchangeable characteristics. As Jean-Paul Sartre and other existentialist philosophers emphasize, we continually make ourselves who we are. Morally speaking, we are more process than product.

As history shows, however, we can *choose* not to be ethical, not to do what is right and just. Hitler and Stalin became reified, fixed in their tyrannical and murderous existence. Putin is on the same path. Junior partner

19. Goldberg, "Joe Biden Is Too Old" (italics added).

though he may be, Donald Trump belongs in this pantheon of tyrants. He disrespects truth and cares much more about his personal power and wealth than about his country and its citizens. He disrespects and demoralizes American democracy. Fortunately, not all of his supporters are cut from the same cloth; some may have left the door to dialogue open, at least a crack. Ways must be found to narrow gaps between them and those who seek the defeat of Trump and Trumpism. Although the schism between those supporting a growing autocracy and those defending the rule of law is wide, it is still bridgeable. Dialogue is certainly not the end point of resistance to Trumpism, but it remains valuable. Indeed it is essential for addressing the divisiveness that imperils our democracy.

When I speak of resistance in the public square—voting and rallying, for example—I am not merely adding activities to supplement dialogue. Each mode of resistance in the public square embodies numerous dimensions. Voting, for instance, is more than merely one among many ways to resist those who would destroy democracy. Democrats have learned the hard way about how much damage organized voting blocs can do. Trumpist Republican efforts to control school boards and election procedures as well as city and state governments are as threatening as they are successful. Well-organized Republican voters have given "antidemocrats" power and made them majorities in state legislatures. Local judiciaries are also overwhelmingly Republican. Grassroot organizing affects the landscape of national politics. Trumpist Republicans have employed the tools of democracy to hasten its destruction. Democrats need to organize resisting movements that bring their voters to local, state, and federal polling places in overwhelming numbers.

"Power must be denied to antidemocratic and authoritarian rule," you say, and I agree. *How* we deny such power is a crucial question. The public square, as I understand it, is also the locus of nonviolent actions that take their cue from the civil rights movement of the late 1950s and 1960s, as well as from the more recent protest movements demanding equal rights for the LGBTQ+ community. In mentioning "rallies" in the public square, I include acts of civil disobedience. Nonviolent actions, like those of civil rights workers in Selma and Birmingham decades ago, may well be needed to counter Trumpism. The public square is not only a physical site where protests occur; it is also a symbol of resistance on a wide continuum beginning with donations to social justice organizations and extending to active nonviolent protests on a massive scale. I look for ways to support acts of civil disobedience that defend democracy against autocracy. Symbolically and physically putting our bodies on the line in nonviolent civil disobedience may be necessary to preserve American democracy.

Finally, I agree that it took superior military power to defeat Nazi Germany. The same is true regarding the defeat of Russian imperialism during the current war in Ukraine. The Holocaust teaches us about the evil that human action can produce. All post-Holocaust generations need to know about that. You cite the Holocaust and Putin's war as examples of evil that resists well-meaning but futile attempts at peacemaking through dialogue. How would human thought and action have to be different, you ask, to make the prospects better for dialogue to resist the present-day evils of Trumpism effectively?

Study of the Holocaust gives us some openings to reflect on responses to your question. The Holocaust warns us not to ignore the fact that human beings can produce radical evil. But the Holocaust also challenges us to remember that even in treacherous circumstances human beings can do what is right and good. Holocaust rescuers, for instance, chose at great risk to hide Jews in numbers beyond what could have been anticipated. These resisting rescuers were not always rescuers; they were not fated to do that work. When they decided to do what they could to get Jews out of harm's way, they changed. Their decisions reveal and support changes for good.

Holocaust rescuers challenge us to reexamine traditional notions of human persons as self-serving beings who always look out for "number one." Typically, Holocaust rescuers did not say that they had done anything more than "the right thing." Holocaust rescuers show that indifference and bystanding are neither inevitable nor acceptable when injustice and untruth try to seize control. They show that people can change; they can even become extraordinarily good. If our democracy is to be preserved, Trumpism's quest for power will have to be denied. One way for that to happen is for Trumpists to change. They could change for the better, and they might do so. Defenders of democracy must not disrespect or dismiss that possibility.

Holocaust rescuers bear witness to possibilities of goodness that preclude total despair about Trumpism's relentless craving for antidemocratic power. It must not be overlooked or forgotten that some of the most effective resistance to MAGA Republicanism comes from Republicans themselves, as Liz Cheney and Adam Kinzinger testify. Holocaust rescuers and resisting Republicans—they help Americans to imagine a future in which at least some Trumpists change their ways, respond favorably to forms of resistance detailed in this chapter, and heed the call for inclusive, pluralistic American democracy.

John's Reflections

Americans must take at least seven steps to rescue and restore our democracy. Law and legislation, let alone political parties, won't ensure that the steps will be taken. That's because the needed steps go deep down. They are fundamentally ethical. A story from the Holocaust advances them.

No longer under a Nazi death sentence after the liberation of Auschwitz on January 27, 1945, Primo Levi became a writer with unsurpassed insight about the Holocaust. A key source of his insight was Lorenzo Perrone, the person Levi credited with saving his life. Not a Jew but an Italian civilian, Lorenzo, a skilled bricklayer, was conscripted by the Germans to help build an industrial plant that they were constructing near Auschwitz. Workers like Lorenzo were not prisoners. They had privileges unknown to Levi and his fellow inmates but also obligations to do the Germans' bidding. Levi saw that Lorenzo "hated Germans, their food, their language, their war," but Lorenzo still took pride in work well done. Levi was struck by the fact that Lorenzo, a quiet, "sensitive man, almost illiterate but really sort of a saint," laid his bricks for the Germans "straight and solid, not out of obedience but out of professional dignity."[20] After meeting Levi as they labored at the construction site in late June 1944, Lorenzo decided to help his fellow Italian. For months and at significant risk, Lorenzo got Levi extra food, which was the physical difference between life and death.

"I believe that I owe it to Lorenzo if I am alive today," Levi would write, underscoring that Lorenzo's help meant much more than food alone. What also sustained him was that Lorenzo "constantly reminded me by his presence, by his natural and plain manner of being good, that a just world still existed outside ours, something and someone still pure and whole, not corrupt, not savage, unconnected to hatred and fear: something difficult to define, a remote possibility of good, but for which it was worth surviving."[21]

When liberation came, Levi lost track of Lorenzo. They reconnected in Italy after the war, but soon Lorenzo died. Levi's recollections of him are memorable. Lorenzo "was not religious," Levi said. "He didn't know the gospel, but instinctively he tried to rescue people, not for pride, not for glory, but out of a good heart and for human comprehension. He asked me once in very laconic words: 'Why are we in the world if not to help each other?'"[22] At one of their postwar meetings, Levi learned that he was not the only Auschwitz prisoner whom Lorenzo had helped, but Levi's friend

20. See Levi's 1985 interview with Motola: Levi, "Primo Levi."

21. Levi, *If This Is a Man*, 115.

22. See Levi, "Primo Levi." See also Philip Roth's "Conversation with Primo Levi," 179.

had rarely told that story. In Lorenzo's view, wrote Levi, "we are in the world to do good, not to boast of it."[23]

Primo Levi never forgot Lorenzo and the dignity his lifesaving gifts restored. Lorenzo despised hatred and fear. So did Levi. Resisting savagery and corruption, they both defended justice. But what about Lorenzo's telling Levi that we are in this world to do good? Was Lorenzo naïve? Was he gullible—even stupid? Anyone who yearns for American democracy to regain health should hope not.

Lots of good must be done to reform and renew American democracy. If we Americans are not in the world to act that way, then dismal chapters will tragically end our nation's history. So, what does "doing good" to revitalize democracy most fundamentally require of us Americans—not only the powerful and influential but citizens of all kinds—in the 2020s and beyond? The following steps are among the most important.

Respect Truth

Before witnesses testify in legal proceedings, a question confers an essential duty upon them: "Do you solemnly swear that the testimony you will give will be the truth, the whole truth, and nothing but the truth, so help you God?" If the response is the expected "I do," then deliberately failing to tell the truth about pertinent matters may be a felony called *perjury*. Lying under oath is a serious matter because the entire system of justice in the United States and everywhere depends on truth-telling. That point can truthfully be expanded: Democracy, indeed human civilization itself, depends on seeking and respecting truth. Failure to pursue and honor truth undercuts and betrays what is good and right.

How different American democracy would be in the 2020s if Donald Trump and his followers sought and respected truth. How different our character would be if Americans persistently and utterly condemned Rudy Giuliani's corruptly nonsensical and cynical Trumpist claim that "truth isn't truth."[24] How different the country would be if every American citizen told the truth and followed where tested evidence leads. The nation not only

23. Levi, "Return of Lorenzo," 1408. Despite the medical assistance that Levi arranged for him, Perrone, wracked by tuberculosis and alcohol, died in 1952. Significantly, Levi's daughter, Lisa Lorenza, and his son, called Renzo, were named after Perrone. On June 7, 1998, Perrone was recognized by Yad Vashem, the State of Israel's memorial to the victims of the Holocaust, as one of the Righteous Among the Nations, a special honor for non-Jews who rescued Jews during the Holocaust. For more detail on Perrone, see Yad Vashem, "Stories of Six."

24. Perrigo, "Here's How Rudy Giuliani Explains."

would have been spared the Big Lie that the 2020 election was stolen by voter fraud—it was not—but also Trump and his acolytes and successors would never have gained the power that egregiously degrades American democracy. Tyranny, authoritarianism, hostility to democracy, from Hitler to Putin and Trump—and with a long, tortured history preceding them—all depend on lying, on disrespecting truth, on willful failure to seek and respect it. If we Americans are in the world to do good for our democracy, nothing is more important than seeking, respecting, and defending truth.

That commitment requires believing in truth, affirming that it exists. And that work requires taking facts seriously. Doing so may be hard and contrary to our wishes, but we do it all the time. Unless we are blind and stupid, we have no other choice because facts are stubborn. They can be suppressed, ignored, and denied, but they do not go away, and democracy's survival depends on fidelity to them.

Stubborn facts: This book exists. Lenny and John wrote it. Moreover, the words that state those facts are true. Donald Trump fairly lost the 2020 presidential election. That, too, is a fact, and the words that state it are true. A Supreme Court decision—*Dobbs v. Jackson Women's Health Organization*—that enables the Ohio legislature to condemn a ten-year-old girl to give birth to her rapist's child is cruel and wrong.[25] That's another stubborn fact, and the words that state it are true. Denial to the contrary notwithstanding, the world's climate crisis intensifies and worsens natural disasters—storms, heat waves, droughts, fires—that kill. The truth of reality is that the baseball-inspired mantra is right: "Nature bats last and owns the stadium too."

As the historian Timothy Snyder wisely says in *On Tyranny*, an essential guidebook, "To abandon facts is to abandon freedom. If nothing is true, then no one can criticize power, because there is no basis upon which to do so."[26] Snyder tells how truth dies. Hostility to verifiable reality lets inventions and lies become "facts." Then blunt and endless repetition of those inventions and lies makes "the fictional plausible and the criminal desirable." Snyder's warning is that "post-truth is pre-fascism."[27] With Hitler in mind and also Putin and Trump, he continues:

> Fascists despised the small truths of daily existence, loved slogans that resonated like a new religion, and preferred creative

25. Mayer, "State Legislatures Are Torching Democracy."

26. Snyder, *On Tyranny*, 65 [56]. A graphic edition of Snyder's book, brilliantly illustrated by the artist Nora Krug, appeared in 2021. Quotation citations for the 2021 edition appear in brackets after the page numbers for citations from the 2017 edition. For a perceptive biographical article about Snyder, see Baird, "Timothy Snyder."

27. Snyder, *On Tyranny*, 71, [63].

> myths to history or journalism. They used new media, which at the time was radio, to create a drumbeat of propaganda . . . And now, as then, many people confused faith in a hugely flawed leader with truth about the world we all share.[28]

If we Americans are in the world to do good for our democracy, we cannot, must not accept the rank ignorance, astonishing stupidity, and relentless lying that will plunge the United States into a post-truth culture where nothing is true, might makes right, and anything goes.

Support Freedom of the Press

In rallies, tweets, and confrontations with reporters, Donald Trump repeatedly maligns the press and misleads his followers to think that its truthful and critical reporting is "fake news." He slanders diligent journalists. They are, he lies, enemies of the people, dishonest, corrupt, "low life reporters," "human scum," and "some of the worst human beings you'll ever meet." Exempting his Fox News and Newsmax accomplices from those canards and heaping praise on them instead, Trump draws on the tyrant's playbook, which always calls for control of the media by smashing journalistic opposition and by promoting the actual "fake news" that promotes autocratic schemes and antidemocratic agendas.

Especially in the 2020s, Americans should be grateful that freedom of the press is enshrined in the First Amendment to the US Constitution. We ought to defend that freedom, not abstractly but by supporting courageous investigative reporting. Absent the daily diligence of journalists at publications such as the *New York Times* and the *Washington Post*, the *Atlantic* and the *New Yorker*, the newscasts provided by CNN and MSNBC, or reporting from Project Censored, Politico, and Axios, for example, Americans would be in the dark. American democracy would truly be beyond repair because, as the *Washington Post*'s motto rightly says, Democracy Dies in Darkness.

Unfortunately, as shown by the defamation suit brought by Dominion Voting Systems against Fox News—Fox lost the case in 2023—much of the darkness that threatens American democracy results from craven abuse of freedom of the press. Fox News amps up that abuse with immensely destructive cynicism whenever its major stars—Tucker Carlson, Sean Hannity, and Laura Ingraham among them—knowingly, repeatedly, and by their own private admission spread lies about election fraud in the 2020 presidential election, doing so to please their Trumpist followers, maintain viewership

28. Snyder, *On Tyranny*, 71, [63].

rankings, and sustain the value of the Fox stock that rewards them.[29] Support for freedom of the press must not be blind or uncritical. To be free, the press has to expose corruption that can infect it. That corruption is at its worst when the press goes the way of Fox News—willingly, knowingly, and by its private but not public admission lying for power and profit.

To do good for American democracy, Americans have to subscribe to what our best journalists discover and share. We have to read, listen, watch, debate, criticize, think twice, and act accordingly. Our best journalists do not embrace conspiracy theories; they expose and debunk them. Nor do those sources transmit misinformation or deceive with disinformation. Instead, they support the truth by unmasking deception and uncovering lies. At their best, they maintain professional ethics, which means that they admit mistakes and correct them. They welcome being held to exacting standards by Americans who know that responsible freedom of the press is absolutely necessary for democracy's vigor.

Affirm That Evidence Matters

In June 2022, the Gallup organization asked Americans "how proud are you to be an American—extremely proud, very proud, moderately proud, a little proud or not at all proud?"[30] At the time, the country reeled from mass shootings in Buffalo, New York, and Uvalde, Texas. Those eruptions of gun violence took fifty lives, including nineteen Texas schoolchildren. The Supreme Court had not yet overturned *Roe v. Wade*, but that decision was only days away.

The Gallup poll found that 65 percent of Americans expressed very high degrees of pride about their American identity, but the 38 percent who said they are extremely proud to be American was the lowest since Gallup started polling on the question in 2001. The June 2022 readings were below the trend averages since 2001, which show 55 percent of Americans to be extremely proud about being American and 80 percent extremely or very proud.

Assuming that the Gallup pollsters have sound data, which way should we Americans want our "pride trend" to go? That's a more complicated question than it looks at first because false pride exists. Uncritical and arrogant, it is as dangerous as it is unjustified, as toxic as it is widespread. We should be proud about being American to the extent that good reasons exist for feeling that way. Evidence matters. For instance, should Americans

29. Peters and Robertson, "Fox Stars"; Stelter, "Fox News."

30. Brennan, "Record-Low 38% Extremely Proud."

be proud because we have about 4 percent of the world's population but more than 40 percent of the world's civilian-owned firearms? Should we be proud that more than fifty Americans die each day from gun violence?[31] Should we be proud of a gun-culture country where in 2021 alone more than 1,500 American children and teenagers younger than eighteen were killed in homicides and accidental shootings?[32] Should we be proud that 56 percent of Americans favor banning semiautomatic weapons?[33] Should we be proud of our Supreme Court or our Congress or a feckless Republican Party and a too-often ineffectual Democratic Party? Should we be proud that Rudy Giuliani and Sidney Powell are American lawyers? Should we be proud that Donald Trump served as our forty-fifth president, corrupting the nation's Secret Service to aid and abet his coup attempt? Should we be proud that he is running for president in 2024?

If yes is the answer to any of those questions, then the pride is false because evidence hasn't mattered, and thus the danger signs for American democracy are lit up urgently. If no is the answer to such questions, then not only does evidence matter, but also it should stir us to change our ways and to cast our votes in the way that the former Republican Tom Nichols urges when he writes, "The institutional Republican Party must be weakened enough so that it can't carry out the larger project of undermining our elections and curtailing our rights as citizens."[34]

American democracy can't survive false pride. That's what the evidence shows. Evidence matters. We fail to make those affirmations at our peril.

Build Character

George Washington's 1796 Farewell Address stressed that "virtue or morality is a necessary spring of popular government."[35] He did not say ethical conduct is sufficient to sustain democracy, but lack of it always ravages good government and the freedom, equality under law, and justice that support and depend upon it.

Consider what ethics comprises and why Washington thought it necessary but not sufficient for democracy. Ethics is civilization's keystone. What defines ethics is the intention to encourage human action that fits sound understanding about what is *right* and *wrong*, *just* and *unjust*, *good*

31. Ingraham, "There Are More Guns Than People."
32. Fuller, "Stupefying Tally."
33. Orth and Frankovic, "After Recent Mass Shootings."
34. Nichols, "Confessions."
35. Washington, Farewell Address.

and *evil*, *virtuous* and *corrupt*. At its best, ethics emphasizes careful deliberation about the difference between right and wrong, commitment not to be indifferent toward that difference, cultivation of virtuous character, and action that defends what is right and resists what is wrong.

Defending democracy requires character-building, the cultivation of virtues, good habits of thought and action. The key virtues that Americans need to cultivate—through good parenting, sound education, genuine religion, spirited but respectful dialogue, insistent accountability—include truth-seeking and truth-telling, courage and curiosity, realistic senses of limitation and fallibility and yet a willingness to break new ground for justice and refusal to give up pursuing what is right and good in spite of doubt and despair.

The latter qualities are crucial because ethics and virtue are fragile. Politics, power, and privilege can manipulate, rationalize, neutralize, override, and relativize them into irrelevance, or subvert them by repurposing key ethical concepts—duty and responsibility, conscience and loyalty—into "ideals" that legitimate corruption, injustice, and violence in ways that destroy democracy. For example, no one in recent American history insisted on loyalty more than Donald Trump. But he subverted and corrupted that virtue to such an extent that he and his followers were disloyal to the Constitution.

With character-building at stake, Snyder says "be as courageous as you can."[36] Lorenzo could not help everyone, but he saved Primo Levi. None of us Americans can do everything needed to restore democracy, but even small deeds and modest actions are significant. Think of voting or teaching in that way. If we take responsibility for each other, if we protect human rights and fundamental freedoms as best we can, good prospects for democracy are not guaranteed but they are improved.

Ask Questions

Fragile though they are, ethics and virtue are also persistent and resilient, if we do not abandon them. Question-asking, a key virtue, bears witness to that. Is this policy or that act good? Is this decision or that plan just? Is my loyalty justified? Am I doing the best I can? Are we? When we acknowledge that the most trustworthy responses to such question may well be no, we discern that it is important to revise and reform our ways so that we can answer yes responsibly and truthfully.

36. Snyder, *On Tyranny*, 115, [107].

Best known for her play *The Vagina Monologues*, V (formerly Eve Ensler) believes in questions. They can ignite needed change; they are fundamental for resistance to oppression and tyranny. So she began a response to the overturning of *Roe v. Wade* by asking, "How did you feel when it happened? When they came to take away the rights to our bodily autonomy? When they said 12-year-old girls would be forced to carry to full-term, and then go through excruciating labor to deliver, babies with the faces of their rapists?"[37]

How do we Americans feel? What and how do we Americans think? Can our responses stand scrutiny? What is most important to us? What are our Constitution and our democracy for? What do they support and promote? Why are they worth saving and defending? Are some things—the antiquated Electoral College, for example—not worth saving? What needs to change, what needs to happen for us to do better and be better?

Questions hold us accountable. They produce inquiry. Inquiry finds evidence. Evidence points toward truth. When truth informs us, when our lives embody it, we move closer to what is good, right, and just. That movement can produce solidarity that shows why our Constitution deserves protection and that resists the demise of democracy.

Be Patriotic

Being patriotic differs from being nationalistic. A nationalist says, "My country right or wrong," or "My nation's might makes right." By contrast, as Timothy Snyder observes, a patriot "wants the nation to live up to its ideals, which means asking us to be our best selves."[38] Our best selves want to be better, much better, than our worst impulses and actions. Our best selves resist decisions and policies like those that led to the Holocaust or genocidal war in Ukraine or conspiracy to overturn fair and free elections in the United States. Our best selves reject antisemitism and racism; they oppose hypocrisy and autocracy. Our best selves hold lying leaders accountable; they bring tyrants to justice. Our best selves neither take human rights away nor allow one right (arms-bearing, for example) to run roughshod over others. Instead, our best selves shield rights, wrestle with complex relationships between them, and expand them. Our best selves stand with the nearly-ninety naturalist Jane Goodall, who reminds us that "without hope, all is lost. It is a crucial survival trait that has sustained our species from the time of our Stone Age ancestors . . . Please believe that, against all odds, we

37. V (formerly Eve Ensler), "I Reject the US Abortion Ruling."

38. Snyder, *On Tyranny*, 111, [103].

can win out, because if you don't believe that, you will lose hope, sink into apathy and despair—and do nothing." Our best selves do not do that; they hope instead, understanding that hope "requires action and engagement."[39] Our best selves never give up trying to be our best.

Take Nothing Good for Granted

Doing good depends on taking nothing good for granted.[40] So quickly, and in such devastating ways, Hitler's Holocaust, Putin's war in Ukraine, Trump's relentless corruption swept away so much that is right and just, good and true. Doing good in our times requires us Americans to stand with Primo Levi's lifesaving friend Lorenzo, to be our best selves as patriots who believe in truth and defend democracy as courageously as we can. No law or legislation, no legal proceeding or executive order will create or ensure the resistance required to take back our democracy and make it strong again, but if we Americans take the seven steps of resistance outlined here, we will head in good directions.

Lenny's Questions

I like your choice of seven steps we must take to preserve our democracy. I also agree that these steps are requisite because they are inherently ethical. Lorenzo's claim "that we are in this world to do good" speaks to the very foundation of democratic life. You say, convincingly, that if we disregard this call to live ethically, democracy is doomed. "Dismal chapters," you believe, could "tragically end our nation's history." Your seven imperatives are calls to action at a time when we are living through one such dismal chapter. You implore us, living in an age that reminds us of Germany in the 1930s, to undo the culture of lies that undermines a democratic way of life.

Respecting truth, your first imperative, is not merely one of seven steps, but—in my view and, I believe, your own—the foundation upon which others rest. Lying dissolves all that grounds our being. In the words of Hannah Arendt, "consistent lying . . . pulls the ground from under our feet and provides no other ground on which to stand . . . The experience of a trembling, wobbling motion of everything we rely on for our sense of direction and reality is among the most common and most vivid experiences of men

39. Goodall and Abrams, *Book of Hope*, xiii–xiv, 232.

40. For more on this theme and others related to it, Roth, *Sources of Holocaust Insight*, especially 257–60.

under totalitarian rule."[41] In the spirit of Arendt, you argue that "democracy, indeed civilization itself, depends on seeking and respecting truth." Hitler, Putin, Trump—all tyrants—need a post-truth world to enforce their corrupt schemes and to empower their autocratic regimes.

"When truth informs us," you say, "when our lives embody it, we move closer to what is good, right, and just." For me, the key phrase in this sentence is "when our lives embody it." How, concretely, do we *live* truth to resist Trumpism? You speak in general terms about "taking responsibility for one another" and about the need to "protect human rights." Your most concrete guidance is found in brief references to actions such as voting against Trumpist Republicans and seeking to cultivate key virtues through "sound teaching" and "good parenting." What might be some examples of the "sound teaching" that could motivate our students to pursue "what is right and good"? What are some ways of parenting that might provide our children with the means to be their best selves and take responsibility for one another? What might we do in the face of such unjust Supreme Court decisions as the recent ruling against abortion rights? Scholars like us protest through the written word, certainly an important mode of resistance. But, given the immense suffering of women and girls that will ensue from the *Dobbs* decision, is writing enough? Is it the end point of our responsibility? Examples of resistance through what you deem "small deeds and modest actions" would be valuable.

As Americans face growing fascism, Holocaust scholars like us can find inspiration in Jewish resistance during that catastrophe. As the noose tightened around their necks, Europe's Jews, herded into ghettos and camps and without hope of rescue from outside, resisted as best they could to save Jewish lives and traditions. Like Lorenzo, the gentile who nourished Primo Levi, many Jews resisted evil by sharing their meager food rations with those worse off, thus keeping some fellow prisoners alive. In your study of Jewish resistance during the Holocaust, what has especially moved you to resist current threats to our democracy? Might there be one or more instances of resistance *then* that inspire you *now*?

Finally, you say that protecting democracy requires "refusal to give up pursuing what is right and good in spite of doubt and despair." This virtue, a kind of courage, is critically important. In the 2020s, the daily news is full of reports about the unraveling of our democratic fabric. Those who work to safeguard fragile democracy face "doubt and despair" repeatedly. How do we fortify ourselves against despair? What counsel can you offer that will help us withstand bouts of discouragement as we witness blow after blow

41. Arendt, "Truth and Politics," 253.

to our democracy? How are we to pick ourselves up to re-enter the fray and continue working to preserve our cherished democracy? How do we resist the temptation to abandon what may seem like fruitless resistance?

John's Response

Your questions ask me to specify how to *live* resistance against Trumpism, how to teach and parent in ways that make resistance more than a concept in written reflection. My response begins with a Holocaust survivor, Joseph Rebhun, an esteemed doctor and a longtime, inspiring friend. With deep gratitude and respect for our friendship, I will call him Joseph.

Joseph was born and raised in the Polish city of Przemysl. During World War II, it was under Soviet control for a time, but the Germans took the city in late June 1941. Soon, the Jews were ghettoized, and then deportations to Auschwitz began. At the age of twenty-two, he and his sixty-eight-year-old mother (the Germans had already killed his father) jumped from their train. He never saw his mother again, but after escaping an Auschwitz death, Joseph managed to get an identity card naming him a Polish Catholic. He survived the Holocaust, met Marie, a survivor of twelve concentration camps who became his wife, and eventually settled in Claremont, California, after arriving in the United States via Ellis Island.

This doctor embodied resistance. He refused the Auschwitz death that awaited him and repeatedly eluded danger. His postwar medical training in Austria took courage, because his teachers included former Nazi doctors. When I asked him if they knew that he, one of their students, was Jewish, he said yes, adding with an ironic smile I have not forgotten, "they treated me with courtesy and respect." He resisted disease and suffering by practicing medicine. He resisted antisemitism and racism by teaching. He and Marie resisted genocide by having children and raising a family. He loved America and democracy.

Joseph taught in my courses on the Holocaust. He was patient and gentle with the students, almost parenting them as a caring grandfather would do, but intensity grew when he explained what he hoped to accomplish by teaching them about the Holocaust and his personal experience in it. He hoped that his testimony would *inoculate* them—his word, I remember it—against antisemitism and racism. By implication, he was also hoping to provide, even to be, a vaccine against threats to democracy. Joseph knew that such inoculations and vaccines do not exist, but his point was neither naïve nor lost. His resistance encouraged and inspired my students and me to find ways to honor his example.

When I think of Joseph Rebhun, I also remember my friend Michael Berenbaum, an eminent scholar whose resistance includes building museums and producing films that teach people about the Holocaust and the crushing of German democracy, which was a necessary condition for that genocide. None of his many Holocaust insights is more important and challenging than his proposition that the Holocaust is a "negative absolute."[42] Even if people are skeptical that rational agreement can be obtained about what is right, just, and good, the Holocaust testifies that what the Nazis intended for Joseph Rebhun, what happened at Auschwitz and Treblinka was wrong, unjust, and evil—period, full stop. The Holocaust, in my view, demolishes moral relativism and rightly so. With the Holocaust as a moral compass that orients my attention, guides my priorities, and directs my discernment about what's right and wrong, I affirm that the conditions and powers necessary for the Holocaust must also be denounced and resisted as wrong, unjust, and evil.

Antisemitism and racism, lying and subservience to liars, authoritarianism and hostility to pluralism, seeking power and wealth at the expense of justice and equality—these conditions only start a list that's as discouraging as it is long. How can Americans resist those antidemocratic threats? The first step is to believe that we can, that the threats do not paralyze and doom us. People can help one another to take that step, which can alert them to find ways to resist—individually and together—in our communities, families, and workplaces. Nine examples illustrate what those ways can include:

- casting votes and giving money to support candidates and causes that defend democracy, including the rights of women and girls, who are besieged by cruel courts and misogynistic legislatures
- defending policies that provide American military support to defeat Putin's aggression in Ukraine
- sustaining NGOs that progressively defend democracy (For older folks like me, a worthy candidate is the environmentalist Bill McKibben's Third Act.)[43]
- standing up for comprehensive and humane immigration reform

42. Berenbaum, "Who Owns the Holocaust?," 60.

43. In the 2020s, some ten thousand Americans reach the age of sixty every day. Third Act, an organization for Americans who are sixty and beyond, says that it is "determined to change the world for the better. We muster political and economic power to move Washington and Wall Street in the name of a fairer, more sustainable society and planet. We back up the great work of younger people, and we make good trouble of our own" (https://thirdact.org). See also Third Act, "Third Act: Who We Are."

- respecting science and its public health policies
- advancing critical judgment about the assets and liabilities of social media, which entails rejecting conspiracy theories
- supporting the findings of the US House Select Committee to Investigate the January 6th Attack on the United States Capitol, taking its findings seriously, and acting accordingly
- encouraging US attorney general Merrick Garland, special counsel Jack Smith, and the Department of Justice to prove that no American is above the law by successfully prosecuting Donald Trump and his minions for crimes they have committed against the United States and its democracy
- heeding Adam Kinzinger's urgent warning on July 21, 2022, at the end of the Select Committee's eighth public hearing about the January 2021 insurrection: "If January 6th has reminded us of anything," said Kinzinger, "I pray it has reminded us of this: laws are just words on paper. They mean nothing without public servants dedicated to the rule of law, and who are held accountable by a public that believes oaths matter more than party tribalism and the cheap thrill of scoring political points. We the people must demand more of our politicians and ourselves. Oaths matter. Character matters. Truth matters. If we do not renew our faith and commitment to these principles, this great experiment of ours, our shining beacon on a hill, will not endure."[44]

Americans can renew that faith and commitment. Witnesses from the Holocaust can help us testify to that. Lorenzo Perrone's aid for Primo Levi resisted Nazism, its lies and power. Primo Levi survived and defended democracy. Joseph Rebhun did not give up when all seemed lost. He turned harsh treatment and the threat of death into commitment to heal and help. He cared for his patients, some of them strangers when he first met them. He taught students he had never seen before. He reached out, spoke out, making his presence felt through the values he defended, the risks he took, the hopes he encouraged, the truths he lived. He became my friend, profoundly influencing and nurturing me in the process. Such actions are necessary to protect democracy. If there are enough of them, they will do so.

Discouragement won't go away because the threats that desolate democracy are strongly entrenched—so much so that despair remains an option. But "the essence of being Jewish," insisted Elie Wiesel, is "never

44. Kinzinger, Closing Remarks.

to give up—never to yield to despair."[45] At our best, Americans are Jewish in that way. Such resistance does not guarantee that democracy will be preserved, but never giving up, never yielding to despair is indispensable. The cost of failing to do so is beyond calculation.

The journalist and historian Anne Appelbaum urges Americans to choose friends and allies carefully. Only by doing so, she wisely observes, "is it possible to avoid the temptations of the different forms of authoritarianism once again on offer"; she adds that "the fight against them requires new coalitions."[46] With whom should and will Americans stand in solidarity? With Donald Trump or Elie Wiesel? With Mitch McConnell or Primo Levi? With Dr. Oz or Dr. Rebhun? With Ted Cruz or Lorenzo Perrone? With Marjorie Taylor Greene or Sarah Kofman? With Ginni Thomas or Sonia Sotomayor? With Jim Jordan or Michael Berenbaum? If Americans choose friends and allies carefully, standing in solidarity with people who resisted the Holocaust, we can find the courage needed to restore our democracy.

Postscript

As Vladimir Putin's war against Ukraine slogged on, the journalist Masha Gessen wrote in August 2022 about the unrelenting and limitless crimes that Russian forces are beyond-cruelly inflicting on Ukrainian civilians and military personnel. Gessen indicated that Ukrainian prosecutors have "identified about twenty-five thousand possible war crimes," a toll that had nearly tripled six months later.[47] In addition to indiscriminate attacks on hospitals and schools, gratuitous murder, and rape as a weapon of war, the Russian atrocities, crimes against humanity (starvation, deportation, separation of families), mount and spread to the point of genocide. The immensity of Russian crimes means that no justice or punishment exists to rectify them. Americans who love democracy should remember where attempts to destroy democracy can lead and what resistance against them may entail.

American weapons continued to flow to Ukraine in 2023, bolstering president Volodymyr Zelenskyy's vow that Ukrainians won't stop until they liberate the last Ukrainian village from Russian control. Overall, however, American attention focused less on Ukraine and more on matters closer to home. Amid record-setting heat waves, lethal floods, and epic wildfires, all intensified by uncontrolled climate change, Americans approached the 2022 midterm elections disgruntled by stubborn inflation and distressing

45. Wiesel, *Jew Today*, 164.
46. Appelbaum, *Twilight of Democracy*, 188.
47. Gessen, "Prosecution of Russian War Crimes"; Sly, "66,000 War Crimes."

gas prices. With the November 2022 midterm elections about three months away, more than 75 percent of Americans—whatever their political party, region, race, or age—saw the United States heading in the wrong direction.[48] A July 2022 report issued by the Violence Prevention Research Program at the University of California, Davis, found that an alarming 50.1 percent of Americans agreed that "in the next several years, there will be civil war in the United States."[49] While war and war crimes raged in Ukraine, Donald Trump's Washington, DC, speech on July 26, 2022, poured fuel on domestic fires. To rectify the nation's problems, he urged, right-acting American should prepare to "be tough and be nasty and be mean."[50]

That same day something crucial happened for the defense of democracy and the rule of law: NBC's Lester Holt interviewed US attorney general Merrick Garland. Perhaps scheduled to counter Trump's blustery lawlessness, this interview deserves attention because it offered glimmers of hope about justice.

Garland told Holt that the Department of Justice (DOJ) plans to prosecute anyone who was "criminally responsible for interfering with the peaceful transfer of power from one administration to another."[51] Holt pressed the issue: Would the DOJ indict Trump if the evidence supported such action? "The indictment of a former president, and a likely candidate for president in 2024, would arguably tear the country apart," Holt said. "Is that your concern as you make your decision down the road here, do you have to think about things like that?"

Tear the country apart—Holt didn't say "civil war," but the thought was likely on his mind. It may have been on Garland's too, but he courageously replied: "Look, we pursue justice without fear or favor. We intend to hold everyone, anyone who was criminally responsible for the events surrounding Jan. 6, for any attempt to interfere with the lawful transfer of power from one administration to another, accountable. That's what we do. We don't pay any attention to other issues with respect to that."

Holt wasn't satisfied. What if Trump was running for president again? Wouldn't that "change your schedule," he asked Garland, "or how you move forward or don't move forward?" No, Garland calmly and firmly reiterated, "I'll say again that we will hold accountable anyone who was criminally responsible for attempting to interfere with the transfer,

48. Page et al., "Exclusive"

49. University of California, Davis, Violence Prevention Research Program, "Survey Finds Alarming Trend."

50. Sprunt, "Trump Paints a Grim Picture."

51. Dilanian and Siemaszko, "Merrick Garland."

legitimate, lawful transfer of power from one administration to the next." Later the same day, July 26, the Pulitzer Prize–winning Carol Leonnig and her colleagues at the *Washington Post* reported what could be tipping-point news: "The Justice Department is investigating President Donald Trump's actions as part of its criminal probe of efforts to overturn the 2020 election results."[52] A few weeks later, DOJ revelations about Trump's treachery and lies about classified documents he illegally held at Mar-a-Lago made clear that his criminal liability kept growing.

Investigating actions is a long way from indicting persons, let alone convicting them of crimes. But Garland and the DOJ, with significant assistance and pressure from the Select Committee to Investigate the January 6th Attack on the United States Capitol, have taken steps to prove that the United States is a nation of laws and that no American citizen is above the law—bedrock principles for protecting and sustaining democracy.

Without fear or favor—Garland's guiding, north-star phrase should do more than identify how he and the DOJ must act with regard to the pursuit of justice. It should define how all democracy-loving Americans should act in pursuing the conditions that are inseparable from democracy and in resisting the powers that demoralize it. Without fear or favor—seek truth, be patriotic, do what is right. Without fear or favor means having courage, giving encouragement, and doing so in ways that resist bending the knee to corruption, kissing the rings of liars, bowing to greedy autocracy, or collaborating with criminal tyrants through complicity and indifference. If enough Americans act that way—insistently and persistently—we can rescue our democracy, help Ukrainians to defend theirs, and help democracies everywhere to resist powers that undercut them.

52. Leonnig et al., "Justice Dept. Investigating."

8

Remembering for the Future

"THE DAM HAS BEGUN to break," said the patriotic Liz Cheney on July 21, 2022, as she opened the eighth public hearing of the January 6 Congressional Committee's investigation of the narrowly averted coup d'état led by Donald Trump and his confederates.[1] She hoped that a growing flood of condemning testimony and incontrovertible evidence, mainly from loyal Republican supporters of the former president, would drown Trump's chances of ever being trusted again with governmental authority in the United States.

Revitalizing American democracy depends on that step. But was Cheney too hopeful? Breaking dams can be shored up by those who don't want them to fail. Even if the dams aren't repaired or repairable, the torrent unleashed might not change the political landscape enough. MAGA Republicans and Trumpism remain determined to have their way. Already in the summer before the 2022 elections, the America First Policy Institute (AFPI) financed and staffed by Trump loyalists, plotted comeback plans and policies for the ex-president.[2] Not even Trump's demise or death will deter his zealous followers from advancing Trumpism. They could prove to be even more threatening to American democracy than Trump himself.

The astute journalist and historian Anne Appelbaum sheds valuable light on such matters. "Given the right conditions," she insightfully observes, "any society can turn against democracy. Indeed, if history is anything to go by, all of our societies eventually will."[3] As the 2024 presidential election approaches, whether Donald Trump, Ron DeSantis, or some other Republican is running for that office, democracy itself will be on the ballot amid conditions that threaten and doom it unless we recover and reform,

1. Cheney, Opening Remarks.
2. McGraw, "Trump Returns to D.C."
3. Applebaum, *Twilight of Democracy*, 14.

revise and renew our best north-star vision about what democracy in the United States can and should be.

Appelbaum understands that Trump and his legacy poison such hopes. "Trump," she underscores, "has no knowledge of the American story and so cannot have any faith in it. He has no understanding of our sympathy for the language of the founders, so he cannot be inspired by it. Since he doesn't believe American democracy is good, he has no interest in an America that aspires to be a model among nations."[4] The AFPI touts that its "guiding principles are liberty, free enterprise, national greatness, American military superiority, foreign-policy engagement in the American interest, and the primacy of American workers, families, and communities."[5] That word salad masks the fact that Trumpism is defined by grievance, conspiracy theories, and oppositions—to immigration, for example, and to racial and gender diversity. Trump himself testified to that on July 26, 2022. Returning to Washington, DC, for the first time since snubbing Joe Biden at his inauguration in January 2021, Trump delivered a ninety-minute harangue at AFPI's summer conclave. "Our country," he seethed, "is now a cesspool of crime . . . There is no higher priority than cleaning up our streets, controlling our border, stopping the drugs from pouring in, and quickly restoring law and order in America." He attacked transgender rights. He repeated the Big Lie that he won the 2020 election but voter fraud cost him the victory he deserved.[6]

AFPI's "mission" to the contrary notwithstanding, Trump and his legacy are backward-looking. They inspire no vision of a future worth having because, as Applebaum sees, their outlook is grounded in an America "created by white skin, a certain idea of Christianity, and an attachment to land that will be surrounded and defended by a wall."[7] But misguided though it is, that antidemocratic outlook still has sufficient power to ruin American democracy because, Applebaum warns, "the appeal of authoritarianism is eternal."[8]

Americans can and must be better than that. Countless resources and voices in our heritage offer the needed insight and encouragement. Read aloud, for example, the preamble to the US Constitution.

4. Applebaum, *Twilight of Democracy*, 154.

5. See the America First Policy Institute website (https://americafirstpolicy.com/about).

6. See Smith, "Self-Awareness in Short Supply."

7. Applebaum, *Twilight of Democracy*, 158.

8. Applebaum, *Twilight of Democracy*, 56.

> We the People of the United States, in Order to form a more perfect Union, establish Justice, insure domestic Tranquility, provide for the common defense, promote the general Welfare, and secure the Blessings of Liberty to ourselves and our Posterity, do ordain and establish this Constitution for the United States of America.

Heard and felt, taken to heart, those words, especially the aspirations and questions they contain, can intensify commitment to democracy and to the acts of resistance required to save and sustain it. The preamble speaks between its lines as well as in the words it explicitly contains. Think, it says, about what needs to happen, and what must be stopped from happening, to make the preamble's meaning what it ought to be in the 2020s and beyond. Then act accordingly.

Take heart too from American women who defend democracy by resisting the overturning of *Roe v. Wade* and by giving decisive testimony during the January 6 congressional committee's hearings. Liz Cheney spoke especially about former White House aide Cassidy Hutchinson:

> She sat here alone, took the oath, and testified before millions of Americans. She knew all along that she would be attacked by President Trump, and by the 50-, 60-, and 70-year-old men who hide themselves behind Executive Privilege. But . . . she has courage, and she did it anyway. Cassidy, Sarah [Matthews], and our other witnesses including Officer Caroline Edwards, Shaye Moss and her mother Ruby Freeman, are an inspiration to American women, and to American girls.[9]

They inspired American men as well, including old ones like us, Lenny and John. And the inspiration does not stop with them. It extends to every American who holds that our flag and Constitution are for democracy and freedom, not for authoritarianism and tyranny; for rights, not for mob violence; for equality and pluralism—ethnic, racial, religious, cultural, gendered.

As Anne Appelbaum rightly urges, the best American patriotism rejects blood-and-soil nationalism. It refuses and refutes the exclusionary and false claim that "a single ethnic identity with a single origin in a single space" grounds American distinctiveness and character.[10] But such matters are far from settled. They are and will be contested. So Appelbaum is right again: "It

9. Cheney, Opening Remarks.

10. Applebaum, *Twilight of Democracy*, 144.

is possible that we are already living through the twilight of democracy; that our civilization may already be heading for anarchy or tyranny."[11]

"Possible" and "may already be"—Appelbaum's words are wisely chosen because they foretell what could be coming but do not foreclose other options, other meanings for "possible" and "may already be." What if Americans who care deeply about democracy do not give up the struggle to save and strengthen it? What if Americans take seriously Joe Biden's July 25, 2022, anticipation of Trump's AFPI lies: "You can't be pro-insurrection and pro-cop. You can't be pro-insurrection and pro-democracy. You can't be pro-insurrection and pro-American."[12] What if Donald Trump is indicted and convicted for crimes he has committed? What if we take to heart that Trumpism is incompatible with democracy at its best and support the coalitions necessary to ensure that Trumpism never again gets the corrupting power it seeks? The warnings in this book begin and end with such questions. They do not remove, let alone eliminate, dialogue. To the contrary, dialogue can both persuade democracy's opponents to change and give democracy's proponents lucidity about what's required to resist authoritarianism and minority rule.

Convinced that democracy still has an American future that can be inclusive and strong, we use this concluding chapter to remember for the future, to take stock and look forward by asking, What are the most important things we've said? What do we most want our readers to remember? What needs to be said that we haven't said before?

Lenny's Reflections

As I look back at what John and I have written thus far, I think about our book's title: *Warnings*. If we have succeeded in communicating with our readers, it is because you hear the alarms we're sounding. Too many of us Americans have been slumbering while essential pillars of democracy have begun to fall. I do not exempt myself from this charge. As a young person, I was taught—and reassured as I matured—that America's founding institutions would preclude such collapse. The United States has a Constitution, including a Bill of Rights, and I assumed that the Constitution would be upheld, honored, and protected. Emphasis on checked and balanced powers among the executive, legislative, and judicial branches meant that we were well fortified against the rise of autocracy. I presumed democracy was here to stay; it was self-justifying and self-perpetuating.

11. Applebaum, *Twilight of Democracy*, 185.

12. See Baker, "Biden Lashes Trump" (italics added).

I should have awakened sooner from that falsely assuring stupor. But if doubts arose about whether we were truly impervious to the rise of those fascist powers that had appeared elsewhere, they were rapidly dismissed by my immersion in our myth of exceptionalism. As a younger person, I was living in "a shining city on a hill."

I should have known better even then. As a scholar of the Holocaust, and as the descendant of grandparents, aunts, and uncles murdered by Nazi killing squads, I was well aware of the demise of German democracy—and of German civilization itself—at the hands of a brutal dictator and his followers. Although Nazism arose in a post–World War I era with its own particularity, Germans of the 1930s were heirs to a culture of seldom-matched enlightenment. Descendants of some of the West's most renowned artists, writers, composers, and philosophers gave passive—and often active—support to Hitler's genocide against the Jews. The Holocaust warns us not to take civilized existence and democratic government for granted. Democracy is fragile. We must nurture it unceasingly.

I joined John in coauthoring this book to remind readers, and myself as well, that not everyone believes democracy is a fundamental human value. We Americans currently live in crisis mode, not knowing if Trumpism will strengthen its resolve to trample democratic values. Donald Trump and his MAGA Republicans attacked our proud tradition of a postelection peaceful transfer of power. Trump's coup attempt failed, but the call was too close for comfort, and the integrity of future elections may be compromised if Trumpists seize control of them. Commenting before the 2022 midterm elections, journalist and educator Mark Danner rightly noted: "The 2022 election will be the first held in the shadow of an attempted coup d'état—a nearly successful and still unpunished crime against the state . . . And it will be the first in which it is clear that, from Republican legislators' relentless efforts to change who counts the votes, the very character of American governance is on the ballot."[13] Danner's concerns will be at play again in 2024, arguably even more so than in 2022.

This book's wake-up calls include awareness that future generations will judge how well Americans acted in the 2020s. How will we reply when a grandchild or great-grandchild asks, What were you doing while Trumpists tried to destroy our democracy? Did you vote for Trump? Why? Were you a MAGA Republican? Why? Did you resist—I mean really resist—the attempts to destroy American democracy? How or why not? The philosopher and theologian Cornel West insightfully argues that "the age of Trump is a moral crisis. A reckoning will be needed to help fix all that

13. Danner, "We're in an Emergency."

Trumpism has broken . . . The American people need to decide what side of history they will be on."[14]

The warnings we underscore emphasize the dangers of evangelical Christian support for Donald Trump. Religions can heal, but they can also destroy. Today's self-identified Christian nationalists are crusaders engaged in "putting God back in things."[15] *Washington Post* columnist Colbert King rightly observes that "some of these same people can be found professing . . . that Jesus Christ is their Lord and Savior—even as they deify Trump in their heart . . . They like his promise to be their savior, his pledge to make them great again . . . He is theirs. They are his. Together they are joint owners of a changed Republican Party that is incompatible with democracy."[16] As a scholar of the Holocaust, I am reminded of Nazi-era Christian Nationalism. Robert P. Eriksen, a Holocaust scholar who explores religion in Nazi Germany, stresses that there was "broad support for Hitler's rise to power among German Christians and their leaders, some of whom took their devotion to an extreme. Hitler's numerous flaws were often explained away . . . Christians did this even as Hitler exhibited behavior to the contrary—much as Christian nationalists have publicly ignored Trump's attacks on . . . democratic institutions."[17] These observations about German Christians sound all too familiar. We must be on guard against perversions of Christianity and distortions of other religious traditions. Such corruptions threaten our democracy.

Another Holocaust scholar, Yehuda Bauer, can help Americans to remember for the future when he argues that the Ten Commandments should be supplemented by an additional three: "You, your children, and your children's children shall never become perpetrators; You, your children, and your children's children shall never, ever allow yourselves to become victims; and You, your children, and your children's children shall never, *never,* be passive onlookers to mass murder, genocide, or (may it never be repeated) a Holocaust-like tragedy."[18] The third of these imperatives refers to those who know the evil occurring in their time, but who look on or turn away in silence. Elie Wiesel warned repeatedly about the insidious nature of the bystander's indifference, which becomes a form of complicity: "We must always take sides. Neutrality helps the oppressor, never the victim. Silence

14. See DeVega, "Cornel West on Hope and Resistance."

15. Homans, "How 'Stop the Steal' Captured."

16. King, "How Do Trump's Perpetrators and Bystanders."

17. See Jenkins, "Historians of Christian Nationalism." See also Ericksen, *Complicity in the Holocaust*.

18. Bauer, "Speech to the Bundestag," 273 (italics original).

encourages the tormentor, never the tormented."[19] Unfortunately, both Bauer's and Wiesel's warnings have fallen on the deaf ears of many in our own time. Republican compliance and complicity during and after Trump's presidency remain as destructive as they are pervasive. How can so many Americans remain passive and thus complicit in the face of Trump's flouting of truth, his anti-immigrant rants, his expressions of support for such far-right groups as the Proud Boys, his anti-Muslim invective, his embrace of White supremacy? The list goes on. The indifference of so many plays into the hands of Trumpists and imperils our democracy.

Complicity with Trump and Trumpism is further deepened by the more *active* support of extremist, MAGA Republicans, some members of Congress among them. The journalist Mark Leibovich speaks pointedly of Republicans "who made the Trump era work for them, who humored and indulged him all the way down to the last, exhausted strains of American democracy."[20] During his initial campaign for the presidency, Trump was often not taken seriously. Calling to mind some very early characterizations of Hitler as a clown, conservative *New York Times* op-ed writer Bret Stephens confesses that in the beginning, all he saw in Trump was a "bigoted blowhard."[21] Many of Trump's Congressional supporters, according to Leibovich, know that Trump is, "at best, not a serious person or a good president and, at worst, a dangerous and potentially criminal jackass."[22] Most Republican leaders, acting from pure self-interest, have not defied Trump for fear of losing their own power. Even as Trump's criminality becomes increasingly clear, many Republican stalwarts support the twice-impeached former president by remaining silent as their party becomes synonymous with him. Former senator Jeff Flake, a Republican who broke with Trump, adds chilling words to describe Republican loyalty to Trump: "The idea is to just embrace the president and hope he embraces you back . . . And then try to sleep at night."[23] Leibovich concludes his damning critique of Trump's devotees with a much-needed warning that echoes those in this book: "2024 will not be a long way away, and Trump is well positioned to claim his third consecutive Republican presidential nomination . . . Trump will . . . take what he can take. Because really who's going to stop him?"[24] It remains to be seen whether criminal indictments may thwart Trump's ambitions for a

19. Wiesel, "Nobel Acceptance Speech.
20. Leibovich, "Most Pathetic Men."
21. Stephens, "I Was Wrong."
22. Leibovich, "Most Pathetic Men."
23. Leibovich, "Most Pathetic Men."
24. Leibovich, "Most Pathetic Men."

third presidential nomination and a second term, but the question "who's going to stop him?" still looms large.

The grip of Trump and Trumpism on the Republican Party gives Americans plenty of reason to despair. But as Ukrainians resist Vladimir Putin's atrocity-laden war against them, their bravery should help us to see that despair must not be an American option. Ukrainians are fighting to preserve their independence as a democratic state at a time when Russian state media claim that "'Ukronazism' is a greater threat to the world than Hitler's Nazi Party."[25] That's a Putin-style Big Lie. Ukraine's determined resistance against it and Russia's criminally imperial ambitions should embolden Americans to defeat the internal enemies of our democracy. Trump's fake patriotism, his claim to make America great again, stands in pathetic contrast to the authentic patriotism exhibited by Ukrainian leaders and fighters in their struggle against Russia. Americans must enact our version of Ukrainian patriotism. Doing so means heeding Anne Applebaum's admonition: "Take democracy seriously," she implores. "Teach it, debate it, improve it, defend it."[26] Applebaum's warnings resonate with ours.

Finally, I want to complicate my self-critique of falling victim to the myth of American exceptionalism. Aware that I speak as a privileged citizen, I nonetheless believe that America's democratic values, while shared at least in part by other nations, are remarkable. If this were not the case, we—Lenny and John—along with many other thoughtful Americans, would not be working so hard to sustain them. Flawed as these values have been and continue to be in their realization, America's original and ongoing aspirations are, at their best, a vitally important contribution to human flourishing at home and abroad.

Yet, given the corruption of those early aspirations throughout much of our history—and given the moral crisis provoked by Trumpism in the 2020s—how are we to advance democracy at its best? A necessary condition for responding to that question well is that we must lucidly remember that democracy will fail unless it is safeguarded *continually*. Anne Applebaum reminds us always to debate, study, and attempt to improve democracy in whatever condition we find it. The journalist Tom Nichols adds that civic introspection "is an indispensable duty for voters in a democracy, even in good times . . . If we think things are going well, we should ask whether our happiness is shared by enough of our fellow citizens."[27]

25. Joffre, "Russian State Media Claims."

26. Appelbaum, "There Is No Liberal World Order."

27. Nichols, *Our Own Worst Enemy*, 8.

Remember for the future: democracy at its best is more verb than noun. It is a process; it is in process. Its true supporters keep examining and correcting its shortcomings. America's ongoing experiment with democracy will succeed only insofar as its supporters recognize its flaws and keep striving to mend them.

John's Reflections

Writers and publishers can't keep up with the flood of current events and the deluge of breaking news. But they can remember what has happened and probe what the reverberations include and the portents mean. Events unmentioned before, some of them atop news cycles for a time, recall points worth remembering from this book of warnings about endangered American democracy.

1. On September 14, 2022, Ukraine's president, Volodymyr Zelenskyy, saw his country's flag raised in Izyum, a city of forty-five thousand on the Donets River in the northeastern part of the country. A successful Ukrainian counteroffensive freed Izyum after the Russians occupied it in March. The liberation, however, was bittersweet because, as Zelenskyy said, "Russia leaves death everywhere."[28] As in Bucha back in April, so also in Izyum Ukrainian troops found hundreds of bodies at mass burial sites. Tortured and executed soldiers were among the dead, but many of the victims were women, children, and elderly people. War-crimes investigators had work to do. Two months earlier, on July 23, 2022, the historian Timothy Snyder published "Self-Rule and Survival" in his *Thinking About . . .* newsletter, which focuses on Russia's criminal war against Ukraine.[29] The essay made me think about failures of imagination. Americans: Do not underestimate how life would be different if we lose our democratic way. Snyder's essay showed what would be different by reminding us that in an antidemocratic, authoritarian regime like Vladimir Putin's, freedoms that we take for granted do not exist. "Russians," wrote Snyder, "know that they are lied to all the time." Backed by tyrannical power, the lies dictate what people should say and do, and thus "the people make the lies their daily life." Freedom of thought and speech, freedom to assemble and protest are so compromised that they disappear. Elections may be held, but everyone knows they are rigged

28. See Kalin, "Ukraine Exhumes Mass Burial Site."
29. Snyder, "Self-Rule and Survival."

rituals of power. Dissent against the scheming leads to prison or death. So people go along to get along. For a very few, doing so makes them wealthy oligarchs. But as Zelenskyy saw in Bucha and Izyum, Putin's presence means that death is never far behind. Americans: The demise of democracy can happen in the United States. Do not be deceived by failures of imagination. Under Trump and Trumpism, as prescient journalists such as Jonathan Lemire and Dana Milbank show, we have gone dangerously far toward the destruction of our democracy.[30] Democracy depends on never denying or giving up the fact that truth matters. When it doesn't, destruction and death await.

2. On August 2, 2022, voters in conservative Kansas overwhelmingly rebuffed an attempt to strip abortion protections from their state's constitution. Grassroots activism brought out the decisively winning vote in favor of the rights of women and girls. But three days later, on August 5, Indiana's Republican lawmakers passed, and Eric Holcomb, its Republican governor, signed a near-total ban on abortion from the moment of conception. Exceptions exist for some cases of rape and incest, fetal abnormality, and severe risks faced by the pregnant woman. Americans are not in a violent civil war, at least not yet, but we are in a life-and-death struggle about fundamental values and what it means to say that we have "certain unalienable Rights, that among these are Life, Liberty, and the Pursuit of Happiness." Americans: Nothing guarantees the existence of basic rights, which are inseparable from democracy itself. American authoritarians and antidemocrats will restrict them, even take them away, if they obtain the power they crave. Determined resistance will be required to prevent that oppression.

3. A few hours after her Moscow trial ended on Thursday, August 4, 2022. the women's basketball star Brittney Griner got a nine-year prison sentence for entering Russia with a small amount of cannabis. During the trial, she expressed remorse for violating Russian law, which she had done accidentally. Her appeal was unsuccessful. Diplomacy eventually resulted in a prisoner swap that freed her, but she got no justice in Russia. Arrest and trial in Russia result in conviction and punishment 99 percent of the time. The rule of law as Americans know it does not exist under Putin or in any other autocratic regime. Americans: Do not let failures of imagination consign us to tyranny and injustice because we take the rule of law and fair trials too easily and too much for granted.

30. See Lemire, *Big Lie*; Milbank, *Destructionists*.

4. The August 2, 2022, statewide primary elections in Arizona went "full MAGA" on the Republican slate as Trump-endorsed deniers of the 2020 presidential election results swept to victory. But Democrats' hopes prevailed. Kari Lake, Blake Masters, and Mark Finchem—candidates for governor, US senator, and state attorney general, respectively—were defeated, but those three were one election away from gaining power to erode American democracy. Arizona is not a one-off case. From Pennsylvania to Georgia, from Texas to Idaho, MAGA Republicans like Lake, Masters, and Finchem are on the ballot. They do not stand for the inclusive, pluralistic senses of community that democracy at its best requires and sustains. Their campaigns are as well-funded and well-organized as they are antidemocratic and antipluralistic. Americans: Do not be deceived by failures of imagination. Elections and votes are fundamental for democracy, but they can also be used to destroy it. Do not forget how close the decision points between democracy and tyranny can be. Always vote to save and strengthen democracy. That means voting against Republicans until that party surrenders its antidemocratic ways.

5. Social media, including the freedom to send and receive text messages, are inseparable from American democracy in the 2020s. But social media, including deleting as well as sending and receiving text messages, also dishearten American democracy. As investigations about the January 6, 2021, insurrection and Donald Trump's attempted coup expanded and deepened, summer news in 2022 kept breaking about deleted text messages within the Secret Service and the Department of Defense. Not only were these messages government property, protected by law, but probably they also contained information and evidence of seditious conspiracy against American democracy. Their deletion obstructs justice. Their irretrievability aids, abets, and covers up injustice. Antidemocratic autocracy always seeks to control communications—not only what is said, but how that is controlled and, if necessary, silenced. Trumpism abhors transparency. It depends on cover-ups and the shadows of deletion. Americans: Do not let failures of imagination deny that democracy could die in our own darkness. The health of American democracy depends on holding accountable those who betray it.

6. With a properly executed search warrant in hand, FBI agents arrived at Donald Trump's Mar-a-Lago club and residence during the morning of August 8, 2022. Their search resulted in the removal of more than twenty boxes of documents. Eleven of them contained classified

documents, crucial for national security. Earlier the government retrieved fifteen boxes of documents that Trump had improperly taken with him when he left the White House in late January 2020. After talks broke down about getting Trump's cooperation to return the remaining documents that belonged to the government, not to Trump, a subpoena for their return was issued. When it was rebuffed, a search warrant authorized the FBI's seizure of the documents. Not for the first time, Trump's actions violated the law, but his Republican loyalists were instantly furious about the search, vowing to retaliate against the Department of Justice and to defund the FBI. Republicans used to pride themselves on being a party of law and order, but Trumpist Republicans follow their leader and abandon the rule of law to save themselves and their power. If that abandonment prevails, American democracy is more than disrespected. It will be dead and gone. Americans: Defend the rule of law, which includes the time-honored, Fourth Amendment provisions that search warrants can be issued "upon probable cause, supported by Oath or affirmation, and particularly describing the place to be searched, and the persons or things to be seized." The rule of law also includes the Fifth Amendment, which states that a person cannot be "compelled in any criminal case to be a witness against himself." Self-incrimination is prevented by "taking the Fifth," which is a fundamental American right. But "taking the Fifth" does not exonerate a person of wrongdoing or demonstrate innocence. Not always but often that action covers up wrongdoing and suggests guilt. Donald Trump criticized people who "take the Fifth." "The mob takes the Fifth," he liked to say. "If you're innocent," he contended, "why are you taking the Fifth Amendment?"[31] But then in a daylong New York deposition about his corrupt business practices, Trump took the Fifth Amendment more than four hundred times.[32] Doing so, he did not incriminate himself, but what if Trump told the truth instead? Democracy would be better off but Trump not so much. Democracy or Trump and Trumpism? Americans can't have it both ways. Truth favors democracy.

7. As the nation's schools prepared for the start of a new year, police and educators took steps to harden them against mass shootings that target American children. It remains to be seen how effective those actions will be. Meanwhile the *Washington Post* reporter Hannah Natanson had a different but related concern to share on August 3, 2022, when

31. See Haberman and Olson, "'If You're Innocent.'"

32. See Jacobs et al., "Amid Tumultuous Week."

she described the teacher shortage that will harm American girls and boys in 2022–2023 and beyond.[33] Debate swirls around this issue because the reasons for shrinking numbers of qualified teachers, especially in impoverished and racially diverse districts, reflect the turmoil confronting American democracy. COVID-19 and gun violence, inadequate compensation and support, legislative control over what teachers can teach, book-banning—such discouraging conditions cripple recruiting and hinder retaining the best people to teach American youth. For democracy in the United States to be at its best, American schools, teachers, and students must be at their best too. Americans: Make sure not only that our schools are safe from violence but also that they are equipped for learning the full and true history of our country, its promises and perils. If that work is done well, all of us will rightly feel discomfort about national shortcomings and shortfalls. Handled well, that experience can encourage what it takes to protect and sustain the democracy that makes the United States a place that pursues liberty and justice for all.

8. On the evening of August 1, 2022, President Joe Biden addressed the American people to announce that a precision attack in Kabul, Afghanistan, killed Ayman al-Zawahiri, the long-hunted al-Qaeda leader who masterminded the 9/11 terrorist attack that murdered 2,977 Americans. Biden did not mince words: "We make it clear again tonight that no matter how long it takes, no matter where you hide, if you are a threat to our people, the United States will find you and take you out . . . We will never forget . . . We will always remain vigilant, and we will act. And we will always do what is necessary to ensure the safety and security of Americans at home and around the globe . . . We will never—we will never give up."[34] Americans: Let it be so; let us remember that the safety and security of Americans at home requires at least two determinations. We must reject violence against one another but refuse power to parties and people who put grift and greed, lawless ambition and subservience to autocracy ahead of loyalty to the Constitution and patriotic duty at its best.

9. On August 4, 2022, the four-day Conservative Political Action Conference (CPAC) began in Dallas, Texas, with a keynote address by the Hungarian fascist dictator Viktor Orbán. As he inveighed against "the siege of progressive liberals," the assembled Trumpists gave him standing-ovation cheers. To win the culture war against this foe, he

33. Natanson, "'Never Seen It This Bad.'"

34. Biden, "Successful Counterterrorism Operation."

thundered, "it is not enough to know what you are fighting for. You also have to know how you should fight. My answer is: Play by your own rules! But how do you do that? It is as simple as it sounds. You must play to win."[35] Donald Trump closed CPAC with a ninety-minute grievance-laden tirade, which included incendiary lines like these: "America is on the edge of an abyss. And our movement is the only force on Earth that can save it . . . We have to seize this opportunity to deal with the radical left socialist lunatics and fascists. And we have to hit them very, very hard. Has to be a crippling defeat."[36] Orbán and Trump, Hungarian fascism and Republican Trumpism—philosophical and political collaborators. Their creed: might makes right, the end justifies the means. Their mantra: my way or the highway. Americans: Our country can be, must be better than that.

10. On August 3, 2022, the US Senate voted 95–1—election-denying Trumpist Josh Hawley voted against—to approve a treaty that would expand the North Atlantic Treaty Organization (NATO) to include Finland and Sweden, immensely strengthening the alliance against Putin's Russia and fortifying resistance against his criminal war in Ukraine. Trump's bromance with Putin included the intention to pull the United States out of NATO and to crush that alliance. The addition of Finland and Sweden to NATO shows that this time Trump did not get his way. But his cozy relationship with Putin remains, and his affection for strongmen still weakens American democracy. For instance, according to Susan B. Glasser and Peter Baker, martial law appealed to Trump, who wanted "his generals" to be the loyalists that he thought—inaccurately—all of Adolf Hitler's were.[37] General Mark Milley did not resign as chair of the Joint Chiefs of Staff under Trump, but he came close. His undelivered letter of resignation said that Trump was "doing great and irreparable harm to my country. I believe that you have made a concerted effort over time to politicize the United States military."[38] A bedrock principle of American democracy is that the military exists to defend the United States and its Constitution. The president is the commander in chief, but the military is not the tool of any president or political party. Americans: Be sure that this principle is upheld and stays in force.

35. Orbán, "CPAC Speech."
36. Trump, "CPAC Speech."
37. Glasser and Baker, "Inside the War." See also Baker and Glasser, *Divider*.
38. See Glasser and Baker, "Inside the War."

11. On September 15, 2022, Florida governor Ron DeSantis staged a cruel political stunt. Using taxpayer money, he chartered two planes and deported about fifty undocumented migrants, mostly asylum-seeking Venezuelans, to Martha's Vineyard, Massachusetts. Donald Trump was outraged—not because he opposed the abusive policy, but because he was envious that DeSantis upstaged Trump's anti-immigration reputation. A few weeks earlier, on August 7, Caitlin Dickerson showed how much Trump and his xenophobic confederates deserved hideous repute when she published a lengthy, diligently researched, and blockbusting article called "'We Need to Take Away Children.'"[39] It documented the intentional cruelty in Zero Tolerance, the Trump administration's anti-immigration scheme that separated thousands of families. If their children are taken away, the tortured logic of the vile deterrence strategy reasoned, unwanted families would not risk crossing the nation's southern border. Cruelty was the policy's point. Dickerson showed how this corrupt intent spread through the Trump administration, resulting in suffering and injustice that will never be repaired. Americans understandably have different and conflicting views about what immigration policy should be in the 2020s, but no American should ever claim that the child separations entailed by Zero Tolerance were just and good or that the end—restricted immigration—justified the means. The corrupt intent and malevolent policy embodied in the child separations of Zero Tolerance are emblematic of Trumpism's autocratic grievance culture, its xenophobic, antipluralistic "make America great again" plots, and their hypocrisy about "family values." Americans: Do not allow failures of imagination to blind us to the cruelty that can be inflicted in our name. Family-separating brutality is as antithetical to democracy as it is morally abhorrent.

12. In 1947, as the world faced increasing threats of nuclear war, the Bulletin of Atomic Scientists created the Doomsday Clock.[40] It warns how close the world is to midnight, the hour of apocalyptic disaster that would end human life, which is too easily taken for granted. Since 2020, the clock put the world one hundred seconds from midnight, but a 2023 update shortened the reprieve. According to the Doomsday Clock's "most dire prediction ever," midnight is just ninety seconds away. Events in Ukraine required the ominous adjustment.

    Mid-August 2022 reports on the Russian invasion of Ukraine showed that Ukrainian resistance continued to take a significant toll

39. Dickerson, "We Need."

40. See Francis and Dance, "Doomsday Clock."

on Vladimir Putin's forces. Those developments focused attention on the huge Zaporizhzhia nuclear power plant in southern Ukraine. Europe's largest, it had been occupied by the Russians since March. United Nations secretary-general António Guterres expressed grave concern that shelling in the area would create a radiation disaster.[41] Russian nuclear threats have complicated the war from its beginning in late February. Russia's nuclear arsenal is the world's largest, and Putin has not hesitated to make threats about using it, which cannot be regarded as empty, especially if Ukrainian counteroffensives increase the prospect of Russian defeat. On August 1, with such factors in mind, Guterres warned that humanity is "just one misunderstanding, one miscalculation away from nuclear annihilation."[42] Putin's nuclear saber-rattling worsened on September 30, 2022, when Russia illegally annexed four Ukrainian regions—Donetsk, Luhansk, Kherson, and Zaporizhzhia—and Putin vowed to protect them with all the "forces and means" at his disposal. Imagination cannot grasp what a nuclear conflagration would entail, what it would mean, but we can ill afford failures of imagination as humanity confronts this existential threat, which, to say the least, imperils American democracy. Americans: Take the Doomsday Clock seriously. The challenge for those who love democracy is to find a precarious path that refuses to let nuclear threats like Putin's have their way, that keeps deterrent forces strong, and that negotiates as best we can to prevent nuclear conflict and to deescalate its likelihood. Defense of democracy against autocrats like Putin and Trump is one of the necessary conditions for a hopeful future.

13. On September 1, 2022, President Joe Biden addressed the nation from Independence Hall in Philadelphia, where the Declaration of Independence was signed and the US Constitution written and debated. He touted the year's legislative accomplishments. He offered the optimism he loves to proclaim: "no matter where you start in life, there's nothing you can't achieve." He claimed to have "no doubt—none . . . that we'll secure our democracy."[43] Those hopes were less than convincing because the parts of his speech that rang most true consisted of warnings that we ignore at our peril. "As I stand here tonight," said Biden, "equality and democracy are under assault . . . Donald Trump and the MAGA Republicans represent an extremism that threatens the very foundations of our republic." The president said that we're still

41. United Nations, "Ukraine: Gutteres Calls for Safety."

42. See Fassihi and Levenson, "'One Miscalculation Away.'"

43. Biden, "Continued Battle."

a democracy, and he rightly pointed out that not all Republicans are MAGA Republicans, but he was also on target in saying that we're at an "inflection point—one of those moments that determine the shape of everything that's to come after." Our choices and decisions, he insisted, determine which way things will go. Americans: Share Joe Biden's optimism if and only if it makes sense to do so, but take his warnings with the utmost seriousness. Act on them.

14. Between September 18 and 20, 2022, Ken Burns's *The U.S. and the Holocaust* aired on PBS. This three-part docuseries assesses what Americans did and did not do in response to the Nazi persecution and genocide against European Jews.[44] The United States took in more refugees from Nazism than any other nation, but Burns shows that we could have done much more. American antisemitism, xenophobia, racism, indifference, and "America first" nationalism crippled the better angels of our nature. Burns's film about the 1930s and 1940s contains warnings that augment those in this book. He sums them up:

> The story of the Holocaust reminds us of the fragility of democracies but how, as frustrating as they can be, there is nothing more important than maintaining those democracies—constitutional parliamentary, whatever they might be—in the world because we see from human history that the authoritarian regimes have killed by a multitude of 100 more of their own citizens than democracies have. Not that democracies haven't done bad things and will continue to do bad things, but they don't do them on the scale of autocracies.[45]

Americans: Watch *The U.S. and the Holocaust.* You can stream it on PBS. Know that maintaining our democracy is of the utmost importance. The time to do that work is now—before democracy is lost.

15. In Philadelphia on September 17, 1787, thirty-nine American men signed the Constitution of the United States. Two hundred and thirty-five years later, Donald Trump, who repeatedly disrespected the Constitution and betrayed his oath to defend it, spoke to a MAGA Republican rally in Youngstown, Ohio. His hour-long tirade embraced themes in QAnon's baseless conspiracy theories, which are as hostile to democracy as they are false.[46] Earlier that same day, something very

44. Burns et al., dirs., *U.S. and the Holocaust.*

45. See Smith, "Ken Burns."

46. See Feuer and Haberman, "Trump Rally Plays Music"; Klepper and Swenson, "Trump Openly Embraces."

different took place at Ellis Island in New York City. US attorney general Merrick Garland, whose Jewish family includes Holocaust survivors but also members who were murdered in that catastrophe, administered the oath of allegiance for new American citizens and welcomed them to their country. Garland's remarks emphasized the rule of law. It "is the foundation of our system of government," he stressed. The rule of law "means that the law treats each of us alike: there is not one rule for friends, another for foes; one rule for the powerful, another for the powerless; a rule for the rich, another for the poor; or different rules, depending upon one's race or ethnicity or country of origin." But, he added, "the rule of law is not assured. It is fragile. It demands constant effort and vigilance."[47] Americans: Stand with the rule of law, which Trumpism and QAnon will destroy if they can. Be vigilant in protecting and strengthening respect for the rule of law.

16. Recollection of two pairs of dueling speeches from February 2023 further focuses what's at stake for American democracy as the United States moves toward and beyond the crucial 2024 elections. On February 7, 2023, President Joe Biden delivered the State of the Union address. "Though bruised," he said, "our democracy remains unbowed and unbroken . . . I have never been more optimistic about the future of America."[48] After Biden's speech, the recently elected governor of Arkansas, Sarah Huckabee Sanders, presented the Republican rebuttal. Calling Biden captive to "woke fantasies" and "unfit to serve," Sanders held that "the dividing line in America is no longer between right or left. The choice is between normal or crazy."[49]

    Two weeks later, on February 21 in Moscow, Vladimir Putin addressed Russia's Federal Assembly. Depicting Russia as besieged by the United States and the West, Putin blamed them for starting war in Ukraine and maintained that "we used force and continue to use it to stop it."[50] A few hours later in Warsaw, Poland, after returning from his historic visit to Kyiv, days ahead of the first anniversary of Putin's brutal invasion of Ukraine, Joe Biden said: "When Russia invaded, it wasn't just Ukraine being tested. The whole world faced a test for the ages . . . Would we stand up for democracy?" Underscoring that

47. Garland, Remarks.

48. Biden, "State of the Union."

49. See Itkowitz, "Sarah Huckabee Sanders." In contrast to Sanders's fixations and Ron DeSantis's obsession with what he calls "woke-ocracy," see columnist Eugene Robinson's insightful commentary (Robinson, "'Wokeness' Is Winning").

50. See Viser et al., "Biden and Putin."

Ukraine, the United States, and its NATO allies remain committed to doing so, Biden stressed that "there should be no doubt: our support for Ukraine will not waver, NATO will not be divided, and we will not tire . . . But," he added, "we have to be honest and clear-eyed . . . the defense of freedom is not the work of a day or of a year. It's always difficult. It's always important."[51]

Americans: Do not forget that Putin lies about Russia's barbarous assault on Ukraine and democracy. Remember that Biden speaks the truth when he says that Americans must be honest and clear-eyed about what it takes to defend freedom. Americans: Do not forget how close our democracy came to being bowed and broken. Do not be overoptimistic about the future of the United States, but never waver or tire in upholding democracy. Americans: Discern better than Sarah Sanders the difference between normal and crazy, between commitment to democracy at its best and loyalty to lies that betray it and acceptance of authoritarian ways that harm what is right and destroy what is good. Make informed choices, truthful judgments, and decisions that are just and wise.

17. Recalling key points that I hope will be remembered by readers of this book of warnings, my events list could go on and on, but I close it by noting one from antiquity. Named for the ninth day (Tisha) of the month of Av in the Hebrew calendar, Tish'a B'Av for the Hebrew year 5782 took place on August 6–7, 2022. A solemn day, Tish'a B'Av commemorates desolation of the holiest places in ancient Jerusalem. In 586 BCE, Babylonians destroyed the First Temple. In 70 CE, Romans laid waste to the Second Temple. Judaism and Jewish life survived and flourished after those disasters but more followed, including the Holocaust. Though decimated, Judaism and Jewish life survived and flourished after even that catastrophe too. Tish'a B'Av is about remembering for the future. A profound reminder that nothing held dear is exempt from desolation and destruction, that solemn occasion is also a reminder that, short of annihilation, a devastated people not only can rebuild but also can act to mend the world. Americans: Let our versions of Tish'a B'Av—they could include the attack on Pearl Harbor (December 7, 1941), al-Qaeda's terrorism on September 11, 2001, and the Trump-inspired desecration of the nation's Capitol on January 6, 2021—remind us that we can still save democracy and enliven its future in the world.

51. Biden, "Invasion of Ukraine."

Postscript

On July 21, 2022, when Liz Cheney said, "the dam has begun to break," she did not know how events on or about August 12, 2022, would vindicate her judgment. That day may go down in history as a tipping point for American democracy.

On that Friday afternoon, two pivotal documents were unsealed. One was the search warrant signed on August 5 by US magistrate judge Bruce Reinhart, which authorized the FBI to search Donald Trump's Mar-a-Lago estate in Florida and to seize "all physical documents and records constituting evidence, contraband, fruits of crime, or other items illegally possessed in violation of 18 U.S.C §§ 793, 2071, 1519." The second document was a three-page Receipt for Property. Signed by Trump attorney Christina Bobb on August 8, 2022, it notes eleven sets of classified material that Trump illegally took to Mar-a-Lago when he left the White House in January 2021. The precise contents are not identified, but the labeling indicates that they contain confidential, secret, and top-secret documents. Some of the documents are labeled as even more highly classified. According to the *Washington Post*, documents classified as TS/SCI (Top Secret/ Compartmented Information) are "a highly classified category of government secrets."[52] Nuclear weapons and security may be at play. Three major violations of law may ensnare Trump and associates of his as well. The *Washington Post* summed them up.[53]

> Section 793—"Gathering, transmitting or losing defense information"—is known as the Espionage Act. It's a broad law, and violating it does not necessarily mean that someone committed espionage. The law states it is illegal to remove documents or records related to national security from their proper place if it could risk the security of the country.
>
> Section 1519—"Destruction, alteration, or falsification of such records in Federal investigations and bankruptcy"—criminalizes the destruction or hiding of documents to obstruct an investigation.
>
> Section 2071—"Concealment, removal, or mutilation generally"—makes illegal the willful theft or destruction of any government document.

52. See Barrett and Dawsey, "Agents at Trump's Mar-a-Lago." This article includes copies of the search warrant and the receipt for property recovered by the FBI.

53. See Stein, "Trump Search Warrant."

Trump compromised national security. His arrogant irresponsibility, disrespect for law, and violation of trust as well as law betrayed the country. He has failed not only democracy but also the citizens of the United States, including its children.

In a blizzard of misleading statements and falsehoods, Trump and his supplicants howled "hoax" and "witch hunt." Flailing for defenses, they falsely claimed that Trump had declassified everything. Even if he had done so, that irresponsibility would not relieve him of criminal responsibility for taking property that is not his but belongs to the United States government. Trump and his followers advanced lies when they asserted that the FBI planted evidence at Mar-a-Lago to entrap Trump. Meanwhile Trump and his minions used silence to dodge crucial questions: Why did Trump possess these documents at all? What were his plans for them? What has he done with them? Are the Mar-a-Lago documents the only ones that Trump stole, or are their others at his properties outside Florida? Further investigations will be required to determine whether any of the information in the Trump-heisted documents is now possessed by enemies of the United States. But in countless ways, Trump has put our country in a world of hurt.

Newscasts on August 16, 2022, gave an additional telling reminder about the deception and hypocrisy, fraud, corruption, and lying that define Trumpworld. In video clips from six years earlier to the day, then presidential candidate Trump can be seen and heard proclaiming, "On political corruption—we are going to restore honor to our government. In my administration, I'm going to enforce all laws concerning the protection of classified information. No one will be above the law."[54] As has been the case so often, so tragically for American democracy, Trump's own words trap him but not before betraying us. Beyond ironic, they underscore his guilt for doing the utter opposite of what was stated in his worthless promises.

Americans who love democracy should hope that legal walls are closing in on the twice-impeached former president. He could rightly be indicted, prosecuted, and convicted of multiple crimes. Attorney general Merrick Garland, the Department of Justice, and the FBI acted appropriately and decisively with their seizure of the Mar-a-Lago documents. That action, however, is only the first chapter in what must be a longer, ongoing reckoning. If Trump and his accomplices are indicted and convicted for the crimes they have committed, the chances to save American democracy are improved. The trials will be long and hard, but they must take place. If they don't, and past is prologue, Trump "walks," the rule of law is demolished, and so is the American democracy that ought to be. Americans: We must

54. See Teh, "Old Video Surfaces."

not let that happen. Remember for the future what is right and good, true and just. Resist corruption, conspiracy, misguided loyalty to Trumpist Republicanism, and fidelity to lies and liars. Protect the rule of law. Americans We can do these things. The pro-democracy results of the 2022 elections should give us hope. But we should take nothing good for granted. We have to keep defending and expanding democracy lest it becomes too late. Time—the remainder of the 2020s—is running short.

Epilogue

Expand the Blue

The Holocaust grounds this book's warnings and hopes about American democracy. So these exchanges between old friends draw to a close by remembering a wall, a rock, and a hurricane. Their links to the Holocaust contain insights that keep reflection open and ongoing.

The Wall

The Norwegian composer Kim André Arnesen has written a haunting choral setting for words found on a wall:

> I believe in the sun, even when it's not shining.
>
> I believe in love, even when I feel it not.
>
> I believe in God, even when He is silent.[1]

No one knows who wrote those words or when. No one is certain about the precise location of the wall where they were found. But stories from the Holocaust suggest that they came from a Jew—child, woman, man?—who put them on a hiding-place wall in Cologne, Germany. Other versions of the story put the words on the wall of a ghetto, concentration camp, or killing center. Wherever the wall's Holocaust location may have been, its Jewish inscription expressed resistance against Nazi tyranny. Outlasting their author's living, the words still inspire defiance against powers that rob people of hope and joy.

What do we Americans believe in when democracy may die in darkness? What do we believe in when we don't feel that democracy at its best has much of a future? What do we believe in when justice seems abandoned,

1. See Arnesen, "Even When He Is Silent."

and when the noise of lies and liars quashes evidence and silences truth? We can and must do more than write on walls. We have to heed Supreme Court justice Thurgood Marshall, who broke American walls of racism and wrote the words that are the governing epigraph for this book.

> Where you see wrong or inequality or injustice, speak out, because this is your country. This is your democracy. Make it. Protect it. Pass it on.[2]

This is your democracy. Make it. Protect it. Pass it on. That's vital work that complements the resistance written decades ago on a Holocaust wall. Hard as a rock, it's unending work that must be done lest hate, injustice, despair, and death win victories they do not deserve.

The Rock

In August 1942, the novelist and philosopher Albert Camus arrived in the high plateau near Le Chambon-sur-Lignon, a French village in Vichy, the unoccupied region south of the Loire River where the Germans permitted a puppet government under France's World War I hero, Henri Philippe Pétain. Camus hoped the mountain air would bring relief from tuberculosis. By the time he left that area in late 1943, the Germans had occupied Vichy to shore up defenses against Allied gains across the Mediterranean in North Africa. The German occupation meant that few French havens were left for Jews, but Le Chambon and its surroundings remained one of them. A coalition of resisting helpers kept several thousand Jews out of harm's way. Camus knew about the rescue activities while he was writing *The Plague*, his important metaphorical novel of resistance.

Set in the Algerian city of Oran in the 1940s, Camus's novel chronicles the battle that Dr. Bernard Rieux fought against a lethal outbreak of bubonic plague. Its death toll includes Rieux's friend Jean Tarrou, who lives his conviction that "on this earth there are pestilences and there are victims, and it's up to us, so far as possible, not to join forces with the pestilences." Like his friend, Rieux does all he can to fight the plague. Its siege eventually lifts but not forever. "The plague bacillus never dies or disappears for good," the doctor remembers at the novel's end. The fight against it, he concludes, must be "never ending."[3]

That outlook led Camus to contemplate the fate of Sisyphus, the mythical Greek king who loved life and defied fate by impeding death

2. Marshall, "Commencement Address."

3. Camus, *Plague*, 253–54, 308.

itself. The gods condemned the resisting Sisyphus to a ceaseless repetition that required him to push a weighty rock up a mountain only to have it roll back to the bottom as he neared the top.

In *The Myth of Sisyphus*, Camus depicted Sisyphus in ways that fit defending, improving, and expanding American democracy. "At the very end of his long effort," wrote Camus, "Sisyphus watches the stone rush down . . . whence he will have to push it up again toward the summit. He goes back down to the plain. It is during that return, that pause," said Camus, "that Sisyphus interests me . . . If the descent . . . is sometimes performed in sorrow, it can also take place in joy. This word is not too much . . . The struggle itself toward the heights is enough to fill a [person's] heart. One must imagine Sisyphus happy."[4]

Discouragement and despair are real. The successes of antidemocratic authoritarianism intensify those disheartening moods. The failures of resistance against tyranny, incessant lying, and relentless corruption make joy scarce and happiness hard to sustain. While denying none of that, Camus's account of Sisyphus insists that as long as life allows, one can resist autocracy and scorn surrender to injustice. More than that, the struggle for truth, for democracy and human rights, can produce a defiant *in-spite-of* joy, a happiness sustained by solidarity with those who do what is right and good in spite of the fact that such work has no end and may seem to be a forlorn cause.

No American words are better known than the declaration that people have unalienable rights to "Life, Liberty, and the Pursuit of Happiness." The Holocaust, Sisyphus, and Camus show that nothing guarantees those rights. They depend on an uphill, never-ending struggle to defend democracy. In these circumstances, think twice about what *the pursuit of happiness* means and how it works. The most obvious meaning of the phrase is that happiness is a state of well-being or contentment, a condition that one strives to obtain and sustain. The pursuit is the work required to achieve and maintain happiness. But what if happiness is inseparable from ongoing, resisting action that is never done? What if happiness exists most profoundly in pursuing freedom, respect, justice, and democracy, in resisting happiness-robbing powers such as authoritarianism, racism, lying, corruption, and minority rule?

Camus says of Sisyphus, "his rock is his thing."[5] He calls Sisyphus happy because that mythical king embodies the realization that happiness is not the end of a pursuit. Happiness is the never-ending pursuing of what

4. Camus, *Myth of Sisyphus*, 89–90.

5. Camus, *Myth of Sisyphus*, 91.

is right and good, just and true. Without putting more weight on the point than it can bear, Camus thinks that Sisyphus finds joy in the labor not because it reaches successful completion and closure but in spite—in defiance—of the fact that it does not. If Americans can find that the pursuit of happiness produces and even requires an *in-spite-of* joy, a happiness flowing from pursuing and defending what is right and good, then the chances improve to revitalize and expand democracy.

The Hurricane

Philip Hallie admired Camus. He also killed Germans as an artilleryman in Europe during World War II. He knew that the barrages he unleashed were insufficient to stop the Holocaust, but they were necessary to end that plague. Later, this Jewish philosopher wrote about cruelty and also about the lifesaving work at Le Chambon.[6] The preciousness of human life, the unending threats to it, and the complex necessity of uphill and unceasing resistance—those themes appeared repeatedly in his writing.

Hallie's wall might have been inscribed with his motto: "lucidity and passion." He called himself a skeptic. "No ideas but in facts," he liked to say, "no ideas but in things."[7] His skepticism had two parts: a suspicion of abstraction, closure, and finality and a conviction that details, particularities, and facts contain moral insights and have lessons to teach if we pay attention. Hallie knew much about ancient Greek philosophy. He reminded people that the early skeptics were doctors. They helped him to discern that lucidity means getting as clear as possible about what is happening, especially if disease is the focal point. Knowing what is going on is not enough, however, especially if disease is the focal point. Passion has to sharpen the focus. Hallie's skepticism entailed that one must act, get people out of harm's way, and help them. The bedrock of his ethics was that "it is better to help than to hurt," that the "vital center" of ethics is deep-down recognition of "the connection between the preciousness of my life and the preciousness of other lives," and that ethics, at least at its heartfelt best, is about "spreading the joys of living."[8]

6. See Hallie, *Cruelty*; Hallie, *Lest Innocent Blood Be Shed*; and Hallie, *In the Eye of the Hurricane*.

7. Hallie, "Cruelty," 120.

8. Hallie, *Lest Innocent Blood Be Shed*, xviii, 277; Hallie, *In the Eye of the Hurricane*, 175.

Hallie was a small-d democrat. He was also a brilliant philosophical storyteller. One of his favorite stories centered on a hurricane.[9] The storm reached his Connecticut home, where he experienced its havoc. But havoc was not all that Hallie saw. Even while the storm raged, he thought that space for calm and quiet existed within the hurricane's eye. "The eye of the hurricane," he observed, "is in the very middle of destructive power, and that power is always near." Yet, within the eye, Hallie added, "the sky is blue."

Drawn to the blue sky overhead, Hallie had noticed birds that appeared to be "gliding happily high up in the eye of the hurricane," but later a knowledgeable friend told him that the birds "were actually in trouble, fighting to stay aloft in powerful downdrafts. Trapped in the eye, they were reeling from having slammed into the wall of wind surrounding it."

Despite the plight of the struggling birds, Hallie's hurricane experience contained moral insight. "It's the hurricane we're in," said Hallie. "Don't forget it." But he did not see that condition as one that should harbor resignation, indifference, and hopelessness. Ways can be found, he urged, to "expand the blue." Ways must be found, he insisted, "to make a larger space for blue, for peace, for love." Doing that work, Hallie emphasized, "takes power as well as love. It takes force of will. It takes assertion and commitment."[10]

Blue was Hallie's favorite color. It's a prominent, quintessential American color too. Lucidity and passion about that fact are connected to the Great Seal of the United States. Americans do not often think about that emblem, but it appears on official documents and proclamations. We carry versions of it on our passports and one-dollar bills.

On July 4, 1776, immediately after the Continental Congress adopted the Declaration of Independence, it established a committee—including Benjamin Franklin, John Adams, and Thomas Jefferson—to create an official seal to affix on documents and to certify the new nation's independence. Not until June 20, 1782, however, was a design approved. One of its features is the still aspirational motto—*e pluribus unum* (out of many, one)—which underscores the importance of unity in spite of ongoing, contentious divisions.

The seal includes the colors of our country's flag: red, white, and blue. Charles Thomson, a signer of the Declaration of Independence, longtime secretary of the Continental Congress, and co-designer of the Great Seal, explained their meanings. White, he said, symbolizes "purity and innocence." In spite of the fact that the United States never attains those virtues, they remain part of the pursuit of happiness because they

9. See Hallie, *In the Eye of the Hurricane*, vi, 51–56; Hallie, "Cruelty," 128–30.
10. Hallie, "Cruelty," 128–29.

challenge us to do what's right. Red, said Thomson, represents "hardiness and valor." Their place in American history encourages us never to give up doing our best. Blue, said Thomson, stands for "vigilance, perseverance, and justice."[11] That combination makes blue especially important in the 2020s and beyond. Vigilance tracks danger. Perseverance resists when danger threatens the most. Both are much needed to protect and expand justice, which is democracy's lifeblood.

Enlarge and fortify vigilance, perseverance, and justice—that's what Americans can and need to do now to protect and strengthen democracy. It takes force of will, assertion, and commitment to do that never-ending work. How well Americans will do it remains the question, but here's decisive and steadfast guidance for answering that question well: Expand the blue. That's this book's open-ended conclusion.

11. See United States Congress, *Our Flag*, 41–42; Greenstein, "Why the U.S. Flag Is Red, White, and Blue."

Bibliography

Achenbach, Joel. "NASA Unveils First Images from James Webb Space Telescope." *Washington Post*, July 12, 2022. https://www.washingtonpost.com/science/2022/07/11/nasa-james-webb-space-telescope-images/.

———. "Supermassive Black Hole Seen at the Center of Our Galaxy." *Washington Post*, May 12, 2022. https://www.washingtonpost.com/science/2022/05/11/black-hole-milky-way/.

Alfaro, Mariana, et al. "Pence Calls for National Abortion Ban as Trump, GOP Celebrate End of Roe." *Washington Post*, June 24, 2022. https://www.washingtonpost.com/politics/2022/06/24/abortion-supreme-court-trump-pence-republicans-roe/.

Amar, Vikram D. "The Legal Trick That Could Undermine the 2024 Election—If the Supreme Count Doesn't Shut It Down." *Time*, June 30, 2022. https://time.com/6192872/supreme-court-independent-state-legislature/.

America First Policy Institute. "About." https://americafirstpolicy.com/about/.

Anishanslin, Zara. "What We Get Wrong about Ben Franklin's 'a Republic, if You Can Keep It.'" *Washington Post*, October 29, 2019. https://www.washingtonpost.com/outlook/2019/10/29/what-we-get-wrong-about-ben-franklins-republic-if-you-can-keep-it/.

Anti-Defamation League. "ADL Audit Finds Antisemitism Incidents in United States Reached All-Time High in 2021." April 25, 2022. https://www.adl.org/news/press-releases/adl-audit-finds-antisemitic-incidents-in-united-states-reached-all-time-high-in/.

———. "Number of Americans Harboring Extensive Antisemitic Prejudice Doubled Since 2019; Reaches Highest Levels in Decades." January 12, 2023. https://www.adl.org/resources/press-release/number-americans-harboring-extensive-antisemitic-prejudice-doubled-2019/.

Applebaum, Anne. "There Is no Liberal World Order: Unless Democracies Defend Themselves, the Forces of Autocracy Will Destroy Them." *Atlantic*, March 31, 2022. https://www.theatlantic.com/magazine/archive/2022/05/autocracy-could-destroy-democracy-russia-ukraine/629363/.

———. *Twilight of Democracy: The Seductive Lure of Authoritarianism*. New York: Doubleday, 2020.

Arendt, Hannah. "Truth and Politics." In *Between Past and Future*, 223–59. With an introduction by Jerome Kohn. Penguin Classics. New York: Penguin, 2006.

Arnesen, Kim André, composer. "Even When He Is Silent." Track 1 on *Infinity: Choral Works*. Kantorei, conducted by Joel Rinsema. Recorded May 27–30, 2016, at First Plymouth Congregational Church, in Denver, Colorado. Naxos Music Series. Naxos, 8.573788, 2017, 1 compact disc.

Arnsdorf, Isaac, and Josh Dawsey. "'Frustrated and Upset,' Trump Goes Silent, Then Seethes." *Washington Post*, April 4–5, 2023. https://www.washingtonpost.com/politics/2023/04/04/trump-arraignment-speech-2024-campaign/.

Bachrach, Susan D., project dir., and Dieter Kuntz, ed. *Deadly Medicine: Creating the Master Race*. Washington, DC: United States Holocaust Memorial Museum, 2004.

Baird, Robert P. "Putin, Trump, Ukraine: How Timothy Snyder Became the Leading Interpreter of Our Dark Times." *Guardian* (US ed.), March 30, 2023. https://www.theguardian.com/world/2023/mar/30/how-timothy-snyder-became-the-leading-interpreter-of-our-dark-times-putin-trump-ukraine/.

Baker, Peter. "Biden Lashes Trump over Jan. 6, Saying He 'Lacked the Courage to Act.'" *New York Times*, July 25, 2022. https://www.nytimes.com/2022/07/25/us/politics/biden-trump-jan-6.html/.

———. "The Story So Far: Where 6 Investigations into Donald Trump Stand." *New York Times*, September 19, 2022. https://www.nytimes.com/2022/09/19/us/politics/donald-trump-investigations.html/.

Baker, Peter, and Susan Glasser. *The Divider: Trump in the White House, 2017–2021*. New York: Doubleday, 2022.

Baldwin, James. "As Much Truth as One Can Bear." In *The Cross of Redemption: Uncollected Writings*, edited by Randall Kenan, 34–42. New York: Vintage, 2011.

Barrett, Devlin, and Josh Dawsey. "Agents at Trump's Mar-a-Lago Seized 11 Sets of Classified Documents, Court Filing Shows." National Security. *Washington Post*, August 12, 2022. https://www.washingtonpost.com/national-security/2022/08/12/trump-warrant-release/.

Bauer, Yehuda. "Forms of Jewish Resistance during the Holocaust." In *The Jewish Emergence from Powerlessness*, 26–40. Toronto: University of Toronto Press, 1979.

———. "Speech to the Bundestag." January 27, 1998. In *Rethinking the Holocaust*, 261–73. Nota Bene. New Haven: Yale University Press, 2000.

Beauchamp, Zach. "The European Country Where 'Replacement Theory' Reigns Supreme." *Vox*, May 19, 2022. https://www.vox.com/2022/5/19/23123050/hungary-cpac-2022-replacement-theory/.

Bella, Timothy, and Sammy Westfall. "'Don't Be 'Putin's Altar Boy,' Pope Warns Russian Orthodox Leader." *Washington Post*, May 4, 2022. https://www.washingtonpost.com/world/2022/05/04/patriarch-kirill-pope-francis-russian-orthodox-church-ukraine/.

Ben-Ghiat, Ruth. *Strongmen: Mussolini to the Present*. New York: Norton, 2020.

Berenbaum, Michael. "Who Owns the Holocaust?" *Moment* 25.6 (2000) 60.

Bergson, Henri. *Mind-Energy: Lectures and Essays*. Translated by H. Wildon Carr. London: Macmillan, 1920.

Biden, Joseph R., Jr. "Inaugural Address." January 20, 2021. The Briefing Room, Speeches and Remarks. The White House (website), https://www.whitehouse.gov/briefing-room/speeches-remarks/2021/01/20/inaugural-address-by-president-joseph-r-biden-jr/.

———. "A Proclamation on Remembering the 1,000,000 Americans Lost to COVID-19." May 12, 2022. The Briefing Room, Presidential Actions. The White House (website), https://www.whitehouse.gov/briefing-room/presidential-actions/2022/05/12/a-proclamation-on-remembering-the-1000000-americans-lost-to-covid-19/.

———. Remarks by President Biden Ahead of the One-Year Anniversary of Russia's Brutal and Unprovoked Invasion of Ukraine," February 21, 2023. https://www.whitehouse.gov/briefing-room/speeches-remarks/2023/02/21/remarks-by-president-biden-ahead-of-the-one-year-anniversary-of-russias-brutal-and-unprovoked-invasion-of-ukraine/.

———. "Remarks by President Biden on the Continued Battle for the Soul of the Nation," September 1, 2022. The Briefing Room, Speeches and Remarks. The White House (website), https://www.whitehouse.gov/briefing-room/speeches-remarks/2022/09/01/remarks-by-president-bidenon-the-continued-battle-for-the-soul-of-the-nation/.

———. "Remarks by President Biden to Military Families on Independence Day," July 4, 2022. The Briefing Room, Speeches and Remarks. The White House (website), https://www.whitehouse.gov/briefing-room/speeches-remarks/2022/07/04/remarks-by-president-biden-to-military-families-on-independence-day/.

———. "Remarks by President Biden on a Successful Counterterrorism Operation in Afghanistan." August 1, 2022. The Briefing Room, Speeches and Remarks. The White House (website), https://www.whitehouse.gov/briefing-room/speeches-remarks/2022/08/01/remarks-by-president-biden-on-a-successful-counterterrorism-operation-in-afghanistan/.

———. "Remarks by President Biden and Vice President Harris in a Briefing to Preview the First Images from the James Webb Space Telescope." July 11, 2022. Briefing Room, Speeches and Remarks. The White House (website), https://www.whitehouse.gov/briefing-room/statements-releases/2022/07/11/remarks-by-President-biden-and-vice-president-harris-in-a-briefing-to-preview-the-first-images-from-the-james-webb-space-telescope/.

———. State of the Union Address. February 7, 2023. https://www.whitehouse.gov/briefing-room/speeches-remarks/2023/02/07/remarks-of-president-joe-biden-state-of-the-union-address-as-prepared-for-delivery/.

Bilefsky, Dan, and Nick Cumming-Bruce. "Ukraine's Prime Minister Says Rebuilding Will Cost $750 Billion." *New York Times*, July 5, 2022. https://www.nytimes.com/2022/07/05/world/europe/ukraines-prime-minister-says-rebuilding-will-cost-750-billion.html/.

Blake, Aaron. "How Clarence Thomas's Recusal Controversy Compares to Others." *Washington Post*, March 28, 2022. https://www.washingtonpost.com/politics/2022/03/28/thomas-ginsburg-past-recusals/.

Blickle, Kristian. "Pandemics Change Cities: Municipal Spending and Voter Extremism in Germany, 1918–1933." *Federal Reserve Bank of New York Staff Reports*, no. 921, May 2020, revised June 2020. https://www.newyorkfed.org/medialibrary/media/research/staff_reports/sr921.pdf.

Boder, David P. *I Did not Interview the Dead*. Urbana: University of Illinois Press, 1949.

Bonhoeffer, Dietrich. "On Stupidity." In *"After Ten Years": Dietrich Bonhoeffer and Our Times*, edited with an introduction by Victoria J. Barnett, 22–23. Translated by Barbara and Martin Rumscheidt. Minneapolis: Fortress, 2017.

Boorstein, Michelle. "Christian Nationalism Is Shaping a Pa. Primary—and a GOP Shift." *Washington Post*, May 16, 2022. https://www.washingtonpost.com/religion/2022/05/16/mastriano-pennsylvania-republican-christian-nationalism/.

———. "Sarah Sanders Tells Christian Broadcasting Network: God Wanted Trump to Be President." *Washington Post*, January 30, 2019. https://www.washingtonpost.com/religion/2019/01/30/sarah-sanders-tells-christian-broadcasting-network-god-wanted-trump-be-president/.

———. "Trump Faith Advisors Condemn Insurrection, but Say Benefits of Presidency Will Last Longer Than 'Controversies.'" *Washington Post*, January 8, 2021. https://www.washingtonpost.com/religion/2021/01/08/evangelical-trump-support-abortion-israel-religious-freedom-regulation/.

Braithwaite, Sharon. "Zelensky Refuses US Offer to Evacuate, Saying 'I Need Ammunition, not a Ride.'" CNN, February 26, 2022. https://www.cnn.com/2022/02/26/europe/ukraine-zelensky-evacuation-intl/index.html/.

Brangham, William. "How Misinformation and the Partisan Divide Drove a Surge in U.S. COVID Deaths." PBS News Hour, May 11, 2022. https://www.pbs.org/newshour/show/how-misinformation-and-the-partisan-divide-drove-a-surge-in-u-s-covid-deaths/.

Brennan, Megan. "Record-Low 38% Extremely Proud to Be American." Gallup Poll, June 29, 2022. https://news.gallup.com/poll/394202/record-low-extremely-proud-american.aspx/.

———. "Satisfaction With U.S. Dips; Biden Approval Steady at 41%." Gallup Poll, May 24, 2022. https://news.gallup.com/poll/393038/satisfaction-dips-biden-approval-steady.aspx.

Brody, David. "'Everything I Said Was Right': Donald Trump Wades into Current Culture Wars." CBN News, May 4, 2022. https://www1.cbn.com/cbnnews/politics/2022/may/news-exclusive-everything-i-said-was-right-donald-trump-wades-into-current-culture-wars/.

Bromwich, Jonah E., et al. "From President to Defendant: Trump Pleads not Guilty to 34 Felonies." *New York Times*, April 4–5, 2023. https://www.nytimes.com/2023/04/04/nyregion/trump-arraignment-felony-charges.html/.

Brown, Sara E., and Stephen D. Smith, eds. *The Routledge Handbook of Religion, Mass Atrocity, and Genocide*. Routledge Handbooks in Religion. London: Routledge, 2022.

Browning, Christopher R. "How Hitler's Enablers Undid Democracy in Germany." *Atlantic*, October 8, 2022. https://www.theatlantic.com/ideas/archive/2022/10/nazi-germany-hitler-democracy-weimar/671605/.

———. *Nazi Policy, Jewish Workers, German Killers*. Cambridge: Cambridge University Press, 2000.

Brugen, Isabel van. "Putin Appointed 'Chief Exorcist' as Kremlin Whips up Satanic Panic." *Newsweek*, October 26, 2022. https://www.newsweek.com/putin-chief-exorcist-kremlin-desatanization-ukraine-security-council-1754912/.

Bryanski, Gleb. "Russian Patriarch Calls Putin Era 'Miracle of God.'" *Reuters*, February 8, 2012. https://www.reuters.com/article/idUKTRE81722Y20120208/.

Buber, Martin. *I and Thou*. Translated by Ronald Gregor Smith. Scribner Classics. New York: Macmillan/Collier, 1987.

———. *Pointing the Way: Collected Essays*. Edited and translated by Maurice S. Friedman. New York: Harper, 1967.

Bump, Philip. "Doug Mastriano Does not Plan to Run from the Middle." *Washington Post*, May 18, 2022. https://www.washingtonpost.com/politics/2022/05/18/doug-mastriano-does-not-plan-run-middle/.

———. "'Genius,' 'Savvy': Trump Reacts to Putin's Moves on Ukraine Exactly as You'd Expect." *Washington Post*, February 22, 2022. https://www.washingtonpost.com/politics/2022/02/22/trump-reacts-putins-invasion-ukraine-exactly-youd-expect/.

———. "If Trump Shot Someone Dead on Fifth Avenue, Many Supporters Would Call His Murder Trial Biased." *Washington Post*, March 14, 2019. https://www.washingtonpost.com/politics/2019/03/14/if-trump-shot-someone-dead-fifth-avenue-many-supporters-would-call-his-murder-trial-biased/.

Burbank, Jane. "The Grand Theory Driving Putin to War." *New York Times*, March 22, 2022. https://www.nytimes.com/2022/03/22/opinion/russia-ukraine-putin-eurasianism.html/.

Burns, Ken. "Ken Burns: 'We're in Perhaps the Most Difficult Crisis in the History of America." Interview by David Smith. *Guardian* (US ed.), September 19, 2022. https://www.theguardian.com/tv-and-radio/2022/sep/19/ken-burns-interview-holocaust-docuseries/.

Burns, Ken, et al. dirs. *The U.S. and the Holocaust.* Starring Peter Coyote et al. Produced by Ken Burns et al. 3 episodes. Aired on Public Broadcasting Service (PBS) September 18–20, 2022. https://www.pbs.org/show/us-and-holocaust/.

Camus, Albert. *The Myth of Sisyphus, and Other Essays.* Translated by Justin O'Brien. New York: Vintage, 1955.

———. *The Plague.* Translated by Gilbert Stuart. Vintage International Series. New York: Vintage, 1991.

Carlisle, Madeleine. "Fetal Personhood Laws Are a New Frontier in the Battle over Reproductive Rights." *Time*, June 28, 2022. https://time.com/6191886/fetal-personhood-laws-roe-abortion/.

Carson v. Makin, 596 U.S. ___ (2022), available at https://www.supremecourt.gov/opinions/21pdf/20-1088_dbfi.pdf/.

Chemerinsky, Erwin. *Worse Than Nothing: The Dangerous Fallacy of Originalism.* New Haven: Yale University Press, 2022.

Cheney, Elizabeth. "Opening Statement at the Eighth Public Hearing of the January 6th Select Committee—July 21, 2022. https://awpc.cattcenter.iastate.edu/2022/08/18/opening-remarks-at-the-eighth-public-hearing-of-the-january-6th-select-committee-july-21-2022/.

Christianity Today. "Dietrich Bonhoeffer: German Theologian and Resister." Christian History. n.d. https://www.christianitytoday.com/history/people/martyrs/dietrich-bonhoeffer.html/.

Citizens United v. FEC, 558 U.S. 310 (2010), available at https://supreme.justia.com/cases/federal/us/558/08-205/concur2.pdf/.

Cohen Center for Modern Jewish Studies and the Steinhardt Social Research Institute. Brandeis University. *American Jewish Population Estimates 2020: Summary & Highlights.* https://ajpp.brandeis.edu/documents/2020/JewishPopulationDataBrief2020.pdf/.

Coppins, McKay. "Republicans' 2024 Magical Thinking." *Atlantic*, January 30, 2023. https://www.theatlantic.com/politics/archive/2023/01/2024-republican-primary-donald-trump-deus-ex-machina/672888/.

C-SPAN. Transcript of "Michael Cohen Testimony before House Oversight Committee, February 27, 2019." https://www.c-span.org/video/transcript/?id=57772/.

Daniels, Eugene, et al. Playbook. "POLITICO Playbook: New Poll Shows Huge Support for Gun Restrictions." *Politico*, May 26, 2022. https://www.politico.com/newsletters/playbook/2022/05/26/new-poll-shows-huge-support-for-gun-restrictions-00035349/.

Danner, Mark. "We're in an Emergency—Act Like It!" *New York Review*, August 18, 2022. https://www.nybooks.com/articles/2022/08/18/were-in-an-emergency-act-like-it-mark-danner/.

Davis, Benjamin. "What Is Education in Russia Like? A U.S. Teacher Investigates." *Russia Beyond*, April 30, 2019. https://www.rbth.com/education/330304-education-in-russia/.

Delbo, Charlotte. *Auschwitz and After*. Translated by Rosette C. Lamont. With introduction by Lawrence A. Langer. New Haven: Yale University Press, 1995.

Demirjian, Karoun, and Toluse Olorunnipa. "White House Rebukes Trump's Suggestions to Suspend Constitution over 2020 Election." *Washington Post*, December 3, 2022. https://www.washingtonpost.com/politics/2022/12/03/trump-constitution-truth-social/.

Dennie, Madiba. "Originalism Is Going to Get Women Killed." *Atlantic*, February 9, 2023. https://www.theatlantic.com/ideas/archive/2023/02/originalism-united-states-v-rahimi-women-domestic-abuse/672993/.

DeVega, Chauncey. "Cornel West on Hope and Resistance in the Age of Trump: We Must Find Joy in the Struggle." *Salon*, November 3, 2019. https://www.salon.com/2019/11/03/cornel-west-on-hope-and-resistance-in-the-age-of-trump-we-must-find-joy-in-the-struggle/.

Dewey, John. "The Ethics of Democracy." In *Philosophical Papers*, 1–28. 2nd ser., no. 1. Ann Arbor: Andrews, 1888. http://www.bit.ly/3loscjy/.

———. *Problems of Men*. New York: Philosophical Library, 1946.

Dickerson, Caitlin. "We Need to Take Away Children." *Atlantic*, August 7, 2022. https://www.theatlantic.com/magazine/archive/2022/09/trump-administration-family-separation-policy-immigration/670604/.

Di Giovanni, Janine. "The Real Reason the Russian Orthodox Church's Leader Supports Putin's War: Homophobia Is at the Heart of Patriarch Kirill's Endorsement." *Foreign Policy*, April 26, 2022. https://foreignpolicy.com/2022/04/26/ukraine-war-russian-orthodox-church-support-patriarch-kirill-homophobia/.

Dilanian, Ken, and Corky Siemaszko. "Merrick Garland Calls Justice Department's Jan. 6 Probe the 'Most Wide-ranging in Its History.'" NBC News, July 26, 2022. https://www.nbcnews.com/politics/2020-election/merrick-garland-not-rule-prosecuting-trump-jan-6-rcna40092/.

Dobbs v. Jackson Women's Health Organization, 597 U.S. ___ (2022), available at https://www.supremecourt.gov/opinions/21pdf/19-1392_6j37.pdf/.

Du Bois, W. E. B. *The Souls of Black Folk*. Signet Classics. New York: New American Library, 1969.

Du Mez, Kristin Kobes. "How Abortion Became a Mobilizing Issue among the Religious Right." Interview by Michel Martin. *All Things Considered*, NPR, May 8, 2022. Transcript. https://www.npr.org/2022/05/08/1097514184/how-abortion-became-a-mobilizing-issue-among-the-religious-right/.

Durkheim, Émile. *Sociology and Philosophy*. Translated by D. F. Pocock. With an introduction by J. G. Peristiany. Reprint with additions. New York: Free Press, 1974.

Edelman, Adam. "Biden Wants to Fix the Nation's Teacher Shortage. Educators Say the Problem Is Worsening." NBC News, June 6, 2021. https://www.nbcnews.com/politics/joe-biden/biden-wants-fix-nation-s-teacher-shortage-%20%20educators-say-problem-n1269340/.

Editorial Board. "After the Pennsylvania Primary, the Threat to U.S. Democracy Rises." *Washington Post*, May 18, 2022. https://www.washingtonpost.com/opinions/2022/05/18/pennsylvania-governor-primary-doug-mastriano-win-threatens-democracy/.

Editorial Board. "No Justification for a Brazen Invasion." *New York Times*, February 23, 2022. https://www.nytimes.com/2022/02/23/opinion/ukraine-biden-putin-invasion.html/.

Egan, Timothy. "Lord of the Lies." *New York Times*, June 9, 2016. https://www.nytimes.com/2016/06/10/opinion/lord-of-the-lies.html/.

Eisen, Norman L., et al. "It's Time to Prepare for a Possible Trump Indictment. *New York Times*, February 17, 2023. https://www.nytimes.com/2023/02/17/opinion/trump-georgia-grand-jury-report.html.

Elliott, Philip. "Koch Political Machine Vows to Fight to Deny Trump GOP Nomination in 2024." *Time*, February 5, 2023. https://time.com/6253038/koch-brothers-trump-gop-nomination/.

Ellison, Ralph. *Invisible Man*. 2nd Vintage ed. New York: Vintage, 1995.

Epstein, Reid J. "Liberal Wins Wisconsin Court Race, in Victory for Abortion Rights Backers." *New York Times*, April 4, 2023. https://www.nytimes.com/2023/04/04/us/politics/wisconsin-supreme-court-protasiewicz.html/.

Ericksen, Robert P. *Complicity in the Holocaust: Churches and Universities in Nazi Germany*. Cambridge: Cambridge University Press, 2012.

Ewing, Eve L. "I'm a Black Scholar Who Studies Race: Here's Why I Capitalize 'White.'" *ZORA*, July 2, 2020. *Medium*. https://zora.medium.com/im-a-black-scholar-who-studies-race-here-s-why-i-capitalize-white-f94883aa2dd3/.

Fackenheim, Emil L. *To Mend the World: Foundations of Post-Holocaust Jewish Thought*. New York: Schocken, 1982.

Farnsworth, Ward. *The Socratic Method: A Practitioner's Handbook*. Boston: Godine, 2021.

Fassihi, Farnaz, and Michael Levenson. "'One Miscalculation away from Nuclear Annihilation': The U.N. Chief Issues a Grim Warning, Citing War." *New York Times*, August 1, 2022. https://www.nytimes.com/2022/08/01/world/europe/nuclear-war-un-guterres.html/.

Feldman, Noah. "The Difference Is That Biden Gave the Documents Back." *Washington Post*, January 17, 2023. https://www.washingtonpost.com/business/the-difference-is-that-biden-gave-the-documents-back/2023/01/17/6261190a-9661-11ed-a173-61e055ec24ef_story.html/.

Filipovic, Jill. "It's Time to Say It: the US Supreme Court Has Become an Illegitimate Institution." *Guardian* (US ed.), June 25, 2022. https://www.theguardian.com/commentisfree/2022/jun/25/us-supreme-court-illegitimate-institution/.

Feuer, Alan, and Maggie Haberman. "Trump Rally Plays Music Resembling QAnon Song, and Crowd Reacts." *New York Times*. September 18, 2022. https://www.nytimes.com/2022/09/18/us/politics/trump-rally-qanon-music.html/.

Forgey, Quint. "Fed Study Ties 1918 Flu Pandemic to Nazi Party Gains." *Politico*, May 5, 2020. https://www.politico.com/news/2020/05/05/fed-study-1918-pandemic-nazi-party-gains-236530/.

Francis, Ellen, and Scott Dance. "Doomsday Clock Hits 90 Seconds to Midnight, Its Most Dire Prediction Ever." *Washington Post*, January 23, 2023. https://www.washingtonpost.com/science/2023/01/23/what-how-doomsday-clock/.

Freire, Paulo. *Pedagogy of the Oppressed*. Rev. ed. Translated by Myra Bergman Ramos. New York: Continuum, 1996.

Friedman, Jonathan, and Nadine Farid Johnson. "Banned in the USA: Rising School Book Bans Threaten Free Expression and Students' First Amendment Rights." PEN America, April 2022. https://pen.org/banned-in-the-usa/.

Friedman, Thomas L. "How Do We Deal with a Superpower Led by a War Criminal?" *New York Times*, April 10, 2022. https://www.nytimes.com/2022/04/10/opinion/putin-russia-ukraine.html/.

Fuller, Thomas. "The Stupefying Tally of American Gun Violence." *New York Times*, May 25, 2022. https://www.nytimes.com/2022/05/25/us/american-gun-violence.html/.

Garland, Merrick B. Remarks at Ellis Island. September 17, 2022. United States Department of Justice, Public Affairs, Justice News. https://www.justice.gov/opa/speech/attorney-general-merrick-b-garland-administers-oath-allegiance-and-delivers/.

Gellman, Barton. "January 6 Was Practice." *Atlantic*, January-February 2022. https://www.theatlantic.com/magazine/archive/2022/01/january-6-insurrection-trump-coup-2024-election/620843/.

Gershberg, Zac, and Sean Illing. *The Paradox of Democracy: Free Speech, Open Media, and Perilous Persuasions*. Chicago: University of Chicago Press, 2022.

Gerson, Michael. "Trump Should Fill Christians with Rage. How Come He Doesn't?" *Washington Post*. September 1, 2022. https://www.washingtonpost.com/opinions/2022/09/01/michael-gerson-evangelical-christian-maga-democracy/.

———. "Trump's Evangelicals Were Complicit in the Desecration of Our Democracy." *Washington Post*, January 7, 2021. https://www.washingtonpost.com/opinions/trumps-evangelicals-were-complicit-in-the-desecration-of-our-democracy/2021/01/07/69a51402-5110-11eb-83e3-322644d82356_story.html/.

Gessen, Masha. *The Future Is History: How Totalitarianism Reclaimed Russia*. New York: Riverhead, 2017.

———. "The Prosecution of Russian War Crimes in Ukraine." *New Yorker*, August 1, 2022. https://www.newyorker.com/magazine/2022/08/08/the-prosecution-of-russian-war-crimes-in-ukraine/.

Glasser, Susan B., and Peter Baker. Letter from Washington. "Inside the War between Trump and His Generals." *New Yorker*, August 8, 2022. https://www.newyorker.com/magazine/2022/08/15/inside-the-war-between-trump-and-his-generals/.

Goldberg, Michelle. "Joe Biden is too Old to Be President Again." *New York Times*, July 11, 2022. https://www.nytimes.com/2022/07/11/opinion/joe-biden-too-old.html.

Goodall, Jane, and Douglas Abrams, with Gail Hudson. *The Book of Hope: A Survival Guide for Trying Times*. New York: Celadon, 2021.

Gorman, Amanda. "The Hill We Climb." Inauguration Day Poem, January 20, 2020. https://www.usatoday.com/story/entertainment/celebrities/2021/01/20/read-amanda-gorman-inauguration-poem-the-hill-we-climb/4231769001/.

Gorski, Philip S., and Samuel L. Perry. *The Flag and the Cross: White Christian Nationalism and the Threat to American Democracy*. New York: Oxford University Press, 2022.

Graham, David A. "The Cases against Trump: A Guide." *Atlantic*, March 23, 2023. https://www.theatlantic.com/newsletters/archive/2023/03/trump-cases-manhattan-doj-guide/673506/.

Greenberg, Irving. "Cloud of Smoke, Pillar of Fire: Judaism, Christianity, and Modernity after the Holocaust." In *Auschwitz: Beginning of a New Era?*, edited by Eva Fleischner, 7–55. New York: Ktav, 1977.

Greenstein, Nicole. "Why the U.S. Flag Is Red, White, and Blue." *Time*, July 4, 2013. https://swampland.time.com/2013/07/04/why-the-u-s-flag-is-red-white-and-blue/.

Grunberger, Richard. *The 12-Year Reich: A Social History of Nazi Germany, 1933–1945*. Boston: Da Capo, 1995.

Gun Violence Archive (website). https://www.gunviolencearchive.org/.

Haass, Richard. *The Bill of Obligations: The Ten Habits of Good Citizens*. New York: Penguin, 2023.

Haberman, Maggie. "Text from Donald Trump Jr. Set Out Strategies to Fight Election Outcome." *New York Times*, April 8, 2022. https://www.nytimes.com/2022/04/08/us/politics/donald-trump-jr-meadows-text-message.html/.

Haberman, Maggie, and Michael C. Bender. "Can Trump Count on Evangelicals in 2024? Some Leaders Are Wavering." *New York Times*, January 19, 2023. https://www.nytimes.com/2023/01/19/us/politics/trump-evangelicals-2024.html/.

Haberman, Maggie, and Carly Olson. "'If You're Innocent, Why Are You Taking the Fifth Amendment?' Trump's Position on Decline to Testify Has Changed ver Time." *New York Times*, August 10, 2022. https://www.nytimes.com/2022/08/10/nyregion/trump-fifth-amendment-comments.html/.

Hallie, Philip P. *Cruelty*. Rev. ed. Middletown, CT: Wesleyan University Press, 1982.

———. "Cruelty: The Empirical Evil." In *Facing Evil: Light at the Core of Darkness*, edited by. Paul Woodruff and Harry A. Wilmer, 119–37. LaSalle, IL: Open Court, 1994.

———. *In the Eye of the Hurricane: Tales of Good and Evil, Help and Harm*. Middletown, CT: Wesleyan University Press, 2001.

———. *Lest Innocent Blood Be Shed: The Story of Le Chambon and How Goodness Happened There*. New York: HarperPerennial, 1994.

———. "Scepticism, Narrative, and Holocaust Ethics." *Philosophical Forum* 16 (1984–85) 33–49.

Hamblet, Wendy C. "A Pathological Goodness: Emmanuel Levinas' Post-Holocaust Ethics." *Minerva—An Internet Journal of Philosophy* 10 (2006) 172–96. http://www.minerva.mic.ul.ie/vol10/Goodness.pdf/.

Hamilton, Alexander. *The Federalist Papers*, No. 78. https://www.gutenberg.org/files/1404/1404-h/1404-h.htm#link2H_4_0078/.

Hamilton, Alexander, et al. *The Federalist Papers*. https://www.gutenberg.org/files/1404/1404-h/1404-h.htm/.

Harris, Taylor. "America Insists It Is Great. It Should Work on Being Decent." *Time*, July 2, 2022. https://time.com/6190395/american-exceptionalism-guns-essay/.

Harrison, Robert Pogue. *The Dominion of the Dead*. Chicago: University of Chicago Press, 2003.

Hart, Bradley W. *Hitler's American Friends: The Third Reich's Supporters in the United States*. New York: Dunne, 2018.

Hatley, James. *Suffering Witness: The Quandary of Responsibility after the Irreparable*. SUNY Series in Aesthetics and the Philosophy of Art. Albany: State University of New York Press, 2000.

Hedges, Chris. *American Fascists: The Christian Right and the War on America*. New York: Free Press, 2008.

———. "Fascists in Our Midst." *The Chris Hedges Report*, June 27, 2022. https://chrishedges.substack.com/p/listen-to-this-article-fascists-in#details/.

Hick, John. "Pluralism Conference." *Buddhist-Christian Studies* 24 (2004) 253–55.

Hitler, Adolf. "The Führer to the German People: 22 June 1941." Translated by Randall Bytwerk. *German Propaganda Archive* (website), Calvin University. https://research.calvin.edu/german-propaganda-archive/hitler4.htm/.

———. *Mein Kampf*. Translated by Ralph Manheim. Boston: Houghton Mifflin, 1971.

———. "Speech to the Reichstag." January 30, 1939. In *Witness to the Holocaust*, edited by Michael Berenbaum, 160–62. New York: HarperCollins, 1997.

Hollis-Brusky, Amanda. *Ideas with Consequences: The Federalist Society and the Conservative Counterrevolution*. Studies in Postwar American Political Development. Oxford: Oxford University Press, 2015.

Homans, Charles. "How 'Stop the Steal' Captured the American Right." *New York Times Magazine*, July 19, 2022. Photographs by Mark Peterson. https://www.nytimes.com/2022/07/19/magazine/stop-the-steal.html/.

———. "Seeking Evangelicals' Support Again, Trump Confronts a Changed Religious Landscape." *New York Times*, March 9, 2023. https://www.nytimes.com/2023/03/09/us/politics/evangelicals-republicans-trump.html/.

Hughes, Langston. "Let America Be America Again." In *American Ground: Vistas, Visions & Revisions*, edited by Robert H. Fossum and John K. Roth, 348–50. St. Paul: Paragon House, 1988.

Ifill, Sherrilyn (@SIfill_). "10. Decide today that you will never give up fighting for the country you want for yourself, your children, your community. Decide it. Then no matter what happens, you won't be swayed or paralyzed." Twitter, June 24, 2022, 1:16 p.m. https://twitter.com/SIfill_/status/1540383431783243778/.

Ingraham, Christopher. "There Are More Guns Than People in the United States, according to a New Study of Global Firearm Ownership." *Washington Post*, June 19, 2018. https://www.washingtonpost.com/news/wonk/wp/2018/06/19/there-are-more-guns-than-people-in-the-united-states-according-to-a-new-study-of-global-firearm-ownership/.

Institute for Health Metrics and Evaluation. "On Gun Violence, the United States Is an Outlier." May 31, 2022. https://www.healthdata.org/acting-data/gun-violence-united-states-outlier.

International Criminal Court (ICC). "Situation in Ukraine: ICC Judges Issue Arrest Warrants Against Vladimir Vladimirovich Putin and Maria Alekseyevna Lvova-Belova," March 17, 2023. https://www.icc-cpi.int/news/situation-ukraine-icc-judges-issue-arrest-warrants-against-vladimir-vladimirovich-putin-and/.

Itkowitz, Colby. "Sarah Huckabee Sanders Goes at 'Woke' Left in State of Union Response." *Washington Post*, February 7, 2023. https://www.washingtonpost.com/politics/2023/02/07/sarah-huckabee-sanders-state-of-the-union-rebuttal/.

Jacobs, Shayna, et al. "Amid Tumultuous Week, Trump Takes the Fifth More Than 400 Times." *Washington Post*, August 10, 2022. https://www.washingtonpost.com/national-security/2022/08/10/trump-deposition-letitia-james/.

James, William. "The Teaching of Philosophy in Our Colleges." *Nation* 23 (1876) 178–79.

Jamieson, Kathleen Hall. *Cyberwar: How Russian Hackers and Trolls Helped Elect a President—What We Don't, Can't, and Do Know*. New York: Oxford University Press, 2018.

Jefferson, Thomas. Letter to George Wythe, August 13, 1786. *Founders Online* (website). United States National Archives. https://founders.archives.gov/documents/Jefferson/01-10-02-0162/.

Jenkins, Jack. "Historians of Christian Nationalism Are Alarmed by Its Appearance in American Pulpits: A Lesson on the Dangers to the United States." *ThinkProgress*, August 21, 2017. https://archive.thinkprogress.org/history-christian-nationalism-e3303b46c3bc/.

Jewish Community Relations Council of San Francisco. "B'Tselem Elokim: All Created in God's Image." In *Who We Are: Mission and Values* (web page). https://web.archive.org/web/20211020100635/https://jcrc.org/who-we-are/mission-and-values/.

———. "Core Values: Building Consensus and Speaking with a Collective Civil Voice." In *Who We Are* (webpage). https://web.archive.org/web/20211020100635/https://jcrc.org/who-we-are/mission-and-values/.

Jimenez, Kayla. "COVID Set Half of US Kids Behind." *USA Today*, February 13, 2023. https://www.pressreader.com/usa/usa-today-international-edition/20230213/281513640319782/.a

Joffre, Tzvi. "Russian State Media Claims 'Ukronazism' Greater Threat to World Than Hitler." *Jerusalem Post*, April 4, 2022. https://www.jpost.com/international/article-703184/.

Kahn, Joseph. "Democracy Challenged." *New York Times*, September 19, 2022. Updated October 3, 2022. https://www.nytimes.com/2022/09/19/briefing/democracy-challenged-threats-elections.html/.

Kakel, Carroll P., III. *The American West and the Nazi East: A Comparative and Interpretive Perspective*. London: Palgrave Macmillan, 2011.

Kalin, Stephen. "Ukraine Exhumes Mass Burial Site in City Retaken from Russians." *Wall Street Journal*, September 16, 2022. https://www.wsj.com/articles/ukraine-exhumes-mass-grave-site-in-northeastern-city-retaken-from-russians-11663339330/.

Kennedy v. Bremerton School District, 597 U.S. ___ (2022), available at https://www.supremecourt.gov/opinions/21pdf/21-418_i425.pdf/.

Kessler, Glen. "Trump Made 30,573 False or Misleading Claims as President. Nearly Half Came in His Final Year." *Washington Post*, January 23, 2021. https://www.washingtonpost.com/politics/how-fact-checker-tracked-trump-claims/2021/01/23/ad04b69a-5c1d-11eb-a976-bad6431e03e2_story.html/.

King, Colbert I. "How Do Trump's Perpetrators and Bystanders Stay Silent?" *Washington Post*, May 7, 2021. https://www.washingtonpost.com/opinions/2021/05/07/trump-his-perpetrators-bystanders-own-republican-party-incompatible-with-democracy/.

Kini, Tara. "Tackling Teacher Shortages: What Can States and Districts Do?" Learning Policy Institute, January 11, 2022. https://learningpolicyinstitute.org/blog/teacher-shortage-what-can-states-and-districts-do/.

Kinnard, Meg. "DeSantis Walks Back 'Territorial Dispute' Remark on Ukraine." *AP News* (website), March 23, 2023. https://apnews.com/article/ron-desantis-ukraine-republicans-2024-f44acc03f772f393b7f8d452ee26508a/.

Kinzinger, Adam. "Donald Trump's Conduct on Jan. 6 Was a Complete Dereliction of Duty to Our Nation." *The News with Shepard Smith.* CNBC Television. Streamed live on July 21, 2022. YouTube video, https://www.youtube.com/watch?v=C4Vzg4D1kQU&t=6s/.

Kissinger, Henry, et al. "ChatGPT Heralds an Intellectual Revolution." *Wall Street Journal*, February 24, 2023. https://www.wsj.com/articles/chatgpt-heralds-an-intellectual-revolution-enlightenment-artificial-intelligence-homo-technicus-technology-cognition-morality-philosophy-774331c6/.

Klein, Ezra. "How We Communicate Will Decide Whether Democracy Lives or Dies." Interview with Sean Illing. *The Ezra Klein Show*, July 26, 2022. https://www.nytimes.com/2022/07/26/opinion/ezra-klein-podcast-sean-illing.html/.

———. Interview with Volodymyr Yermolenko. Transcript. *The Ezra Klein Show*, April 12, 2022. https://www.nytimes.com/2022/04/12/podcasts/transcript-ezra-klein-interviews-volodymyr-yermolenko.html/.

Klepper, David, and Ali Swenson. "Trump Openly Embraces, Amplifies QAnon Conspiracy Theories." *AP News*, September 16, 2022. https://apnews.com/article/technology-donald-trump-conspiracy-theories-government-and-politics-db50c6f709b1706886a876ae6ac298e2/.

Knickmeyer, Ellen. "World Bank Puts Cost of Rebuilding Ukraine at $411 Billion." *AP News* (website), March 22, 2023. https://apnews.com/article/ukraine-russia-war-damage-world-bank-6ecb537d2ab78a3473068836 03e65c33/.

Knowles, Hannah. "Christian Leaders Start to Break from Trump—with an Eye on DeSantis." *Washington Post*, January 21, 2023. https://www.washingtonpost.com/politics/2023/01/20/trump-christians-conservatives-evangelicals-desantis/.

Kofman, Sarah. *Smothered Words.* Translated by Madeleine Dobie. Evanston, IL: Northwestern University Press, 1998.

Kornfield, Meryl. "Trump Takes Victory Lap at Conservative Conference." *Washington Post*, March 4, 2023. https://www.washingtonpost.com/politics/2023/03/04/cpac-trump-speech/.

Lauter, David. "Researchers Asked People Worldwide about Divisiveness. Guess Where U.S. Ranked?" *Los Angeles Times,* October 15, 2021. https://www.latimes.com/politics/newsletter/2021-10-15/us-most-divided-nation-in-worldwide-survey-essential-politics/.

Legal Information Institute, Cornell Law School. "Roe v. Wade (1973)." https://www.law.cornell.edu/wex/roe_v_wade_(1973)/.

Leibovich, Mark. "The Most Pathetic Men in America: Why Lindsey Graham, Kevin McCarthy, and So Many Other Cowards In Congress Are Still Doing Trump's Bidding." *Atlantic*, July 7, 2022. https://www.theatlantic.com/ideas/archive/2022/07/kevin-mccarthy-lindsey-graham-trump-devotion-2024-election/661508/.

———. *Thank You for Your Servitude: Donald Trump's Washington and the Price of Submission*. New York: Penguin, 2022.

Lemire, Jonathan. *The Big Lie: Election Chaos, Political Opportunism, and the State of American Politics after 2020*. New York: Flatiron, 2022.

Leonhardt, David. "'A Crisis Coming': The Twin Threats to Democracy." *New York Times*, September 17, 2022. https://www.nytimes.com/2022/09/17/us/american-democracy-threats.html/.

Leonnig, Carol D., et al. "Justice Dept. Investigating Trump's Actions in Jan. 6 Criminal Probe. *Washington Post*, July 26, 2022. https://www.washingtonpost.com/national-security/2022/07/26/trump-justice-investigation-january-6/.

Lepore, Jill. "The Supreme Court's Selective Memory on Gun Rights." *New Yorker*, June 24, 2022. https://www.newyorker.com/news/daily-comment/the-supreme-courts-selective-memory-on-gun-rights/.

———. "The United States' Unamendable Constitution." *New Yorker*, October 26, 2022. https://www.newyorker.com/culture/annals-of-inquiry/the-united-states-unamendable-constitution/.

———. "What the January 6th Report Is Missing." *New Yorker*, January 9, 2023. https://www.newyorker.com/magazine/2023/01/16/what-the-january-6th-report-is-missing/.

Levi, Primo. *If This Is a Man*. Translated by Stuart Woolf. In *The Complete Works of Primo Levi*, edited by Ann Goldstein, 1:1–193. 3 vols. New York: Liveright, 2015.

———. *Other People's Trades*. Translated by Antony Shugaar. In *The Complete Works of Primo Levi*, edited by Ann Goldstein, 3:2009–52. 3 vols. New York: Liveright, 2015.

———. "Primo Levi: The Art of Fiction No. 140." Interview from 1985 by Gabriel Motola. *Paris Review* 37 (1995) 201–20. https://www.theparisreview.org/interviews/1670/primo-levi-the-art-of-fiction-no-140-primo-levi/.

———. "The Return of Lorenzo." In *Lilith and Other Stories*, translated by Ann Goldstein. In *The Complete Works of Primo Levi*, edited by Ann Goldstein, 2:1401–8. 3 vols. New York: Liveright, 2015.

———. *Survival in Auschwitz: The Nazi Assault on Humanity*. Translated by Stuart Woolf. 1987. Reprint, 1st Touchstone ed. New York: Simon & Schuster, 1996.

Levinas, Emmanuel. "Being toward Death and 'Thou Shalt not Kill.'" Translated by Andrew Schmitz. In *Is It Righteous To Be? Interviews with Emmanuel Levinas*, edited by Jill Robbins, 130–39. Meridian. Stanford: Stanford University Press, 2001.

———. *Difficult Freedom: Essays on Judaism*. Translated by Sean Hand. Johns Hopkins Jewish Studies. Baltimore: Johns Hopkins University Press, 1990.

———. "Ethics and Politics." In *The Levinas Reader*, edited by Sean Hand, 289–97. Blackwell Readers. Oxford: Blackwell, 1989.

———. "Judaism and Christianity after Rosenzweig." In *Is It Righteous To Be? Interviews with Emmanuel Levinas*, edited by Jill Robbins, 255–67. Translated by Andrew Schmitz. Meridian. Stanford: Stanford University Press, 2001.

———. *Otherwise Than Being, Or Beyond Essence. Translated by Alphonso Lingis*. Pittsburgh: Duquesne University Press, 1998.

Levitsky, Stephen, and Daniel Ziblatt. *How Democracies Die*. New York: Broadway, 2018.

Lewis, John. "Together, You Can Redeem the Soul of Our Nation." *New York Times*, July 30, 2020. https://www.nytimes.com/2020/07/30/opinion/john-lewis-civil-rights-america.html/.

Lincoln, Abraham. Address at Sanitary Fair, Baltimore, Maryland. April 18, 1864. https://quod.lib.umich.edu/l/lincoln/lincoln7/1:665?rgn=div1;singlegenre=All;sort=occur;subview=detail;type=simple;view=fulltext;q1=april+18+1864/.

———. Annual Message to Congress—Concluding Remarks. December 1, 1862. *Abraham Lincoln Online* (website). https://www.abrahamlincolnonline.org/lincoln/speeches/congress.htm/.

———. First Inaugural Address. March 4. 1861. *Avalon Project* (website) of the Lillian Goldman Law Library at Yale University Law School. https://avalon.law.yale.edu/19th_century/lincoln1.asp/.

———. Gettysburg Address. November 19, 1863. *Library of Congress* (website), https://www.loc.gov/resource/rbpe.24404500/?st=text/.

———. Second Inaugural Address. *Abraham Lincoln Online* (website). https://www.abrahamlincolnonline.org/lincoln/speeches/inaug2.htm/.

Lucey, Catherine. "Upholding Roe v. Wade Is Supported by Most Americans, WSJ Poll Finds." *Wall Street Journal*, June 2, 2022. https://www.wsj.com/articles/upholding-roe-v-wade-is-supported-by-most-americans-wsj-poll-finds-11654162200/.

Lynch, David J. "Casualties from War in Ukraine Include Millions of the World's Poor." *Washington Post*, July 7, 2022. https://www.washingtonpost.com/business/2022/07/07/ukraine-war-poverty-undp/?utm_campaign=wp_the7&utm_/.

Mackenzie, Hannah. "Hundreds Gather to Hear Former VP Mike Pence Speak at Pro-Life Gala in Spartanburg, SC." WLOS News, May 5, 2022. https://wlos.com/news/local/former-vp-mike-pence-to-speak-at-fundraising-event-carolina-pregnancy-center-roe-wade-supreme-court-abortion/.

MacLeish, Archibald. "The Young Dead Soldiers Do Not Speak." Library of Congress, Washington, DC, 1940. *Library of Congress* (website), https://www.loc.gov/item/rbpe.24204400/.

Maddow, Rachel. *Rachel Maddow Presents: Ultra*. MSNBC podcast. 2022. 8 episodes. https://www.msnbc.com/rachel-maddow-presents-ultra/.

Madison, James. *The Federalist Papers*, No. 10. *Avalon Project* (website) of the Lillian Goldman Law Library at Yale University Law School. https://avalon.law.yale.edu/18th_century/fed10.asp/.

Main, Thomas J. *The Rise of Illiberalism*. Washington, DC: Brookings Institution Press, 2021.

Marche, Stephen. *The Next Civil War: Dispatches from the American Future*. New York: Avid Reader, 2022.

Marcus, Ruth. "Originalism Is Bunk. Liberal Lawyers Shouldn't Fall for It." *Washington Post*, December 1, 2022. https://www.washingtonpost.com/opinions/2022/12/01/originalism-liberal-lawyers-supreme-court-trap/.

Marimow, Ann E., et al. "How the Supreme Court Ruled in the Major Decisions of 2022." *Washington Post*, June 30, 2022. https://www.washingtonpost.com/politics/interactive/2022/significant-supreme-court-decisions-2022/.

Marshall, Thurgood. "Commencement Address at the University of Virginia." University of Virginia, May 21, 1978. https://news.virginia.edu/sites/default/files/photos/Marshall.pdf/.

Mayer, Jane. "How Russia Helped Swing the Election for Trump." *New Yorker*, September 24, 2018. https://www.newyorker.com/magazine/2018/10/01/how-russia-helped-to-swing-the-election-for-trump/.

———. "State Legislatures Are Torching Democracy." *New Yorker*, August 6, 2022. https://www.newyorker.com/magazine/2022/08/15/state-legislatures-are-torching-democracy/.

McGraw, Meridith. "Trump Returns to D.C. This Week. These Former Advisers Are Plotting the Comeback." *Politico*, July 25, 2022. https://www.politico.com/news/2022/07/25/trump-america-first-policy-institute-think-tank-00047634/.

McKenzie, Robert Tracy. *We the Fallen People: The Founders and the Future of American Democracy*. Downers Grove, IL: IVP Academic, 2021.

McKibben, Bill. *The Flag, the Cross, and the Station Wagon: A Graying American Looks Back at His Suburban Boyhood and Wonders What the Hell Happened*. New York: Holt, 2022.

Menand, Louis. "American Democracy Was Never Designed to Be Democratic." *New Yorker*, August 15, 2022. https://www.newyorker.com/magazine/2022/08/22/american-democracy-was-never-designed-to-be-democratic-eric-holder-our-unfinished-march-nick-seabrook-one-person-one-vote-jacob-grumbach-laboratories-against-democracy/.

Messer-Kruse, Timothy. "The Unbearable Whiteness of Ken Burns." *Chronicle of Higher Education*, April 20, 2022. https://www-chronicle-com.ccl.idm.oclc.org/article/the-unbearable-whiteness-of-ken-burns/.

Milbank, Dana. *The Destructionists: The Twenty-Five-Year Crack-Up of the Republican Party*. New York: Doubleday, 2022.

———. "A Hero of the Trump Right Shows His True Colors: White Only." *Washington Post*, July 27, 2022. https://www.washingtonpost.com/opinions/2022/07/27/viktor-orban-cpac-conservatives-welcome-racism/.

Mitropoulos, Ariel. "For Red and Blue America, a Glaring Divide in COVID-19 Death Rates Persists 2 Years Later." ABC News, March 28, 2022. https://abcnews.go.com/Health/red-blue-america-glaring-divide-covid-19-death/story?id=83649085/.

Mooney, Michael J. "Trump's Apostle." *Texas Monthly*, August 2019. https://www.texasmonthly.com/news-politics/donald-trump-defender-dallas-pastor-robert-jeffress/.

Movement Advancement Project (MAP). *Under Fire: The War on LGBTQ People in America*. February 2023. https://www.mapresearch.org/under-fire-report/.

Müller, Ingo. *Hitler's Justice: The Courts of the Third Reich*. Translated by Deborah Lucas Schneider. Cambridge: Harvard University Press, 1992.

Murray, Mark. "NBC News Poll: 57% of Voters Say Investigations into Trump Should Continue." NBC News, August 21, 2022. https://www.nbcnews.com/meet-the-press/first-read/nbc-news-poll-57-voters-say-investigations-trump-continue-rcna43989/.

Natanson, Hannah. "'Never Seen It This Bad': America Faces Catastrophic Teacher Shortage." *Washington Post*, August 3, 2022. https://www.washingtonpost.com/education/2022/08/03/school-teacher-shortage/.

Nechepurenko, Ivan, and Anton Troianovski. "A War the Kremlin Tried to Disguise Becomes a Hard Reality for Russians." *New York Times*, March 2, 2022. https://www.nytimes.com/2022/03/02/world/europe/russia-ukraine-war-casualties.html/.

New Republic. "TNR Poll: Americans Agree Democracy Is Doomed, but Not About Why." *New Republic*, April 14, 2022. https://newrepublic.com/article/166027/democracy-poll/.

New York State Rifle & Pistol Association, Inc. v. Bruen, 597 U.S. ___ (2022), available at https://www.supremecourt.gov/opinions/21pdf/20-843_7j80.pdf/.

New York Times. "Tracking the States Where Abortion Is Now Banned." https://www.nytimes.com/interactive/2022/us/abortion-laws-roe-v-wade.html/.

Nichols, Tom. "Confessions of a Conservative Apostate." *Peacefield* newsletter, *Atlantic*, July 20, 2022. https://newsletters.theatlantic.com/peacefield/62d74c4e30d04800225b7346/republican-party-trump-conservatism/.

———. "The January 6 Attack Is Not Over." *Peacefiefld* newsletter, *Atlantic*, January 6, 2023. https://www.theatlantic.com/newsletters/archive/2023/01/the-january-6-attack-is-not-over/672671/.

———. *Our Own Worst Enemy: The Assault from Within on Modern Democracy*. New York: Oxford University Press, 2021.

Niebuhr, Reinhold. *The Irony of American History*. New York: Scribner, 1952.

North Atlantic Treaty Organization (NATO). "Finland Joins NATO as 31st Ally," April 4, 2023. https://www.nato.int/cps/en/natohq/news_213448.htm/.

NPR/Ipsos. "Seven in Ten Americans Say the Country Is in Crisis, at Risk of Failing." Poll, January 3, 2022. https://www.ipsos.com/sites/default/files/ct/news/documents/2022-01/Topline-NPR-Ipsos-poll.pdf/.

O'Donnell, Lawrence. "Lawrence Asks: 'Is a Vote for Republicans a Vote to Destroy Democracy?'" *The Last Word*, MSNBC, April 20, 2022. https://www.msnbc.com/the-last-word/watch/lawrence-asks-is-a-vote-for-republicans-a-vote-to-destroy-democracy-138191429920/.

Orbán, Viktor. "CPAC Speech." August 4, 2022. https://miniszterelnok.hu/speech-by-prime-minister-viktor-orban-at-the-opening-of-cpac-texas/.

Orth, Taylor, and Kathy Frankovic, "After Recent Mass Shootings, a Majority of Americans Desire Stricter Gun Control Laws." *YouGovAmerica* (website), February 1, 2023. https://today.yougov.com/topics/politics/articles-reports/2023/02/01/majority-americans-support-gun-control-poll/.

Orwell, George. *1984: A Novel*. New York: New American Library, 1983.

Packer, George. "I Worry We'll Soon Forget about Ukraine." *Atlantic*, April 10, 2022. https://www.theatlantic.com/ideas/archive/2022/04/ukraine-america-democracy-russification/629521/.

Page, Susan, et al. " Exclusive: 100 Days before Vote, Americans not Happy." *USA Today*, July 28, 2022, 1A, 3A. https://www.usatoday.com/story/news/politics/2022/07/28/voters-biden-trump-100-days-midterms/10148278002/.

Paine, Thomas. *Common Sense*. https://www.gutenberg.org/files/147/147-h/147-h.htm/.

———. *The Rights of Man*. In *Common Sense, The Rights of Man and Other Essential Writings of Thomas Paine*, 133–292.With an introduction by Sidney Hook and a new foreword by Jack Fruchtman Jr. New York: Signet, 2003.

Park, Alice. "Why Ukraine's COVID-19 Problem Is Everyone's Problem." *Time*, March 2, 2022. https://time.com/6153254/ukraine-russia-war-covid-19/.

Patterson, David. "Reflections on the Nazi Assault on Death." In *Facing Death: Confronting Mortality in the Holocaust and Ourselves*, edited by Sarah K. Pinnock,

128–40. The Stephen S. Weinstein Series in Post-Holocaust Studies. Seattle: University of Washington Press, 2017.

———. *When Learned Men Murder: Essays on the Essence of Higher Education.* Bloomington, IN: Phi Delta Kappa Educational Foundation, 1996.

Paybarah, Azi. "Trump Warns of 'Big Problems' if Indicted, Says He'd Still Run for Office." *Washington Post*, September 15, 2022. https://www.washingtonpost.com/politics/2022/09/15/trump-justice-department-investigation-fbi-search/.

Penn State College of Medicine. "U.S. Gun Violence Increased 30% during COVID-19 Pandemic." *PennState Health* (website), October 21, 2021. https://pennstatehealthnews.org/2021/10/u-s-gun-violence-increased-30-during-covid-19-pandemic/.

Perrigo, Billy. "Here's How Rudy Giuliani Explains His 'Truth Isn't Truth' Comment." *Time*, August 20, 2018. https://time.com/5371650/rudy-giuliani-truth-isnt-truth/.

Peters, Jeremy W., and Katie Robertson. "Fox Stars Privately Expressed Disbelief about Election Fraud Claims. 'Crazy Stuff.'" *New York Times*, February 16, 2023. https://www.nytimes.com/2023/02/16/business/media/fox-dominion-lawsuit.html/.

Pilkington, Ed. "The 'Stench' of Politicization: Sonia Sotomayor's Supreme Court Warning." *Guardian* (US ed.), December 4, 2021. https://www.theguardian.com/us-news/2021/dec/04/us-supreme-courrt-sonia-sotomayor-abortion/.

Plummer, Brad, and Raymond Zhong. "Stopping Climate Change Is Doable, but Time Is Short, U.N. Panel Warns." *New York Times*, April 4, 2022. https://www.nytimes.com/2022/04/04/climate/climate-change-ipcc-un.html/.

Pomerantsev, Peter. *Nothing Is True and Everything Is Possible: The Surreal Heart of the New Russia.* 1st paperback ed. New York: PublicAffairs, 2015.

Posner, Sarah. "The Southern Baptist Convention's Deal with the Devil." *Nation*, September 12, 2022. https://www.thenation.com/article/society/southern-baptists-roe-gop-dobbs/.

Priestley, J. B. *An Inspector Calls.* In *J. B. Priestley: An Inspector Calls and Other Plays, 157–220.* London: Penguin, 2000.

Project Censored and the Media Revolution Collective. *The Media and Me: A Guide to Critical Media Literacy for Young People.* Fair Oaks, CA: Censored Press; New York: Seven Stories, 2022.

Public Religion Research Institute (PPRI). "Religious Affiliation Updates and Trends: White Christian Decline Slows, Unaffiliated Growth Levels Off." April 27, 2022. https://www.prri.org/spotlight/prri-2021-american-values-atlas-religious-affiliation-updates-and-trends-white-christian-decline-slows-unaffiliated-growth-levels-off/.

Putin, Vladimir. "Address by the President of the Russian Federation," February 21, 2022. http://en.kremlin.ru/events/president/news/67828/.

Quinnipiac University. "Nearly 3 Out Of 4 Support Raising Legal Age To Buy Any Gun, Quinnipiac University National Poll Finds; Support For Assault Weapons Ban Hits A Low." June 8, 2022. https://poll.qu.edu/poll-release?releaseid=3848/.

Rakove, Jack. "James Madison's Critique of the Senate Still Holds." *Wall Street Journal*, September 16, 2022. https://www.wsj.com/articles/james-madisons-critique-of-the-senate-still-holds-11663335204/.

Raskin, Jamie. "We Must Fight for Democracy Itself." Epilogue to *The January 6th Report*, by the Select Committee to Investigate the January 6th Attack on the United States Capitol, 717–24. New York: Celadon, 2022.

Reagan, Ronald. Farewell Address to the Nation. January 11, 1989. https://www.reaganfoundation.org/media/128652/farewell.pdf/.

Reiner, Rob (@robreiner). "It couldn't be more simple. A vote for Republicans is a vote to destroy democracy." Twitter, April 20, 2022, 8:03 a.m. https://twitter.com/robreiner/status/1516749404434092041/.

Remnick, David. Preface to *The January 6th Report*, vii–xxviii. *The January 6th Report*, by the Select Committee to Investigate the January 6th Attack on the United States Capitol, 717–24. New York: Celadon, 2022. New York: Celadon, 2022.

Reyes, Juliana Feliciano, and Andrew Seidman. "Doug Mastriano Embodies a Christian Nationalist Movement as He Runs for Governor: 'We Have the Power of God.'" *Philadelphia Inquirer*, May 20, 2022. https://www.inquirer.com/politics/doug-mastriano-governor-christian-nationalism-qanon-20220504.html/.

Robinson, Eugene. "Michigan State Shootings Are a Reminder: We Must Take the Guns Away." *Washington Post*, February 14, 2023. https://www.washingtonpost.com/opinions/2023/02/14/michigan-state-shooting-response-gun-control/.

———. "'Wokeness' Is Winning." *Washington Post*, March 27, 2023. https://www.washingtonpost.com/opinions/2023/03/27/woke-values-survey-norc-university-of-chicago/.

Robinson, Kali. "What Is U.S. Policy on the Israeli-Palestinian Conflict?" Council on Foreign Relations, May 27, 2021. https://www.cfr.org/backgrounder/what-us-policy-israeli-palestinian-conflict/.

Robinson, Marilynne. *Gilead*. New York: Farrar, Straus & Giroux, 2004.

Roosevelt, Franklin D. "Address at Dedication of Great Smoky Mountains National Park." September 2, 1940. *The American Presidency Project* (website), University of California, Santa Barbara. https://www.presidency.ucsb.edu/documents/address-dedication-great-smoky-mountains-national-park/.

Rosen, Alan. *The Wonder of Their Voices: The 1946 Holocaust Interviews of David Boder*. New York: Oxford University Press, 2010.

Roth, John K. "Ethics." In *The Oxford Handbook of Holocaust Studies*, edited by Peter Hayes and John K. Roth, 722–36. Oxford: Oxford University Press, 2010.

———. *The Failures of Ethics: Confronting the Holocaust, Genocide, and Other Mass Atrocities*. Oxford: Oxford University Press, 2015.

———, ed. *Genocide and Human Rights: A Philosophical Guide*. New York: Palgrave Macmillan, 2005.

———. "The Holocaust and Philosophy." In *Lessons and Legacies III: Memory, Memorialization, and Denial*, edited by Peter Hayes, 41–44. Evanston, IL: Northwestern University Press, 1999.

———. *Private Needs, Public Selves: Talk about Religion in America*. Public Expressions of Religion in America. Urbana: University of Illinois Press, 1997.

———. *Sources of Holocaust Insight: Learning and Teaching about the Genocide*. Eugene, OR: Cascade Books, 2020.

———. "What Teaching Teaches Me: How the Holocaust Informs My Philosophy of Education." In *Inspiring Teaching: Carnegie Professors of the Year Speak*, edited by John K. Roth, 199–210. Bolton, MA: Anker, 1997.

———. "What We Know and What We Still Need to Know." In *The Routledge Handbook of Religion, Mass Atrocity, and Genocide*, edited by Sara E. Brown and Stephen D. Smith, 461–66. Routledge Handbooks in Religion. New York: Routledge, 2022.

Roth, Philip. "A Conversation with Primo Levi." In *Survival in Auschwitz: The Nazi Assault on Humanity*, by Primo Levi, 175–87. Translated by Stuart Woolf. 1st Touchstone ed. New York: Simon & Schuster, 1996.

Ruane, Michael E. "Cut Off from Food, Ukrainians Recall Famine under Stalin, Which Killed 4 Million of Them." *Washington Post*, March 12, 2022. https://www.washingtonpost.com/history/2022/03/12/holodomor-famine-ukraine-stalin/.

Rucker, Philip. "Trump Escalates Baseless Attacks on Election with 46-Minute Video Rant." *Washington Post*, December 2, 2020. https://www.washingtonpost.com/politics/trump-election-video/2020/12/02/f6c8d63c-34e8-11eb-a997-1f4c53d2a747_story.html/.

Russell, Catherine. "War in Ukraine Has Left Nearly 1,000 Children Killed or Injured." UNICEF. United Nations. August 22, 2022. https://www.unicef.org/press-releases/war-ukraine-has-left-nearly-1000-children-killed-or-injured#/.

Saad, Lydia. "Americans Still Glum about State of the Union in Most Areas." *Gallup* (website), February 2, 2023. https://news.gallup.com/poll/469241/americans-glum-state-union-areas.aspx/.

Said-Moorhouse, Lauren, and Oleksandra Ochman. "This Is What the 'Russification' of Ukraine's Education System Looks Like in Occupied Areas." CNN, May 16, 2022. https://www.cnn.com/2022/05/16/europe/russia-ukraine-education-intl-cmd/index.html/.

Sands, Tommy, singer-songwriter, with Moya and Fionan. *Let the Circle Be Wide*. Appleseed Recordings, APR CD 1114, 2009, 1 compact disc.

———. *The Songman: A Journey in Irish Music*. Dublin: Lilliput, 2005.

Scheindlin, Shira A. "Trump's Judges Will Call the Shots for Years to Come. The Judicial System Is Broken." *Guardian* (US ed.), October 25, 2021. https://www.theguardian.com/commentisfree/2021/oct/25/trump-judges-supreme-court-justices-judiciary/.

Schmidt, Michael S., and Luke Broadwater, "Jan. 6 Panel Has Evidence for Criminal Referral of Trump, but Splits on Sending." *New York Times*, April 10, 2022. https://www.nytimes.com/2022/04/10/us/politics/jan-6-trump-criminal-referral.html/.

Schwartzman, Bryan. "Reconstructionist Affiliates, Rabbis Push for a More Just Immigration System." *Reconstructing Judaism* (website), July 15, 2019. https://www.reconstructingjudaism.org/news/reconstructionist-communities-immigration-justice/.

Schwarz, Ryan. "Brian Williams Channels Frank Sinatra ('Regrets, I've Had a Few . . .') in Farewell to NBC News—Watch Goodbye Speech." *TVLine*, December 10, 2021. https://tvline.com/2021/12/10/brian-williams-leaving-msnbc-not-returning-farewell-speech-statement-video/.

Seidel, Andrew L., et al. *Christian Nationalism and the January 6, 2021, Insurrection*. Washington, DC: Baptist Joint Committee for Religious Liberty (BJC), 2022. https://static1.squarespace.com/static/5cfea0017239e10001cd9639/t/6203f007e07275503964ab4d/1644425230442/Christian_Nationalism_and_the_Jan6_Insurrection-2-9-22.pdf/.

Shanes, Joshua. "Volodymyr Zelenskyy Is the Antisemites' New Soros." *Haaretz*, March 28, 2022. https://www.haaretz.com/world-news/.premium-zelenskyy-is-the-antisemites-new-soros-1.10703375/.

Shelby County v. Holder, 570 U.S. 529 (2013), available at https://supreme.justia.com/cases/federal/us/570/529/.

Siegel, Reva. "The Trump Court Limited Women's Rights Using 19th-Century Standards." *Washington Post*, June 25, 2022. https://www.washingtonpost.com/outlook/2022/06/25/trump-court-limited-womens-rights-using-19th-century-standards/.

Sly, Liz. "66,000 War Crimes Have Been Reported in Ukraine. It Vows to Prosecute Them All." *Washington Post*, January 29, 2023. https://www.washingtonpost.com/world/2023/01/29/war-crimes-ukraine-prosecution/.

Smith, David. "Self-Awareness in Short Supply as Trump Calls for Law and Order in DC." *Guardian* (US ed.), July 26, 2022. https://www.theguardian.com/us-news/2022/jul/26/donald-trump-washington-dc-speech-america-first/.

Snyder, Timothy. *Bloodlands: Europe between Hitler and Stalin*. New York: Basic Books, 2010.

———. *On Tyranny: Twenty Lessons from the Twentieth Century*. New York: Duggan, 2017.

———. "Putin Has Long Fantasized about a World without Ukrainians. Now We See What That Means." *Washington Post*, March 23, 2022. https://www.washingtonpost.com/opinions/2022/03/23/putin-genocide-language-ukraine-wipe-out-state-identity/.

———. *The Road to Unfreedom: Russia, Europe, America*. New York: Duggan, 2018.

———. "Russia's Eugenic War." *Thinking About*, January 8, 2023. https://snyder.substack.com/p/russias-eugenic-war?utm_source=substack&utm.

———. "Russia's Genocide Handbook." *Thinking About*, April 8, 2022. https://snyder.substack.com/p/russias-genocide-handbook/.

———. "Self-Rule and Survival." *Thinking About*, July 23, 2022. https://snyder.substack.com/p/self-rule-and-survival/.

———. "We Should Say It. Russia Is Fascist." *New York Times*, May 19, 2022. https://www.nytimes.com/2022/05/19/opinion/russia-fascism-ukraine-putin.html/.

———, with illustrations by Nora Krug. *On Tyranny: Twenty Lessons from the Twentieth Century*. Graphic ed. New York: Ten Speed, 2021.

Span, Paula. "For Older Americans, the Pandemic Is Not Over." *New York Times*, https://www.nytimes.com/2023/02/11/health/covid-pandemic-seniors.html/.

Sprunt, Barbara. "Trump Paints a Grim Picture and Pence Tries to Look Ahead in Dueling D.C. Speeches." NPR, July 26, 2022. NPR. https://www.npr.org/2022/07/26/1113637898/trump-paints-a-grim-picture-and-pence-tries-to-look-ahead-in-dueling-d-c-speeche/.

Stafford, William. *The Way It Is: New & Selected Poems*. St. Paul: Graywolf, 1998.

Stanley, Jason. *How Fascism Works: The Politics of Us and Them*. 2020 Random House trade paperback ed. New York: Random House, 2018.

Stein, Perry. "The Trump Search Warrant Focuses on Classified Information. What You Need to Know." *Washington Post*, August 13, 2022. https://www.washingtonpost.com/national-security/2022/08/13/trump-warrant-classified-answers/.

Steinberg, Neil. "Trump v. Jesus: Christians Can't Follow Both." *Chicago Sun-Times*, October 10, 2019. https://chicago.suntimes.com/columnists/2019/10/10/20908102/trump-jesus-christians-evangelicals-religion-jim-wallis-steinberg/.

Steinweis, Alan E., and Robert D. Rachlin, eds. *The Law in Nazi Germany: Ideology, Opportunism, and the Perversion of Justice*. New York: Berghahn, 2025.

Stelter, Brian. "I Never Truly Understood Fox News until Now." *Atlantic*, February 17, 2023. https://www.theatlantic.com/ideas/archive/2023/02/fox-news-dominion-voting-lawsuit-2020-election-conspiracy/673111/.

Stephens, Bret. "I Was Wrong about Trump Voters." *New York Times*, July 21, 2022. https://www.nytimes.com/2022/07/21/opinion/bret-stephens-trump-voters.html/.

Stewart, Katherine. “Christian Nationalists Are Excited about What Comes Next.” *New York Times*, July 5, 2022. https://www.nytimes.com/2022/07/05/opinion/dobbs-christian-nationalism.html/.

———. *The Power Worshippers: Inside the Dangerous Rise of Religious Nationalism*. New York: Bloomsbury, 2019.

———. “The Rise of Spirit Warriors on the Christian Right.” *New Republic*, January 23, 2023. https://newrepublic.com/article/170027/rise-spirit-warriors-christian-right-politics/.

Suri, Jeremi. *Civil War by Other Means: America's Long and Unfinished Fight for Democracy*. New York: PublicAffairs, 2022.

Teach for America. Website: http://www.teachforamerica.org/.

Teh, Cheryl. “Old Video Surfaces of Trump Vowing in 2026 to Enforce Regulations on Classified Information: ‘No One Will Be above the Law.’” *Yahoo News*, August 16, 2022. https://www.yahoo.com/news/old-video-resurfaces-trump-vowing-070935167.html/.

Third Act. “Third Act: Who We Are” (webpage). https://vimeo.com/620222538/.

Trochev, Alexei, and Olga Schwartz. *The Rule of Law in Russia: Power of Rulers, Power of Rules; Russia's Legal Dualism in Action*. The Rule of Law in Context. London: Hart, 2022.

Troianovski, Anton. “Putin Aims to Shape a New Generation of Supporters, through Schools.” *New York Times*, July 16, 2022. https://www.nytimes.com/2022/07/16/world/europe/russia-putin-schools-propaganda-indoctrination.html/.

Trump, Donald. “CPAC Speech.” August 6, 2022. *Rev Blog* (blog). https://www.rev.com/blog/transcripts/former-president-donald-trump-speaks-at-cpac-8-06-22-transcript/.

———. “Full Text: 2017 Donald Trump Inauguration Speech Transcript.” *Politico* (website).” January 20, 2017. https://www.politico.com/story/2017/01/full-text-donald-trump-inauguration-speech-transcript-233907/.

———. “President Donald J. Trump Is Protecting America's Founding Ideals by Promoting Patriotic Education.” November 2, 2020. Fact Sheets. https://trumpwhitehouse.archives.gov/briefings-statements/president-donald-j-trump-protecting-americas-founding-ideals-promoting-patriotic-education/.

United Nations. “Convention of the Prevention and Punishment of the Crime of Genocide.” December 9, 1948. https://www.un.org/en/genocideprevention/documents/atrocity-crimes/Doc.1_Convention%20on%20the%20Prevention%20and%20Punishment%20of%20the%20Crime%20of%20Genocide.pdf/.

———. “Ukraine: Gutteres Calls for Safety and Security of Zaporizhzhia Nuclear Plant.” *UN News*, September 6, 2022. https://news.un.org/en/story/2022/09/1126131#:~:text=Guterres%20gravely%20concerned&text=I%20remain%20gravely%20concerned%20about,in%20Ukraine%2C%20could%20spell%20catastrophe/.

———. UN High Commissioner for Refugees. “Ukraine, Other Conflicts Push Forcibly Displaced Total Over 100 Million for First Time.” May 23, 2022. https://www.unhcr.org/en-us/news/press/2022/5/628a389e4/unhcr-ukraine-other-conflicts-push-forcibly-displaced-total-100-million.html/.

———. UNESCO. “Proclamation of a World Philosophy Day.” General Conference, 33rd, July 29, 2005. https://unesdoc.unesco.org/ark:/48223/pf0000140277_eng/.

United States Congress. Joint Committee on Printing. *Our Flag*. Washington, DC: US Government Printing Office, 2007. https://www.govinfo.gov/content/pkg/CDOC-109sdoc18/pdf/CDOC-109sdoc18.pdf/.

———. Select Committee to Investigate the January 6th Attack on the United States Capitol. *The January 6th Report*. New York: Celedon, 2022.

United States Holocaust Memorial Museum. "Introduction to the Holocaust." *Holocaust Encyclopedia*. https://encyclopedia.ushmm.org/content/en/article/introduction-to-the-holocaust/.

———. "Stanisławów." *Holocaust Encyclopedia*. https://encyclopedia.ushmm.org/content/en/article/stanislawow/.

United States Library of Congress, and the Congressional Research Service. *Constitution Annotated: Analysis and Interpretation of the U.S. Constitution* (website). https://constitution.congress.gov/.

———. "Textualism and Interpreting the Constitution." *Constitution Annotated: Analysis and Interpretation of the U.S. Constitution*. https://constitution.congress.gov/browse/essay/intro.7-2/ALDE_00001303/.

United States National Archives. Constitution of the United States. https://www.archives.gov/founding-docs/constitution-transcript/.

University of California, Davis. Violence Prevention Research Program. "Survey Finds Alarming Trend Toward Political Violence." *UC Davis Health* (website), July 20, 2022. https://health.ucdavis.edu/news/headlines/survey-finds-alarming-trend-toward-political-violence/2022/07/.

V (formerly Eve Ensler). "I Reject the US Abortion Ruling. I Vow to Defend the Sovereignty of Women's Bodies." *Guardian* (US ed.), July 2, 2022. https://www.theguardian.com/us-news/2022/jul/02/multitudes-us-decision-abortion-supreme-court-women-revolt-questions/.

Verhagen, Dave. *How White Evangelicals Think: The Psychology of White Conservative Christians*. Eugene, OR: Cascade Books, 2022.

Viser, Matt, et al. "Biden and Putin Deliver Dueling Fiery Speeches on Ukraine." *Washington Post*, February 21, 2023. https://www.washingtonpost.com/politics/2023/02/21/biden-poland-proclaims-natos-unity-against-russia/.

Vlamis, Kelsey. "Christians against Christian Nationalism Say That Ideology Distorts Both American and Christian Values." *Business Insider* (website), September 4, 2022. https://www.businessinsider.com/christian-nationalism-distorts-american-and-christian-values-group-2022-9/.

Walter, Barbara F. *How Civil Wars Start: And How to Stop Them*. New York: Crown, 2022.

Wang, Amy B., and Caroline Kitchener. "Graham Introduces Bill to Ban Abortions Nationwide after 15 Weeks." *Washington Post*, September 13, 2022. https://www.washingtonpost.com/politics/2022/09/13/abortion-graham-republicans-nationwide-ban/.

Warnock, G. J. *Contemporary Moral Philosophy*. New Studies in Ethics. London: Macmillan, 1967.

Warnock, Raphael (@ReverendWarnock). "Democracies don't die overnight. They slowly erode before completely dismantling. We can't let that happen. We must change the rules to save voting rights." Twitter, January 11, 2022, 10:35 a.m. https://twitter.com/ReverendWarnock/status/1480926355235737603/.

Washington, George. Farewell Address. September 19, 1796. *Avalon Project* (website) https://avalon.law.yale.edu/18th_century/washing.asp/.

Watad, Mahmoud, and Leonard Grob. *Teen Voices from the Holy Land: Who Am I to You?* Amherst, NY: Prometheus, 2007.

Waxman, Deborah, and Seth Rosen. "We Must Work to Ensure that the January 6th Insurrection Will Not Disrupt American Democracy." *Reconstructing Judaism* (website), January 8, 2021. https://www.reconstructingjudaism.org/news/we-must-work-ensure-january-6th-insurrection-will-not-disrupt-american-democracy/.

Wehner, Peter. "More MAGA Than Ever." *Atlantic*, November 10, 2022. https://www.theatlantic.com/ideas/archive/2022/11/midterms-trump-desantis-dobbs-republicans/672068/.

———. "The Trump Abandonment Has Begun." *Atlantic*, December 19, 2022. https://www.theatlantic.com/ideas/archive/2022/12/republicans-never-trumpers-ye-fuentes-dinner/672477/.

Weinreich, Max. *Hitler's Professors: The Part of Scholarship in German's Crimes against the Jewish People.* New Haven: Yale University Press, 1999.

Weisman, Jonathan, and Reid J. Epstein. "G.O.P. Declares Jan. 6 Attack 'Legitimate Political Discourse.'" *New York Times*, February 4, 2022. https://www.nytimes.com/2022/02/04/us/politics/republicans-jan-6-cheney-censure.html/.

West Virginia v. Environmental Protection Agency, 597 U.S. ___ (2022), available at https://www.supremecourt.gov/opinions/21pdf/20-1530_n758.pdf/.

Whalen, Jeanne. "Russian Orthodox Leader Backs War in Ukraine, Divides Faith." *Washington Post*, April 18, 2022. https://www.washingtonpost.com/world/2022/04/18/russian-orthodox-church-ukraine-war/.

Whitehead, Andrew L. "3 Threats Christian Nationalism Poses to the United States." *Time*, September 26, 2022. https://time.com/6214724/christian-nationalism-threats-united-states/.

Whitehead, Andrew L., and Samuel L. Perry. *Taking America Back for God: Christian Nationalism in the United States.* New York: Oxford University Press, 2020.

Whitman, James Q. *Hitler's American Model: The United States and the Making of Nazi Race Law.* Princeton: Princeton University Press, 2017.

Whitman, Walt. "Song of Myself." In *American Ground: Vistas, Visions & Revisions*, edited by Robert H. Fossum and John K. Roth, 107–8. St. Paul, MN: Paragon House, 1988.

Wiesel, Elie. Foreword. In *Shadows of Auschwitz: A Christian Response to the Holocaust*, by Harry James Cargas, ix–x. Rev. ed. New York: Crossroad, 1990.

———. *A Jew Today.* Translated by Marion Wiesel. New York: Random House, 1978.

———. *Legends of Our Time.* 1968. Reprint, New York: Schocken, 1982.

———. "My Teachers." In *Legends of Our Time*, 8–15. 1968. Reprint, New York: Schocken, 1982.

———. "The Nobel Acceptance Speech." December 10, 1986. https://www.nobelprize.org/prizes/peace/1986/wiesel/acceptance-speech/.

———. "One Must Not Forget." Interview by Alvin P. Sanoff. *US News and World Report*, October 27, 1986, 68.

———. *Open Heart.* Translated by Marion Wiesel. New York: Knopf, 2012.

Williams, Brian, et al. "Transcript: The 11th Hour with Brian Williams, 10/21/21." *MSNBC* (website). https://www.msnbc.com/transcripts/transcript-11th-hour-brian-williams-10-21-21-n1282138/.

Wilson-Hartgrove, Jonathan. "Faith Is Powerful. That's Why Christian Nationalism Is So Dangerous." *Time*, July 28, 2022. https://time.com/6201483/christian-nationalism-threat-democracy/.

Wire, Sarah D. "Jan. 6 Committee Says Trump 'May Have Engaged in Criminal Acts' to Overturn Election." *Los Angeles Times*, March 2, 2022. https://www.latimes.com/politics/story/2022-03-02/house-january-6-select-committee-says-it-believes-former-president-trump-may-have-engaged-in-criminal-acts-to-subvert-2020-election/.

World Health Organization. *WHO Coronavirus (COVID-19) Dashboard* (website). https://covid19.who.int/.

———. "WHO Director-General's Opening Remarks at the Media Briefing on COVID-19." March 11, 2020. http://www.who.int/director-general/speeches/detail/who-director-general-s-opening-remarks-at-the-media-briefing-on-covid-19—-11-march-2020/.

Yad Vashem. "Lorenzo Perrone." *The Stories of Six Righteous among the Nations in Auschwitz* (website). https://www.yadvashem.org/yv/en/exhibitions/righteous-auschwitz/perrone.asp/.

Yaffa, Joshua. "Why Russia Hasn't Cracked Down on COVID-19." *New Yorker*, November 23. 2021. https://www.newyorker.com/news/dispatch/why-russia-hasnt-cracked-down-on-covid-19/.

Yermolenko, Volodymyr. "Ezra Klein Interviews Volodymyr Yermolenko." Interview by Ezra Klein. *The Ezra Klein Show*, April 12, 2022. Transcript. https://www.nytimes.com/2022/04/12/podcasts/transcript-ezra-klein-interviews-volodymyr-yermolenko.html/.

Zapotosky, Matt, and John Wagner. "Judge: Trump 'More Likely Than not' Committed Crime in Trying to Block Biden Win.'" *Washington Post*, March 28, 2022. https://www.washingtonpost.com/politics/2022/03/28/judge-says-trump-more-than-likely-committeed-crime/.

Zelenskyy, Volodymyr. "Full Transcript of Zelensky's Speech Before Congress." *New York Times*, December 21, 2022. https://www.nytimes.com/2022/12/21/us/politics/zelensky-speech-transcript.html/.

———. "Text of President Zelensky's Virtual Address to Congress." *Washington Post*, March 16, 2022. Transcript. https://www.wasshingtonpost.com/politics/2022/03/16/text-zelensky-address-congress/.

Ziemer, George. *Education for Death: The Making of the Nazi*. New York: Farrar, Straus and Giroux, 1969.

Index

www.ingramcontent.com/pod-product-compliance
Lightning Source LLC
LaVergne TN
LVHW091126080826
845145LV00008B/2064
* 9 7 8 1 6 6 6 7 4 3 9 6 8 *